Other Books by Florence and Fred Littauer

THOMAS NELSON
Freeing Your Mind from Memories That Bind
The Promise of Restoration/Healing
Make the Tough Times Count

WORD BOOKS
Silver Boxes
Dare to Dream
Raising Christians Not Just Children
Your Personality Tree (also video album)
Hope for Hurting Women
Looking for God in All the Right Places
Wake Up Women
Wake Up Men

FLEMING REVELL, BAKER BOOKS
Personality Plus (also available in French, German, Spanish)
Personality Puzzle (with Marita Littauer)

HARVEST HOUSE PUBLISHERS
Blow Away the Black Clouds
After Every Wedding Comes a Marriage
It Takes So Little to be Above Average
How to Get Along with Difficult People
Out of the Cabbage Patch

HUNTINGTON HOUSE
Personalities in Power

CLASS BOOKS
Christian Leaders and Speakers Seminar (Tape, album, and manual)
The Best of Florence Littauer

For information on "Promise of Healing" recovery workshops conducted by Fred and Florence Littauer, please call 1-800-433-6633.

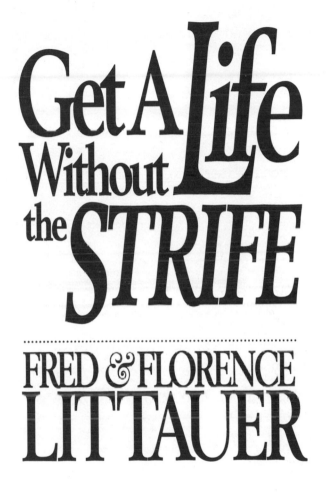

Get A Life Without the STRIFE

FRED & FLORENCE LITTAUER

A
JANET
THOMA
BOOK

Thomas Nelson Publishers
Nashville

Published in Nashville, Tennessee, by Janet Thoma Books, a division of Thomas Nelson, Inc., Publishers, and distributed in Canada by Word Communications, Ltd., Richmond, British Columbia, and in the United Kingdom by Word (UK), Ltd., Milton Keynes, England.

Scripture quotations are from the NEW KING JAMES VERSION of the Bible. Copyright © 1979, 1980, 1982, Thomas Nelson, Inc., Publishers.

Library of Congress Cataloging-in-Publication Data

Littauer, Fred.
    Get a life without the strife / by Fred & Florence Littauer.
      p.   cm.
    "A Janet Thoma book."
    Includes bibliographical references and index.
    ISBN 0-8407-7816-3
    1. Problem solving.   2. Personality and situation.   3. Counseling.   4. Pastoral counseling.   I. Littauer, Florence, 1928–   II. Title.
BF449.L58   1993
158—dc20
                                      93-4673
                                         CIP

Printed in the United States of America.
234567 — 97 96 95 94 93

*"Please let there be no strife
between you and me."*

—Genesis 13:8

CONTENTS

PART ONE

---- ◆ ----

Toward a Life Without the Strife

I've Got a Problem, But I Don't Know What to Do

"**I** don't know what to do with myself," Anne admitted as we sat around a table, eating chocolate cake.

"I know how you feel," answered Karen, a pretty blonde singer who looked so confident when she was on stage. As she stared down at the paper napkin she was folding into little squares she said, "I've about given up on myself. I don't know why I'm so depressed all the time, and when I went to a counselor on Friday he told me he'd need to see me twice a week—at seventy dollars a visit—and it might take about five years."

"And you still won't know what's wrong!" Anne exclaimed. "I've spent thirty thousand dollars on therapy, and I don't know much more now than I did in the beginning. My therapist is a nice Christian lady and she's held me together over the years, but I still don't understand what's wrong with me."

We were sitting with a group of women in a comfortable lodge, relaxing after the Mount Shasta Women's Weekend Retreat. The people who were staying overnight were in no hurry to go to bed. We had taught them about personalities that day, and this focus on understanding themselves had given them permission to be real. Our explanation of the masks some people wear to cover up their pain had allowed these women to share their hurts with each other.

"I guess my problems aren't so bad," piped up Betty, an energetic beauty who had led the morning aerobics. "I just can't stand my husband. I went to the pastor and told him how I felt, and he told me I was lucky to have such a good man, even if he was boring."

"He's right. You've got nothing to complain about." This statement came from the saddest one of the group. Her nametag said 'Joy,' but the name didn't fit her face. "My husband walked out on me and left me with no money and three kids," she said.

Within a few minutes four women had thrown their hurts out on the table.

"I wouldn't mind working on my problems if I could just get my finger on the source," said Karen, the pretty singer. "If only I could find out why I have these headaches and why I have no energy. My doctor gave me some pills, but I don't feel any better."

"Pills don't help in the long run," Anne explained. "They only make you feel better for a while. I know because I've tried 'em all."

Anne was a depressed Melancholy. She was discouraged with counseling and had given up on miracle drugs. She had used up her insurance money and still owed the last counselor thousands of dollars. She saw no hope, no light at the end of the tunnel. If the years of counseling hadn't solved her problems, where should she turn now?

"Medicine doesn't bring your husband back," said Joy. She sighed sadly.

"Or brighten up the one you've got," Betty added. She was able to take control of just about everything in life and she was sure if she had a different husband she would be happy. She didn't think much was wrong with her that new circumstances couldn't fix, and she felt sorry for the others who had real problems. With her Choleric nature she wanted to straighten out other people, but she didn't know where to start with this group. She just looked around the table and shook her head.

"At least I know what's wrong with me," Joy said. "I've been rejected. I thought I'd been a good wife, but my husband left me for another woman."

Joy had given up and didn't know where to turn. As a Phlegmatic she hated to make decisions, and even though her husband had been abusive to her and the children, he had brought a certain perverse stability to her life. Now she was sinking under the weight of double responsibility in the home. Where had her marriage gone wrong?

"You're probably a co-dependent," Betty stated with assurance, even though she'd only known Joy for five minutes. Betty had ready opinions on every subject and had read all the self-help books.

"All I want is to have fun again," Karen said wistfully. "I hate being depressed. When my husband finds out how much I spent shopping trying to cheer myself up, he'll be depressed, too, and then I'll be in real trouble."

Karen was an obvious Sanguine personality. She loved being in the spotlight and appeared to be happy—until she dropped her guard and let us know she was depressed and had chronic headaches. Why was this optimistic woman so pessimistic?

As we observed this group of well-meaning, motivated Christian women who cared enough about their lives to come to the retreat, we wished we had something to hand them that would cover their range of problems and help them sort out their symptoms.

Just as we were thinking about their needs, Betty turned toward us and asked, "Do you have a book that would help us figure out where our problems come from?"

We didn't like to say no, but we didn't have a book that covered the range of problems before us: Anne with her head in her hands, sighing hopelessly; Karen, laughing on the outside, crying on the inside; Betty in firm control of her shapely body and eating habits but unhappily married; and Joy, rejected and wondering where to turn.

As we glanced around the table, Anne asked, "Don't you have one book that will help diagnose our emotional pain? When you're depressed you can't read a lot of books."

We began to explain the thrust of our books, but Betty interrupted. "If you don't have one book to cover all our problems then you'd better write one. Write a book with little tests on a lot of subjects so we can begin to sort out our lives." Betty was thrilled with her idea. "Start with the personalities and work up to more serious subjects."

"I like those little quizzes in magazines that help you find out what kind of a person you are," Karen added.

As we discussed what type of tests they would want, Anne said, "I hope you put in something to help us recall our childhoods. I can't remember anything before I was twelve. My mother says I had a perfect childhood, but if I did why can't I remember it? And why am I such a mess today?"

Joy wanted to make sure we put in something about marriage communication and abuse. "I should have taken a stand a long time ago. Now it's too late."

"I know just how you could do this," Betty said. By now this was *her* book. "You take all the tests you've written on personalities, marriage, and emotional problems and put them in one book. That way readers could go through the questions and find the source of their problems. You could help people get a life without the strife!" Betty was thrilled with her little rhyme. She inferred that her interest in this project was solely to help other people; she would be fine, she believed, if her husband would only shape up.

By the time we all said good night, the catalyst for this book had started to explode in our minds. We would help people think through their problems and find their areas of need; then we would guide them in getting the right kind of help. We would help each person *Get a Life Without the Strife*.

1

What Is My Personality?

For centuries people have been fascinated with analyzing themselves. Quizzes on personality have been singularly popular because many people aren't sure they even have one. Others who think they have one don't like what they've got and wish they were someone else.

During our years of teaching and writing on personalities we have learned that if you give people a tool so simple that they can recognize their strengths, look at their weaknesses, and admit they need to do something about them, they will make the necessary changes. Most of us don't work on our weaknesses because our faults have been pointed out to us by people whose opinions we don't value and whose lives we consider worse than our own. We can always find fault with the fault finders; who are they to tell us what we're doing wrong? Children resist parental instructions, mates get livid at each other over criticism, and friends are lost over an honest word of requested appraisal. If we are left to the comments of parents, mates, and friends we may never take an insightful look at ourselves.

However, if we make it a positive experience, give it an objectivity removed from familial emotions, people eagerly grab on to the system provided. We have learned that people seldom make life-

7

changing choices by their intellect but by their emotions. A humorous view of their personalities is nonthreatening even to those who are usually defensive. Insecure people let down their barriers to change when they are having fun.

Our study of the four personalities, described in our book *Personality Plus,* is light reading on the surface, yet deep enough to move people's emotions into a desire for change. In a report aired by Cable News Network, Roger Johnson, CEO of Western Digital, said at the conclusion of President Clinton's economic summit, "Ultimately all people make decisions based on their emotions—it's how they feel about the economy or whatever."

The original categories of personality division were conceived by a physician who was looking for a way to help his patients understand themselves and see how their emotional differences influenced their health. The system has been renamed and expanded throughout the years but the various personality evaluations are still based on the original terms:

The popular Sanguine who wants to have fun,

The powerful Choleric who wants to be in control,

The perfect Melancholy who wants everything done properly,

The peaceful Phlegmatic who seeks serenity and a stress-free life.

The Taylor-Johnson Temperament Test and the Myers-Briggs Type Indicator, both long-standing psychological evaluations with universal credibility, provide expansions of the four original personalities. Gary Smalley and John Trent, authors of *The Two Sides of Love,* have named the same traits after animals (otter, lion, beaver, and retriever); DISC, a personal profile system, has created new terms; Dr. Edward de Bono has labeled the personalities as different colored hats; and Larry Crabb of the Institute of Biblical Counseling calls them relational skills. Whatever the labels, they all spring from the same origin. The Personality System Comparison Chart shows the terms the different systems use for the same general traits.

Personality System Comparison Chart[1]

Personality:	Popular Sanguine	Powerful Choleric	Perfect Melancholy	Peaceful Phlegmatic
Larry Crabb:	Emotional	Volitional	Rational	Personal
Gary Smalley and John Trent:	Otter	Lion	Beaver	Golden Retriever
DISC Personal Profile System:	Influencing	Dominant	Cautious	Steady
Alessandra and Cathcart:	Socializer	Director	Thinker	Relater
Merrill-Reid Social Styles:	Expressive	Driving	Analytical	Amiable
Dr. Edward de Bono:	Red Hat Intuition and Hunches	Blue Hat Controlling Conductor	Yellow Hat Logical Positives	Black Hat Caution and Danger

Scripture tells us to examine ourselves, put ourselves to the test and judge ourselves that we be not judged. Social scientists have done extensive research in the last decade and agree (a rare happening in itself!) that we are born with a direction of personality; we call it the birth personality. We do not come into the world as blank pages waiting for circumstances to create our behavior and reactions. All we have to do is look at our siblings or at our own children to see that several people with the same parents and upbringing can turn out to be markedly different in personality.

Once we realize that we come into this world with a prepackaged unit of responses to life and relational skills, our aim should be to find out our true natures and to function in our strengths and work prayerfully and humanly to eliminate our weaknesses. Playing a different role from what we were cast to be is like being a character actor in a theatrical production every single day. After a while we are exhausted, and we wonder why.

Oswald Chambers wrote, "The only way we can be of use to God is to let him take us through the nooks and crannies of our own character. It is astounding how ignorant we are about ourselves. We have to get rid of the idea that we understand ourselves, it is the last conceit to go."[2]

Some of us wonder if there's anyone who can guide us. We find a counselor who will at least listen or we question a stranger we met at a seminar or we level with a close friend, but often we don't feel any better afterward. We may even feel worse because we have exposed our own personal doubts, confusion, and confessions to another person.

By taking the Personality Profile Test that follows, each of us can find out who we really are and observe our strengths and weaknesses, laid out clearly before us. And that's not all. We can also understand other people better.

Some relationship problems may have hindered our progress. We just don't understand some people because they don't think at all like we do. As we perceive our strengths and weaknesses we will begin to understand why these difficult people function differently. Suddenly we will say to ourselves, "That's why he reacts like that. I thought he was just out to get me."

For these reasons we recommend that you take the Personality Profile Test. If you have read *The Personality Puzzle* or *Personality Plus* and already know your profile, skip to page 49. Definitions for all the words on the test start on page 12.

PERSONALITY PROFILE TEST

Directions: In *each* of the following rows of *four words across* place an X in front of the *one* word that most often applies to you. Continue through all forty lines. Be sure each numbered line is marked. If you are not sure which word most applies, look at the word definitions that follow the test, or ask a spouse or a friend, or think of what your answer would have been *when you were a child*.

STRENGTHS

1. __ Adventurous	__ Adaptable	__ Animated	__ Analytical
2. __ Persistent	__ Playful	__ Persuasive	__ Peaceful

3. ___ Submissive	___ Self-sacrificing	___ Sociable	___ Strong-willed
4. ___ Considerate	___ Controlled	___ Competitive	___ Convincing
5. ___ Refreshing	___ Respectful	___ Reserved	___ Resourceful

6. ___ Satisfied	___ Sensitive	___ Self-reliant	___ Spirited
7. ___ Planner	___ Patient	___ Positive	___ Promoter
8. ___ Sure	___ Spontaneous	___ Scheduled	___ Shy
9. ___ Orderly	___ Obliging	___ Outspoken	___ Optimistic
10. ___ Friendly	___ Faithful	___ Funny	___ Forceful

11. ___ Daring	___ Delightful	___ Diplomatic	___ Detailed
12. ___ Cheerful	___ Consistent	___ Cultured	___ Confident
13. ___ Idealistic	___ Independent	___ Inoffensive	___ Inspiring
14. ___ Demonstrative	___ Decisive	___ Dry humor	___ Deep
15. ___ Mediator	___ Musical	___ Mover	___ Mixes easily

16. ___ Thoughtful	___ Tenacious	___ Talker	___ Tolerant
17. ___ Listener	___ Loyal	___ Leader	___ Lively
18. ___ Contented	___ Chief	___ Chartmaker	___ Cute
19. ___ Perfectionist	___ Pleasant	___ Productive	___ Popular
20. ___ Bouncy	___ Bold	___ Behaved	___ Balanced

WEAKNESSES

21. ___ Blank	___ Bashful	___ Brassy	___ Bossy
22. ___ Undisciplined	___ Unsympathetic	___ Unenthusiastic	___ Unforgiving
23. ___ Reticent	___ Resentful	___ Resistant	___ Repetitious
24. ___ Fussy	___ Fearful	___ Forgetful	___ Frank
25. ___ Impatient	___ Insecure	___ Indecisive	___ Interrupts

26. ___ Unpopular	___ Uninvolved	___ Unpredictable	___ Unaffectionate
27. ___ Headstrong	___ Haphazard	___ Hard to please	___ Hesitant
28. ___ Plain	___ Pessimistic	___ Proud	___ Permissive
29. ___ Angers easily	___ Aimless	___ Argumentative	___ Alienated
30. ___ Naive	___ Negative attitude	___ Nervy	___ Nonchalant

31.	___ Worrier	___ Withdrawn	___ Workaholic	___ Wants credit
32.	___ Too sensitive	___ Tactless	___ Timid	___ Talkative
33.	___ Doubtful	___ Disorganized	___ Domineering	___ Depressed
34.	___ Inconsistent	___ Introvert	___ Intolerant	___ Indifferent
35.	___ Messy	___ Moody	___ Mumbles	___ Manipulative

36.	___ Slow	___ Stubborn	___ Show-off	___ Skeptical
37.	___ Loner	___ Lord-over-others	___ Lazy	___ Loud
38.	___ Sluggish	___ Suspicious	___ Short-tempered	___ Scatterbrained
39.	___ Revengeful	___ Restless	___ Reluctant	___ Rash
40.	___ Compromising	___ Critical	___ Crafty	___ Changeable

Now transfer all your Xs to the corresponding words on the Personality Profile Scoring Form; then add up your totals.

PERSONALITY TEST WORD DEFINITIONS
(Adapted from *Personality Patterns* by Lana Bateman)

Use these definitions to help you decide which words on the Personality Profile Test most apply to you.

STRENGTHS

1. Animated — Full of life, lively use of hand, arm, and face gestures.

   Adventurous — One who will take on new and daring enterprises with a determination to master them.

   Analytical — Likes to examine the parts for their logical and proper relationships.

   Adaptable — Easily fits in and is comfortable in any situation.

2. Persistent — Sees one project through to its completion before starting another.

   Playful — Full of fun and good humor.

   Persuasive — Convinces through logic and fact rather than charm or power.

Peaceful	Seems undisturbed and tranquil and retreats from any form of strife.
3. Submissive	Easily accepts any other's point of view or desire with little need to assert his or her own opinion.
Self-sacrificing	Willingly gives up his or her own personal well-being for the sake of or to meet the needs of others.
Sociable	One who sees being with others as an opportunity to be cute and entertaining rather than as a challenge or business opportunity.
Strong-willed	One who is determined to have his or her own way.
4. Considerate	Has regard for the needs and feelings of others.
Controlled	Has emotional feelings but rarely displays them.
Competitive	Turns every situation, happening, or game into a contest and always plays to win.
Convincing	Can win you over to anything through the sheer charm of his or her personality.
5. Refreshing	Renews and stimulates others or makes them feel good.
Respectful	Treats others with deference, honor, and esteem.
Reserved	Self-restrained in expression of emotion or enthusiasm.
Resourceful	Able to act quickly and effectively in virtually all situations.
6. Satisfied	A person who easily accepts any circumstance or situation.
Sensitive	Intensively cares about others and what happens.
Self-reliant	An independent person who can fully rely on his or her own capabilities, judgment, and resources.
Spirited	Full of life and excitement.
7. Planner	Prefers to work out a detailed arrangement beforehand for the accomplishment of a project or goal, and prefers involvement with the planning stages and the finished product rather than carrying out the task.
Patient	Unmoved by delay, remains calm and tolerant.
Positive	Knows it will turn out right if he's in charge.
Promoter	Urges or compels others to go along, join, or invest through the charm of his own personality.
8. Sure	Confident, rarely hesitates or wavers.
Spontaneous	Prefers all of life to be impulsive, unpremeditated activity, not restricted by plans.
Scheduled	Makes and lives according to a daily plan, dislikes his plan to be interrupted.
Shy	Quiet, doesn't easily instigate a conversation.

9. Orderly   A person who has a methodical, systematic arrangement of things.

Obliging   Accommodating. One who is quick to do it another's way.

Outspoken   Speaks frankly and without reserve.

Optimistic   Sunny disposition who convinces himself and others that everything will turn out all right.

10. Friendly   A responder rather than an initiator, seldom starts a conversation.

Faithful   Consistently reliable, steadfast, loyal, and devoted, sometimes beyond reason.

Funny   Sparkling sense of humor that can make virtually any story into an hilarious event.

Forceful   A commanding personality whom others would hesitate to take a stand against.

11. Daring   Willing to take risks; fearless, bold.

Delightful   A person who is upbeat and fun to be with.

Diplomatic   Deals with people tactfully, sensitively, and patiently.

Detailed   Does everything in proper order with a clear memory of all the things that happened.

12. Cheerful   Consistently in good spirits and promoting happiness in others.

Consistent   Stays emotionally on an even keel, responding as one might expect.

Cultured   One whose interests involve both intellectual and artistic pursuits, such as theater, symphony, ballet.

Confident   Self-assured and certain of own ability and success.

13. Idealistic   Visualizes things in their perfect form and has a need to measure up to that standard.

Independent   Self-sufficient, self-supporting, self-confident, and seems to have little need of help.

Inoffensive   A person who never says or causes anything unpleasant or objectionable.

Inspiring   Encourages others to work, join, or be involved, and makes the whole thing fun.

14. Demonstrative   Openly expresses emotion, especially affection, and doesn't hesitate to touch others while speaking to them.

Decisive   A person with quick, conclusive, judgment-making ability.

Dry humor   Exhibits "dry wit," usually humorous one-liners that can be sarcastic in nature.

	Deep	Intense and often introspective with a distaste for surface conversation and pursuits.¹
15.	Mediator	Consistently finds himself or herself reconciling differences in order to avoid conflict.
	Musical	Participates in or has a deep appreciation for music, is committed to music as an art form rather than the fun of performance.
	Mover	Driven by a need to be productive, a leader whom others follow; finds it difficult to sit still.
	Mixes easily	Loves a party and can't wait to meet everyone in the room; never meets a stranger.
16.	Thoughtful	A considerate person who remembers special occasions and is quick to make a kind gesture.
	Tenacious	Holds on firmly, stubbornly, and won't let go until the goal is accomplished.
	Talker	Constantly talking, generally telling funny stories and entertaining everyone around, feeling the need to fill the silence in order to make others comfortable.
	Tolerant	Easily accepts the thoughts and ways of others without the need to disagree with or change them.
17.	Listener	Always seems willing to hear what you have to say.
	Loyal	Faithful to a person, ideal, or job, sometimes beyond reason.
	Leader	A natural-born director who is driven to be in charge and often finds it difficult to believe that anyone else can do the job as well.
	Lively	Full of life, vigorous, energetic.
18.	Contented	Easily satisfied with what he or she has; rarely envious.
	Chief	Commands leadership and expects people to follow.
	Chartmaker	Organizes life, tasks, and problem-solving by making lists, forms, or graphs.
	Cute	Precious, adorable, center of attention.
19.	Perfectionist	Places high standards on himself or herself and often on others, desiring that everything be in proper order at all times.
	Pleasant	Easygoing, easy to be around, easy to talk with.
	Productive	Must constantly be working or achieving, often finding it very difficult to rest.
	Popular	Life of the party and therefore much desired as a party guest.
20.	Bouncy	A bubbly, lively personality full of energy.

Bold — Fearless, daring, forward, unafraid of risk.

Behaved — Consistently desires to conduct himself or herself within the realm of what he or she feels is proper.

Balanced — Stable, middle-of-the-road personality, not subject to sharp highs or lows.

WEAKNESSES

21. Blank — A person who shows little facial expression or emotion.

Bashful — Shrinks from getting attention due to self-consciousness.

Brassy — Showy, flashy; comes on strong and too loud.

Bossy — Commanding, domineering, sometimes overbearing in adult relationships.

22. Undisciplined — A person whose lack of order permeates almost every area of his or her life.

Unsympathetic — Finds it difficult to relate to the problems or hurts of others.

Unenthusiastic — Tends to not get excited, often feeling it won't work anyway.

Unforgiving — One who has difficulty releasing or forgetting a hurt or injustice done to him or her; apt to hold on to a grudge.

23. Reticent — Unwilling or struggling against getting involved.

Resentful — Often holds ill feelings as a result of real or imagined offenses.

Resistant — Strives, works against, or hesitates to accept any other way but his own.

Repetitious — Retells stories and incidents to entertain you without realizing he has already told the story several times before; is constantly needing something to say.

24. Fussy — Insistent over petty matters or details, calling for great attention to trivial details.

Fearful — Often experiences feelings of deep concern, apprehension, or anxiousness.

Forgetful — Lack of memory that is usually tied to a lack of discipline and not bothering to mentally record things that aren't fun.

Frank — Straightforward, outspoken, and doesn't mind telling you exactly what he or she thinks.

25. Impatient — A person who finds it difficult to endure irritation or wait for others.

	Insecure	One who is apprehensive or lacks confidence.
	Indecisive	A person who finds it difficult to make any decision at all.
	Interrupts	A person who is more of a talker than a listener, who starts speaking without even realizing someone else is already speaking.
26.	Unpopular	A person whose intensity and demand for perfection can push others away.
	Unpredictable	May be ecstatic one moment and down the next, or willing to help but then disappears, or promises to come but forgets to show up.
	Unaffectionate	Finds it difficult to verbally or physically demonstrate tenderness openly.
	Uninvolved	Has no desire to listen to others or to become interested in clubs, groups, activities, or other people's lives.
27.	Headstrong	Insists on having his or her own way.
	Haphazard	Has no consistent way of doing things.
	Hard to please	A person whose standards are set so high that it is difficult to ever satisfy him or her.
	Hesitant	Slow to get moving and hard to get involved.
28.	Plain	A middle-of-the-road personality without highs or lows and showing little, if any, emotion.
	Pessimistic	While hoping for the best, this person generally sees the downside of a situation first.
	Proud	Someone with great self-esteem who sees himself or herself as always right and the best person for the job.
	Permissive	Allows others (including children) to do as they please in order to keep from being disliked.
29.	Angered easily	One who has a childlike flash-in-the-pan temper that expresses itself in tantrum style and is over and forgotten almost instantly.
	Aimless	Not a goal-setter, with little desire to be one.
	Argumentative	Incites arguments generally because he or she is certain he or she is right no matter what the situation may be.
	Alienated	Easily feels estranged from others, often because of insecurity or fear that others don't really enjoy his or her company.
30.	Naive	Simple and childlike perspective, lacking sophistication or comprehension of what the deeper levels of life are really about.

Negative attitude	One whose attitude is seldom positive and is often able to see only the down or dark side of each situation.
Nervy	Full of confidence, fortitude, and sheer guts, often in a negative sense.
Nonchalant	Easygoing, unconcerned, indifferent.
31. Worrier	Consistently feels uncertain, troubled, or anxious.
Withdrawn	A person who pulls back to himself and needs a great deal of alone or isolation time.
Workaholic	An aggressive goal-setter who must be constantly productive and feels very guilty when resting, is not driven by a need for perfection or completion but by a need for accomplishment and reward.
Wants credit	Thrives on the credit or approval of others. As an entertainer this person feeds on the applause, laughter, and/or acceptance of an audience.
32. Too sensitive	Overly introspective and easily offended when misunderstood.
Tactless	Sometimes expresses himself in a somewhat offensive and inconsiderate way.
Timid	Shrinks from difficult situations.
Talkative	An entertaining, compulsive talker who finds it difficult to listen.
33. Doubtful	Characterized by uncertainty and lack of confidence that it will ever work out.
Disorganized	Lack of ability to ever get his or her life in order.
Domineering	Compulsively takes control of situations and/or people, usually telling others what to do.
Depressed	A person who feels down much of the time.
34. Inconsistent	Erratic, contradictory, with actions and emotions not based on logic.
Introvert	A person whose thoughts and interest are directed inward; lives within himself or herself.
Intolerant	Appears unable to withstand or accept another's attitudes, point of view, or way of doing things.
Indifferent	A person to whom most things don't matter one way or the other.
35. Messy	Living in a state of disorder, unable to find things.
Moody	Doesn't get very high emotionally, but easily slips into low lows, often when feeling unappreciated.
Mumbles	Will talk quietly under the breath when pushed, doesn't bother to speak clearly.

Manipulative	Influences or manages shrewdly or deviously for his own advantage; *will* get his way somehow.
36. Slow	Doesn't often act or think quickly, too much of a bother.
Stubborn	Determined to exert his or her own will, not easily persuaded, obstinate.
Show-off	Needs to be the center of attention, wants to be watched.
Skeptical	Disbelieving, questioning the motive behind the words.
37. Loner	Requires a lot of private time and tends to avoid other people.
Lord over	Doesn't hesitate to let you know that he or she is right or is in control.
Lazy	Evaluates work or activity in terms of how much energy it will take.
Loud	A person whose laugh or voice can be heard above others in the room.
38. Sluggish	Slow to get started, needs push to be motivated.
Suspicious	Tends to suspect or distrust others or ideas.
Short-tempered	Has a demanding, impatience-based anger and a short fuse. Anger is expressed when others are not moving fast enough or have not completed what they have been asked to do.
Scatter-brained	Lacks the power of concentration or attention; flighty.
39. Revengeful	Knowingly or otherwise holds a grudge and punishes the offender, often by subtly withholding friendship or affection.
Restless	Likes constant new activity because it isn't fun to do the same things all the time.
Reluctant	Unwilling to or struggles against getting involved.
Rash	May act hastily without thinking things through, generally because of impatience.
40. Compromising	Will often relax his or her position, even when right, in order to avoid conflict.
Critical	Constantly evaluating and making judgments, frequently thinking or expressing negative reactions.
Crafty	Shrewd, one who can always find a way to get to the desired end.
Changeable	A childlike, short attention span that needs a lot of change and variety to keep from getting bored.

PERSONALITY SCORING FORM

Place an X beside the corresponding words you marked on the Personality Profile Test. For example, if you checked <u>Adventurous</u> on the test, then check <u>Adventurous</u> on the Scoring Form.

Then, giving one point for each X, add up your totals.

STRENGTHS

	Popular Sanguine	Powerful Choleric	Perfect Melancholy	Peaceful Phlegmatic
1	___ Animated	___ Adventurous	___ Analytical	___ Adaptable
2	___ Playful	___ Persuasive	___ Persistent	___ Peaceful
3	___ Sociable	___ Strong-willed	___ Self-sacrificing	___ Submissive
4	___ Convincing	___ Competitive	___ Considerate	___ Controlled
5	___ Refreshing	___ Resourceful	___ Respectful	___ Reserved
6	___ Spirited	___ Self-reliant	___ Sensitive	___ Satisfied
7	___ Promoter	___ Positive	___ Planner	___ Patient
8	___ Spontaneous	___ Sure	___ Scheduled	___ Shy
9	___ Optimistic	___ Outspoken	___ Orderly	___ Obliging
10	___ Funny	___ Forceful	___ Faithful	___ Friendly
11	___ Delightful	___ Daring	___ Detailed	___ Diplomatic
12	___ Cheerful	___ Confident	___ Cultured	___ Consistent
13	___ Inspiring	___ Independent	___ Idealistic	___ Inoffensive
14	___ Demonstrative	___ Decisive	___ Deep	___ Dry humor
15	___ Mixes easily	___ Mover	___ Musical	___ Mediator
16	___ Talker	___ Tenacious	___ Thoughtful	___ Tolerant
17	___ Lively	___ Leader	___ Loyal	___ Listener
18	___ Cute	___ Chief	___ Chartmaker	___ Contented
19	___ Popular	___ Productive	___ Perfectionist	___ Pleasant
20	___ Bouncy	___ Bold	___ Behaved	___ Balanced

SUBTOTALS ___   ___   ___   ___

WEAKNESSES

21 ___ Brassy	___ Bossy	___ Bashful	___ Blank
22 ___ Undisciplined	___ Unsympathetic	___ Unforgiving	___ Unenthusiastic
23 ___ Repetitious	___ Resistant	___ Resentful	___ Reticent
24 ___ Forgetful	___ Frank	___ Fussy	___ Fearful
25 ___ Interrupts	___ Impatient	___ Insecure	___ Indecisive
26 ___ Unpredictable	___ Unaffectionate	___ Unpopular	___ Uninvolved
27 ___ Haphazard	___ Headstrong	___ Hard-to-please	___ Hesitant
28 ___ Permissive	___ Proud	___ Pessimistic	___ Plain
29 ___ Angered easily	___ Argumentative	___ Alienated	___ Aimless
30 ___ Naive	___ Nervy	___ Negative attitude	___ Nonchalant
31 ___ Wants credit	___ Workaholic	___ Withdrawn	___ Worrier
32 ___ Talkative	___ Tactless	___ Too sensitive	___ Timid
33 ___ Disorganized	___ Domineering	___ Depressed	___ Doubtful
34 ___ Inconsistent	___ Intolerant	___ Introvert	___ Indifferent
35 ___ Messy	___ Manipulative	___ Moody	___ Mumbles
36 ___ Show-off	___ Stubborn	___ Skeptical	___ Slow
37 ___ Loud	___ Lord-over-others	___ Loner	___ Lazy
38 ___ Scatterbrained	___ Short tempered	___ Suspicious	___ Sluggish
00 ___ Restless	___ Rash	___ Revengeful	___ Reluctant
40 ___ Changeable	___ Crafty	___ Critical	___ Compromising

___   ___   ___   ___

SUBTOTALS

___   ___   ___   ___

GRAND TOTAL

The Comparison of Strengths and Weaknesses by Personality Type chart shows how the typical strengths and weaknesses of the personality types are revealed emotionally, with friends, and at work.

You'll see from the Comparison of Strengths and Weaknesses by Personality Type that we've added some descriptive adjectives to the

Comparison of Strengths and Weaknesses by Personality Type

STRENGTHS

	Popular-Sanguine	Powerful-Choleric	Perfect-Melancholy	Peaceful-Phlegmatic
E M O T I O N S	Appealing personality Talkative, storyteller Life of the party Good sense of humor Memory for color Physically holds on to listener Emotional and demonstrative Enthusiastic and expressive Cheerful and bubbling over Curious Good on stage Wide-eyed and innocent Lives in the present Changeable disposition Sincere at heart Always a child	Born leader Dynamic and active Compulsive need for change Must correct wrongs Strong-willed and decisive Unemotional Not easily discouraged Independent and self-sufficient Exudes confidence Can run anything	Deep and thoughtful Analytical Serious and purposeful Genius prone Talented and creative Artistic or musical Philosophical and poetic Appreciative of beauty Sensitive to others Self-sacrificing Conscientious Idealistic	Low-key personality Easygoing and relaxed Calm, cool, and collected Patient, well balanced Consistent life Quiet, but witty Sympathetic and kind Keeps emotions hidden Happily reconciled to life All-purpose person
W O R K	Volunteers for jobs Thinks up new activities Looks great on the surface Creative and colorful Has energy and enthusiasm Starts in a flashy way Inspires others to join Charms others to work	Goal oriented Sees the whole picture Organizes well Seeks practical solutions Moves quickly to action Delegates work Insists on production Makes the goal Stimulates activity Thrives on opposition	Schedule oriented Perfectionist, high standards Detail conscious Persistent and thorough Orderly and organized Neat and tidy Economical Sees the problems Finds creative solutions Needs to finish what he starts Likes charts, graphs, figures, lists	Competent and steady Peaceful and agreeable Has administrative ability Mediates problems Avoids conflicts Good under pressure Finds the easy way
F R I E N D S	Makes friends easily Loves people Thrives on compliments Seems exciting Envied by others Doesn't hold grudges Apologizes quickly Prevents dull moments Likes spontaneous activities	Has little need for friends Will work for group activity Will lead and organize Is usually right Excels in emergencies	Makes friends cautiously Content to stay in background Avoids causing attention Faithful and devoted Will listen to complaints Can solve others' problems Deep concern for other people Moved to tears with compassion Seeks ideal mate	Easy to get along with Pleasant and enjoyable Inoffensive Good listener Dry sense of humor Enjoys watching people Has many friends Has compassion and concern

WEAKNESSES

	Popular-Sanguine	Powerful-Choleric	Perfect-Melancholy	Peaceful-Phlegmatic

E M O T I O N S	Compulsive talker
	Exaggerates and
	  elaborates
	Dwells on trivia
	Can't remember names
	Scares others off
	Too happy for some
	Has restless energy
	Egotistical
	Blusters and complains
	Naive, gets taken in
	Has loud voice and laugh
	Controlled by
	  circumstances
	Gets angry easily
	Seems phony to some
	Never grows up
		Bossy
		Impatient
		Quick-tempered
		Can't relax
		Too impetuous
		Enjoys controversy and
		  arguments
		Won't give up when losing
		Comes on too strong
		Inflexible
		Is not complimentary
		Dislikes tears and emotions
		Is unsympathetic
			Remembers the negatives
			Moody and depressed
			Enjoys being hurt
			Has false humility
			Off in another world
			Low self-image
			Has selective hearing
			Self-centered
			Too introspective
			Guilt feelings
			Persecution complex
			Tends to hypochondria
				Unenthusiastic
				Fearful and worried
				Indecisive
				Avoids responsibility
				Quiet will of iron
				Selfish
				Too shy and reticent
				Too compromising
				Self-righteous

W O R K	Would rather talk
	Forgets obligations
	Doesn't follow through
	Confidence fades fast
	Undisciplined
	Priorities out of order
	Decides by feelings
	Easily distracted
	Wastes time talking
		Little tolerance for
		  mistakes
		Doesn't analyze details
		Bored by trivia
		May make rash decisions
		May be rude or tactless
		Manipulates people
		Demanding of others
		End justifies the means
		Work may become his god
		Demands loyalty in the
		  ranks
			Not people oriented
			Depressed over
			  imperfections
			Chooses difficult work
			Hesitant to start projects
			Spends too much time
			  planning
			Prefers analysis to work
			Self-deprecating
			Hard to please
			Standards often too high
			Deep need for approval
				Not goal oriented
				Lacks self-motivation
				Hard to get moving
				Resents being pushed
				Lazy and careless
				Discourages others
				Would rather watch

F R I E N D S	Hates to be alone
	Needs to be center
	  stage
	Wants to be popular
	Looks for credit
	Dominates conversations
	Interrupts and
	  doesn't listen
	Answers for others
	Fickle and forgetful
	Makes excuses
	Repeats stories
		Tends to use people
		Dominates others
		Decides for others
		Knows everything
		Can do everything
		  better
		Is too independent
		Possessive of friends
		  and mate
		Can't say, "I'm sorry"
		May be right, but
		  unpopular
			Lives through others
			Insecure socially
			Withdrawn and
			  remote
			Critical of others
			Holds back affection
			Dislikes those in
			  opposition
			Suspicious of people
			Antagonistic and
			  vengeful
			Unforgiving
			Full of contradictions
			Skeptical of
			  compliments
				Dampens enthusiasm
				Stays uninvolved
				Is not exciting
				Indifferent to plans
				Judges others
				Sarcastic and teasing
				Resists change

personality types: Popular Sanguine, Perfect Melancholy, Powerful Choleric, and Peaceful Phlegmatic. We find that these terms help people remember which characteristics are typically associated with those personality types. And while we call some of those character-istics *strengths*, it's important to note that, when carried to extremes, these traits *can* become weaknesses—or even compulsions, as shown in the Strengths Carried to Extremes chart.

Strengths Carried to Extremes

		Natural strengths	Strengths carried to extremes	Compulsions
P O P U L A R	S A N G U I N E	Magnetic personality Entertaining storyteller Loves to go shopping Life of the party	Depends on charm and wit Constantly talking Buys and charges irrationally Too loud, too wild	Can become a con artist, bigamist Must be talking to feel secure Becomes a debt-laden shopaholic Makes fool of self, becomes party animal
P E R F E C T	M E L A N C H O L Y	Schedule oriented Knowledge of health and nutrition Neat, immaculate dresser Wants things done perfectly	Can't function without schedule Constant physical attention Can't go out until perfect Wants others to be perfect	Obsessed with punctuality May become hypochondriac Constant washing; has fetish about looks Nitpicks and criticizes constantly
P O W E R F U L	C H O L E R I C	Born leader Decisive Quick and active Loves to work	Angry if people buck authority Decides for everyone Makes impulsive choices Works beyond the norm	Obsessed with power Manipulates own way Becomes irrational Becomes a workaholic
P E A C E F U L	P H L E G M A T I C	Low-key emotions Easy-going Cooperative Low motivation	Hides emotions Lets others decide Compromises standards Becomes lazy and laid back	Blocks out all feeling Can't make any decisions Easily becomes a pawn Refuses to budge

After you have transferred your checked words from the Personality Profile Test to the Personality Scoring Form, calculate your score and see which personality you score highest in. If you do not feel right about your results, consider these possibilities that may have distorted the profile:

1. You may have taken the test incorrectly. You should have made one check on each of forty lines (twenty strengths and twenty weaknesses). Sometimes people check no response or more than one response on each line, or they check only one response in each vertical column rather than on each horizontal line.

2. You transferred your responses incorrectly. For instance, instead of putting an X by the word *adaptable* on the scoring form you may have put the check in the same position on the scoring sheeting as it was on the test, instead of on the same word.

3. You scored yourself as you would like to be, as others always wanted you to be, or as good Christian people should be instead of how you really are.

4. You are somewhat confused about who you really are and you need help interpreting the score.

An explanation of the results should clear up your confusion. And anyone who took the test will want to understand how to fully interpret the results.

UNDERSTANDING YOUR PERSONALITY PROFILE SCORES

One Dominant Personality

If you scored strongly in one area, such as a 36 in Choleric, you don't need to be concerned about the other scores. They will have minimal influence on your behavior.

The complete Choleric, for instance, will be a dedicated, in-charge worker but a little too bossy in relationships. The strongly

Sanguine will be hilarious in storytelling but very poor on follow-through. The straight Melancholy will do everything perfectly but frequently will be moody, depressed, and nitpicky with others. The extreme Phlegmatic will be so relaxed and pleasant that he or she may appear to be close to death. As one lady said, "My husband is so Phlegmatic that he's just one step above furniture!" Another added, "When we got married, my husband and the couch became one."

Combinations of Two Personalities

The majority of you will be combinations of two personalities. One will be your dominant personality and the other will be your secondary. Almost everyone has a dominant and a secondary, but the numbers may vary greatly. For example 32 Choleric with 8 Melancholy would be described as a very strong Choleric with some Melancholy traits.

However, it is also quite possible to have more evenly balanced scores in two columns. One or two checks in the remaining two columns can generally be ignored as insignificant. Any test such as this can be assumed to have a 10 percent margin of error because the words simply represent how you perceive yourself.

Normal healthy patterns are usually characterized by similar scores of strengths and weaknesses within a single column. Sometimes, however, a person will have all Sanguine strengths and all Choleric weaknesses. There is nothing wrong with this but it would be helpful for you to go back and put a second check on each line of the test. This will give you eighty responses instead of forty, and you will probably be balanced evenly on strengths and weaknesses of the two personalities.

WHAT ARE THE NORMAL HEALTHY PATTERNS?

Natural combinations of personalities are:

Sanguine/Choleric   Choleric/Melancholy
Phlegmatic/Sanguine   Melancholy/Phlegmatic

The Sanguine/Choleric combination is a person who likes to have fun while getting the job done. These people are best in leadership and relational positions. They are at ease in front of people and can motivate others to action, making the whole process sound like fun.

The Choleric/Melancholy blend is a person who wants things done perfectly in his or her own way. They are goal oriented, strong in organizational skills, and relatively demanding of others. They are outstanding in business and management where drive and accuracy are important.

The Melancholy/Phlegmatic person wants things to be done perfectly but also wants to avoid any kind of conflict. These people are gentle with high standards. They are constantly debating in their minds: *If I push to get this done right, will I upset anyone?* They are excellent in mediation and in personnel matters where balanced discussion and appraisal are needed.

The Phlegmatic/Sanguine combination is the most easygoing and fun-loving of all. These people are not highly motivated and don't worry if things aren't done on time. Their relaxed and friendly attitude makes them well liked and inoffensive. They have the highest relationship skills but it is better that they not be involved in financial details.

Unnatural Combinations

Now let's look at personalities that are combinations of two opposites. Two of these combinations are not natural, although they are sometimes seen:

1. Sanguine/Melancholy

2. Choleric/Phlegmatic

Either of these two appearing on the scoring form in significant numbers is evidence of a "personality mask" because they are diametrically opposite. They are inevitably (1) the result of outside forces working in your life to make you conform to someone else's concept of who you should be, or (2) "put on" in childhood to survive a difficult or dysfunctional family living situation.

If you come out to be a combination of Sanguine/Melancholy, you probably live an existence of extremes. You are up one minute and down the next. Your children check to see what mood you're in before they ask for favors. Your friends know by your voice on the phone whether or not you are in a good mood today. You go from wanting to go shopping with friends to locking yourself away from people. You go from entertaining those in line at the supermarket to having a panic attack in the produce department. Have you ever wondered why you don't seem to balance out like other people?

If you seem to be a Choleric/Phlegmatic, your ups and downs are in the area of control. One minute you are compulsively in charge of all you survey and the next you shrink back and wonder how in the world you got into this situation. People don't know why you have bursts of energy and then need to take a nap. You don't understand your drastic changes either. Do you wonder if you have to live like this forever?

These opposite combinations always indicate that there is some form of masking of the real personality.

Combination of Three

Any combination of three personalities indicates that one must be a mask. Generally, the "center" of the three is the natural personality and one of the "ends" is a mask. For example, if a person scores relatively evenly in Sanguine/Choleric/Melancholy, the Choleric is generally the natural personality and either the Sanguine or the Melancholy is the mask.

Frequently a person who knows you well can objectively review the two columns in question and help you select the word that they feel describes you better. Or you can think back to how you would have answered as a child before life's experiences distorted your perception of yourself. Such a review of the words you selected will frequently cause you to transfer enough of your responses to another column to clearly define your correct and natural birth personalities.

Combination of Four

It is unusual for anyone to come out with even scores on all four of the personalities, but it does happen occasionally. Either you somehow took the test incorrectly, you had trouble with the definitions of the words, you couldn't make up your mind about which word applied, or you are Phlegmatic and have trouble with decisions. The more serious explanation is that you are "double masked." You have a natural-personality combination with two masks. Somehow your life experiences have so distorted your self-perception that you have trouble knowing who you really are. Remember, it takes a great deal of energy to wear a mask and live in a personality role that is not naturally yours. Our goal should be to take off the mask and live life to the fullest.

If any of these masking situations seem to apply to you, the following section of explanation may help you understand the problem.

ARE YOU WEARING A MASK?

"Do you think I'm wearing a mask?" questioned Karen, the blonde singer at the Mount Shasta retreat. As we sat with the group around the table late that night, all eyes turned toward Karen.

"How did your Personality Profile score come out?" we asked. "That's the first place to look."

"Well, I think I'm Sanguine but I had a lot of Melancholy too."

"You—Melancholy?" the women all scoffed at once.

Karen had all the visual traits of the Sanguine. Even in a casual setting she wore a sequined T-shirt and rhinestone earrings. She had the casual hit-or-miss hairstyle that effervescent Sanguines can get away with. If any of the rest of us tried to carry it off, someone would surely comment, "I see you didn't have time to comb your hair today!" One of the women had already labeled Karen's look as "glittery casual."

We looked at her score: 22 Sanguine and 18 Melancholy. Since none of us are born with direct opposites in our personalities, this combination is always a sign of a distorted self-image: Somewhere along the line something has warped our concept of ourselves. Are you like Karen, not exactly sure who you really are?

The first thing we did was look at those items Karen had checked in the Melancholy column: perfectionist, depressed, moody, sensitive, resentful. How could a Sanguine have all those Melancholy traits? Were there some logical reasons for her depression and sensitivity?

Everyone began to analyze Karen. Those who weren't any better off than she was asked questions and gave words of wisdom. Joy, depressed and rejected herself, felt led to tell Karen she'd always appeared a little phony to her and Choleric Betty told her to get hold of herself and stop whining. Neither of these remarks helped Karen in her search for worth and value. We listened to the comments and then asked, "What were you like as a child?"

"My mother says I was very bad and wouldn't sit still," Karen answered.

"What was your mother's personality?"

"She was Choleric and Melancholy. She ruled with an iron hand and everything had to be perfect. She told me over and over that she didn't know where I had come from." Karen burst into tears at the memory of her mother's comment.

"What about your father?"

"He was a pastor and told me from the time I was little that if I made any noise in church, he'd lose his job and we'd have no place to live and we might starve." Karen cried again at her fear that the welfare of the entire family had depended on her behavior in church.

As we discussed these issues, we could all see Karen as a Sanguine who had put on a Melancholy mask because of legalistic, well-meaning parents who had controlled her fun-loving nature by threats of disaster. They had put undeserved blame on her, had made her feel like an outsider, and had set perfection as the norm in life. Karen, as a Sanguine trying hard to please so she'd be accepted, had worked throughout her childhood to become what her parents so clearly wanted: a perfect child. Unable to do so, she felt she had failed her parents and ultimately was a disappointment to God.

Karen had married a Melancholy man who continued the pattern of perfection and told her frequently, "You don't have a brain in your head." Poor Karen, born to have fun, desperate to be loved and accepted as she was, and yet so discouraged, so tired, so lacking in hope.

We have learned over the years how closely our bodies and our emotions are tied together. When we are not functioning in our real God-given personalities, we put our bodies under physical stress and sooner or later we wear out. Karen had headaches and low energy, especially for a Sanguine. One doctor told her she had the "bored housewife syndrome" and she should get a job. Another gave her mood-elevating drugs (that had the opposite effect). Her pastor told her she had a spiritual problem and needed to study more. This pastor made her feel ashamed of herself just as her pastor father had so successfully done.

Karen's whole life was one of manipulation and guilt-laden response to "perfect people" who wanted her to be like them. None of them understood her personality, and none appreciated her natural bubbly optimistic nature. They turned her strengths into weaknesses and caused her to play a false role that had sapped her energy and wiped out her joy.

Until that weekend Karen had no tools to use to analyze herself and her background, but once she saw her personality split, she found the cause of her low self-worth, her headaches, and her sensitivity. She realized she didn't need to be perfect to please parents she seldom saw anymore. She realized that she had allowed her husband to put her down because she felt she deserved no better.

That night we all prayed for Karen to take off her mask, to realize she was God's special child, and to know that He loved her exactly as He had created her to be. What a smile came over her as she relaxed in the knowledge that she didn't need to strive to become perfect any longer.

She wrote us later to say, "When I told my husband I had been wearing a mask, he said he always thought there was something phony about me. I let him know I was created to be outgoing, optimistic, and fun-loving, and that's what I intended to be from here on. He let me know that's what he liked about me in the first place. Now when I do something dumb, he just shrugs. Even if he does say I'm stupid, I brush it off and move on."

In contrast to Karen's situation, both Bonnie and Jack understand their personalities and function in them. They came to our Personality Plus seminar, and as Bonnie puts it, "Now our life is like a daily soap opera and it's fun to watch it unfold."

Bonnie is a vivacious, delightful Sanguine with a little of the Choleric drive. Her husband Jack is Melancholy with some Phlegmatic. What a perfect combination! Bonnie loves to watch the Miss America Pageant but Jack thinks it is trivial and a waste of time. This year Bonnie decided she didn't want to watch the pageant alone, so she did what the Sanguine finds natural—she decided to have a Miss America party. She set up TV snack trays like desks for the guests, provided score sheets, scratch paper and pens, and added calculators for the Melancholies. Bonnie made the whole group listen to the rules when they were given to the judges on TV and they all agreed to abide by them. The Sanguines casually chose candidates that appealed to them. They played their hunches and did it in a most unscientific fashion. The rest of the time they had fun talking, annoying the Melancholies who were deep into statistical analysis.

Bonnie saw that Jack was making neat little boxes on his score sheet using the TV remote control as a ruler. Each person was given ten pages to write on to cover all the categories. This quantity wasn't enough for some Sanguines, but Jack got his total works onto one page in tiny print. He calculated his selections down to the nearest tenth of a point and decided that if you were forced into watching something as trivial as the Miss America pageant, this Melancholy manner was the only way to make the whole thing meaningful. He came up with his top five finalists and was almost excited over his professional, systematic selections.

When the winners were announced, Jack had only one in the top five, and much to his amazement Bonnie, in her hit-or-miss Sanguine way, had three. While the others celebrated their correct choices, Jack sat in deep analysis trying to figure out where his statistics had gone wrong and how he could do it better next year.

Think about your situation for a minute. Are you and your family functioning in your real personalities? Are you having fun together as you observe your differences? Or are some of you not quite sure who you really are? Ask yourself the following questions.

1. What kind of masks are there?

2. When do people start wearing masks?

3. What caused you to cover up your birth personality?

This test and the discussion following it may help you discover if you are wearing a mask—and why.

ARE YOU WEARING A MASK?

	Yes	No
1. Did you have trouble taking the Personality Profile Test?	——	——
2. Were you uncertain on many of the words and not sure which one to choose?	——	——
3. Did you feel you needed someone else's opinion to help you decide?	——	——
4. Do you lack assurance that the way your scores came out is the real you?	——	——
5. Do you come out differently each time you do the profile test?	——	——
6. Do you feel confused as to who you really are?	——	——
7. Have you been insecure about your self worth for as long as you can remember?	——	——
8. Do you think you were one person as a child and someone different as an adult?	——	——
9. Do you sometimes wonder if people can see through you?	——	——
10. Do you often wish you were someone else?	——	——

If you came out with three or more in the yes column, you may be wearing a mask. This is not your fault! We don't put on a mask on purpose. We don't say to ourselves, *I think I'll become a phony.* No, we put one on to survive some set of circumstances and after a while we're not sure which one is real. Life seems to become a staged tragedy.

In his play, *Hamlet,* Shakespeare said, "This above all—to thine own self be true; ... thou canst not then be false to any man."

If you think you are wearing a mask, go through the following list to see if you can identify the mask you are wearing.

TYPES OF MASKS

Sanguine

Mask of Popularity and Humor
Put on by anyone not a Sanguine in hopes of becoming the life of the party. These people want to be popular and use attempted humor to cover up pain. *If only we could all be happy...,* they say to themselves. Sometimes parents demand that non-Sanguines be cute and adorable to show off for their friends. They then put on the Sanguine mask and try to be funny.

Melancholy

Mask of Perfection and Pain
Put on by non-Melancholies who perceive that perfection is the only standard in their families, or who learn through being domineered or abused that life is painful. *If only I could be perfect...,* these people say to themselves. "Survivors may be successful on the external level," said therapist Linda Schiller, describing these mask-wearers. "It's called 'defensive competence.' They try to be perfect to keep their lives as intact as possible on the outside, but at great inner cost."

Choleric

Mask of Power and Control
Put on by anyone not a Choleric who is moved into a position where he or she has to take control, perhaps because of an absent parent or a high degree

of dysfunction. *Somebody's got to take charge here...,* this person thinks. He or she wins the position by default.

Phlegmatic	**Mask of Peace and Submission** Put on by anyone not a Phlegmatic who realizes that trying to offer an opinion or take charge is futile. His or her attitude is, Just keep your mouth shut, agree with them, and learn not to care. These people say to themselves, *If I can just stay out of trouble....* This mask is frequently worn by suppressed Cholerics who have learned to pull back and not make waves.

CAUSES OF MASKING

Now that you have identified the mask you may be wearing, you need to ask yourself, *Why? What has caused me to disguise my natural personality?* We have identified ten causes of masking.

1. A Domineering Parent

A parent who constantly requires the child to conform to the personality he or she wants the child to have forces the child to wear a mask. A Melancholy parent, for example, tries to make a spontaneous Sanguine child into a meticulously neat Melancholy. A highly motivated Choleric parent tries to make his low-key placid Phlegmatic child into a dynamic super-achiever, or in Karen's situation, a religious parent insisted on having a perfect child and made her wear a Melancholy mask.

Another example is Monica, whose Choleric father put a Choleric mask on her. Monica grew up in a broken home and was left living with her father, who was confined to a wheelchair. Her brother and sister, who were older than she was, were free to come and go as they wished, but Monica's whole purpose in life was to please her father and make him happy.

"From the time I was seven years old I was given the responsibility to be Daddy's girl, to be smart, to be good, to run and clean a four-bedroom house, to be everything my brother and sister would never be," Monica told us. "By the time I was thirteen I was confused about my identity and wanted some fun in life. For five years I was involved with boys and was using and selling drugs. As I look back I see I was a Phlegmatic wearing the Choleric mask of hard work. I became compulsive in trying to please my father. From that it was easy to shift compulsions and get into drugs." Monica is now a believing Christian and she is in the process of removing the Choleric mask put upon her as a child.

It is not easy to relax from compulsive workaholic behavior without being gripped by guilt and constantly thinking, *I can't sit here. I should be doing something!* But when you see this as a solvable problem and don't need acclaim for your works as your measure of self-worth, you can lay down the mask and become real.

If you had a domineering parent (stepparent, foster parent, or grandparent), put a check here __.

2. A Domineering and Controlling Spouse

This type of spouse can have a similar effect as a domineering parent in childhood. For example, a strong Melancholy/Choleric husband may try to change a Sanguine wife into his concept of what his wife should be. After a period of such control she may perceive herself to be Melancholy/Phlegmatic, when in fact her misconception is nothing more than a mask to cope or survive in the marriage.

Often the domineering influence in childhood carries over into marriage because those who were victimized in any way tend to marry a victimizer. Karen, the blonde singer, had well-meaning parents who didn't realize their control was obliterating their child's natural personality. Although well-educated, her parents had no knowledge of the basic personalities and they thought working on this child constantly to make her perfect was the right and godly thing to do. They liked Karen's husband because he was a moral person and they felt his pressure on Karen was necessary to keep their "wild and flighty" daughter on the "straight and narrow." Poor Karen didn't have a chance to take off her mask with all these perfectionists directing her.

How about you? If you are making over someone to suit your desires, realize the devastation you may be causing and let them relax. Put a check here if you are the one being domineered, nitpicked, or made over: ___.

3. An Alcoholic Parent

A child who has an alcoholic parent feels unnatural pressures to perform or contribute to the household, often assuming parental roles not natural for the child or his or her God-given birth personality.

Frequently children growing up in an alcoholic or drug-dependent home feel responsible for the chaos around them. Even when they don't understand what's happening, they sense that if they were different in some way the problems would cease. (The results vary according to the particular situation, the age of the child, and the child's position in the birth order.) For example the Sanguine child may perceive, *If only I could be perfect Daddy wouldn't abuse me.* This child puts on the Melancholy mask of perfection and begins a lifetime of playing an unnatural role that may end in a series of psychosomatic ailments.

As the Sanguine struggles to be perfect, the Melancholy may feel that what the family needs is a light touch: *How can I make them all happy? I'll try to be cute and say funny things. Will that make Mommy smile?* On goes the Sanguine mask.

The Choleric may try to take charge and find his or her efforts are shot down every time. After a while this person gives up, believing, *If they want to live in disaster I'll let 'em. I'll just take care of my own life and offer no opinions.* He or she shuts down, puts on the Phlegmatic mask, and pretends not to care. The Choleric sublimated at home is open to exerting any kind of domination or power outside. He or she would be the natural candidate to lead a street gang.

The Phlegmatic whose tendency is to stay out of trouble and look the other way may find himself in such turmoil that he has no

choice but to step in and take charge. When little sister is screaming, he finally feeds her. When mother passes out, he covers her.
When Dad is beating up Mom, he stands between them. When
Dad is gone (off on a drunk, in jail, living with another woman,
divorced, or dead) he is told, "You are now the man of the house."
He pulls himself up and forces himself to be in charge. This
unnatural demand on his emotional resources splits his personality,
and he puts on a Choleric mask.

In any dysfunctional family there will be enough masked people
to stage a costume ball. Even though you may think you grew up in
a "normal family," if you had even one alcoholic or drug-dependent
parent, check here: __.

4. *A Legalistic Religious Household*

In this type of family, everyone is expected to be a spiritual giant,
living up to the letter of the law. Amazingly enough, great saints of
the faith (Christians who would be in shock over the sight of a glass
of champagne or a pack of cigarettes in a friend's home and who
have not had a lustful thought in a lifetime of dull Sundays) can still
produce a religiously dysfunctional home. In this setting children
are so sanctified and sterilized that no natural personality, no matter
what it may have started out to be, can ever come to any natural
maturity.

Sanguines are totally unacceptable in this home, and their humor
is considered a tragic weakness that must be confessed and eliminated. Cholerics who offer opinions slightly left of doctrinal extremes are in deep trouble, too, and they soon learn to feign piety
until that great day in the future when they can run away. No matter
what they started out to be, all the children in this family are likely
to become passive and perfectionistic. They put on Phlegmatic and
Melancholy masks for survival.

If you grew up in a legalistic home, check here: __.

5. Strong Feelings of Rejection in Childhood

A child can grow up in a home with highly educated parents, with a private, well-decorated bedroom, and with plenty of money and still feel rejected by one or both parents.

Often parents are so busy earning money that they have little eye-to-eye contact with their children. They perceive that the giving of money and gifts satisfies the children's need for love. These parents mean well but the things of the world take precedence over reading "Little Red Riding Hood" or cutting out paper dolls or gluing together a model airplane. These children know that Mommy and Daddy must love them but somehow they don't feel loved. Children from dysfunctional homes frequently feel rejected by at least one parent. Sometimes the other parent overprotects the child or depends on that child for his or her happiness. All children who are abused in any form also have feelings of rejection. They tell themselves, *If I'd been a decent person, they wouldn't have done this to me.*

If you ever felt rejected as a child, check here: ___.

6. Feelings of Rejection as an Adult

Adults suffer feelings of rejection due to loss of a job, friends, mate, or children. Other causes include put-downs, feelings of exclusion, and inferences of stupidity.

People who are rejected as children tend to feel that way as adults. No one seems to like them; people ignore them at work or church, and they don't feel attractive or well-dressed. Their insecurity causes them to test people's love, and after a while those being tested do what is most feared: They reject them.

For instance, parents may have a desperate need for their children to need them. When the children show any independence, the parents may sink into rejection. Or a wife may be suspicious of her husband's fidelity and keep checking on him and following him around. One day she spots him with another woman, assumes the worst, and knows he has rejected her. We know one woman,

Cheryl, who was still living in the pain from her Sanguine sister's flip comment when the sister introduced Cheryl to her new boy-friend years ago, saying, "Cheryl is really a great person once you get beyond her face." Every time Cheryl looked in the mirror that condemnation flashed across her forehead like a neon sign.

If you have felt rejected or left out by anyone as an adult, check here: __.

7. A Single-Parent Home

A child reared in a single-parent home, especially a first-born, may often be required to fulfill some of the roles of the absent parent. When these functions are not consistent with the child's natural personality, he or she is apt to put on a mask, which he or she generally continues to wear in adult life.

The best single parent in the world cannot be two parents. This statement does not condemn single parents but merely explains why children growing up with one parent tend to wear a mask over their pain. If they are moved back and forth between parents in a divorce situation their feelings of rejection are renewed each week. The confusion will be even greater if one parent has one set of standards that is drastically different from the other's. The child is forced to put on a mask with at least one of them, if not both.

If you grew up in a single-parent home, even an exceptional one, check here: __.

8. Any Form of Verbal, Emotional, or Physical Abuse

One of the surest ways to put a mask on a child is to abuse him or her with harsh and critical words, with implied feelings of worthlessness, or with severe physical abuse that far exceeds what the infraction deserves. Many parents who consider themselves to be loving disciplinarians are in fact taking out their own insecurities and anger on their children. Many have such a high anger level from their own abuse that they quickly lash out at the first child who makes a wrong move.

Sometimes people feel if they weren't hurt in a physical way, no harm was done; however, when a child is ridiculed or pointed out as a bad person, especially in front of friends, this can have lifelong effects of emotional devastation. Sanguine Susan told us her father never took her or her sisters anywhere, thus causing them to feel rejected. One day he surprised her and took them to the lake swimming:

"I was so happy that my daddy wanted to take us somewhere to have a good time and be with *us* for a change!" she told us. "Daddy had a bar of soap. I asked him what he was doing. He said, 'I'm taking a bath in the lake. Do you want to wash off too?'

"I thought, *This is neat! I'm taking a bath in the lake. This is a lot more fun than being in an old bathtub!* As I reached down to wash my legs under the water, the bar of soap slipped through my fingers. Daddy said, 'Where's the soap?'

"I replied, 'I accidentally dropped it.'

"He retorted, 'You better find it.' I felt around the bottom of the lake, frantically searching for the lost bar of soap.

"After a few minutes, my father announced to everyone that it was time to go. We all got out of the lake, dried off, and got into the car. Daddy then appeared from out of the bushes with a switch in his hand. He ordered me out of the car and switched my bare legs because he said I had 'carelessly lost the bar of soap.'"

Susan remembers this incident clearly today. At another time she made the mistake of laughing loudly when her father was taking a rest after golfing all day.

"Daddy called me into his bedroom," she recalled. "He folded a newspaper in half and placed it on the floor beside his bed. He told me since I had not heeded his warning about being quiet so he could rest, I could stand on the newspaper until he finished his nap. He said, 'If you make a noise, I'll get up out of this bed and whip you!' So like a dog in obedience school, I stood still and quiet (hoping I wouldn't have to cough) for forty-five minutes while Daddy napped."

Both of these tales of uncalled-for punishment are examples of emotional abuse. The results of this type of abuse do not disappear when the child grows up and leaves home; unfortunately they usually are passed down to the next generation. By then the individual has so masked the abuse that the adult child doesn't realize what he or she is doing. Statistics show that those who were abused as children are more likely to abuse as adults. Those who grew up in alcoholic homes are more apt to become alcoholics or to marry them.

As you think about this area of abuse ask yourself if this applies to you. If you grew up with at least one adult who used vulgar or insulting language, who put down your talent and emotions, or who punished you severely, check here: ___.

9. Childhood Sexual Interference

Sexual interference is any form of touching the child in a sexual way or having the child touch the adult in an inappropriate manner.

Either type of violation is inevitably a cause of masking, particularly when perpetrated by a parent or a person playing the parental role. The child subconsciously rationalizes, *Maybe if I would just be good enough, he would leave me alone.* This is especially true when the knowledge of these childhood experiences has been completely suppressed and is unknown in adult life. This is frequently seen in a person with a high score in Melancholy weaknesses without a comparable number of Melancholy strengths, or in a person with a high number of Sanguine strengths without balancing Sanguine weaknesses.

Caryn is an example of a Sanguine/Choleric child who was a victim of incest and who put on a Melancholy mask of pain. From a happy toddler Caryn turned into a depressed and withdrawn child who hated her own body.

One of the ways Caryn manifested her mask was in her clothing, even though she didn't realize this herself. She wore dark, conservative dresses that somehow didn't look right on her. When she came to a CLASS (Christian Leaders and Speakers Seminar) seminar and heard the lesson on how to dress, she suddenly realized her choice of clothing did not represent how she really felt about herself. Way down inside was a Sanguine waiting to get out. When she approached us about removing her Melancholy mask, she said she hated her clothes. We told her it was not the clothes but herself that she didn't like. Caryn thought about it and said, "You're right. I don't like myself or my clothes, but I see now that I don't have to live this way any longer. I've always been jealous of the way Sanguines dressed, not realizing that I was a closet Sanguine."

Caryn explained to us that she had been praying specifically that the Lord would restore her to what He originally planned for her to be, but she hadn't realized she was wearing a Melancholy mask. As we looked at her she changed. Her eyes began to twinkle, she stood up tall, and she giggled, "I'm going to be *me*!"

The next day when she came into CLASS she handed us a note that said:

> I went shopping last night and for *the very first time* (I'm not exaggerating!) I chose clothes that fit a Sanguine—and I had fun! And I did it all myself except for some help from a cute saleswoman choosing a blouse. She kept encouraging me, saying, "Go girl, go girl!" I even chose "hang down" earrings! Another first for me! I bought a skirt *above my knees*—another first!
>
> This morning my seven-year-old said, "Mom you look so cute. I thought you didn't like hang down earrings!" My Phlegmatic husband laughed (out of pleasure) and said, "I like the new you." I said "Tell me I did a good job picking out these things!"
>
> Previously I would have felt "dressed up" and even fake or not myself. But when the Lord works on the *inside*, the work is whole and complete.
>
> I'm sure you've both "heard it all" in the many years you've done CLASS, but I wanted you to know that the small things you teach may seem at times insignificant, but they are life changing.
>
> P.S. Florence, if you look for me, I'm the one with the adorable outfit, dangly earrings, hair up, extra makeup, shoulders back, head up, and a huge smile on my face. But then again, maybe I just blend right in with all the other Sanguines!

What a difference a day makes when you throw off your mask and become real!

Caryn knew what had happened to her, but the majority of victims have blocked out the abuse. Just because there is no recollection of the incident does not eliminate the symptoms.

The first time bright and bubbly Christine took the Personality Profile Test she came out Melancholy. There was such a contrast between her score and her looks that we were sure she was wearing a mask. Since she wanted to find out who she really was, we suggested she read our book *Freeing Your Mind from Memories That Bind*. As she worked through the questions, she felt there was abuse in her childhood and she asked to meet with Fred in the office. After a few minutes Fred said, "Christine, you are not Melancholy. You are Sanguine." Later she wrote about that moment: "As soon as he spoke those words I felt a warmth in my chest, and involuntary tears streamed down my face. For the first time in thirty years I felt free. A great weight/burden was lifted and the charade that I had been living unaware was over."

She told us, "I know now that I was born Sanguine but I have been masking Melancholy nearly all my life. I've tried to earn favor by being perfect—so organized, so analytical."

She continued her search for wholeness, prayed for her suppressed memories, and spent time with a counselor who understood the pain of childhood sexual abuse. By her own study, the removing of her mask, and her memory retrieval prayer (see Part 4 of this book), Christine is a new person today, a true Sanguine who knows and enjoys who she really is.

We will discuss this issue more fully after the Survey of Emotions and Experiences in Chapter 11. For the moment, however, if you know you were sexually interfered with or you feel you might have been, check here __.

10. Abuse Received as an Adult

This may be any type of abuse—verbal, emotional, physical, or sexual—received after the age of eighteen. If you felt hurt and ashamed when it happened, it was abuse.

Many of us hope to get married and live happily ever after, but this dream often fails to come true. Instead of finding someone who will spend the rest of his or her life meeting your needs, complimenting you daily, and loving you unconditionally, some of you may have experienced abuse from the person you married. Perhaps you denied it was really abuse. "He doesn't really mean what he says." "She doesn't realize how her comments hurt." "Don't all men treat their wives like this?" Perhaps when you had bruises on your body you lied and said you fell down the stairs. When you are denying and even lying you are putting on a mask of survival to fool yourself as well as others.

In our experience we have never found a person who accepted adult abuse for any period of time that had not been abused in a similar way as a child. Emotionally stable people will not allow themselves to be victimized more than one or two times before taking action. The person who was abused as a child usually will not go for help until the seventh major attack, according to reports from spouse abuse centers. If you have been victimized in any way as an adult, check here: __.

Go back now and look at the checks you have made. Can you see clearly where your confusion about your personality came from? By doing so you may save yourself months of counseling and expense because this is what has caused your low self-worth and other emotional problems.

If you completed this discussion of the causes of masking without checking any statements, chances are that you are clear about your identity. If you checked statements at the end of reasons 1 and 2, your problems come from being domineered by others who have made you insecure about yourself. Numbers 3 and 4 refer back to dysfunctional families. Numbers 5 and 6 deal with rejection (as all of them do in a way). Number 7 represents the single-parent home. Numbers 8, 9, and 10 alert you to the fact that you are suffering today because of some type of abuse. As you continue reading, testing, and searching, you may be able to diagnose your own problems.

IS THERE ANY HOPE?

Heather and her husband attended a leadership weekend where we spoke about the personalities, and they bought several of our books. When Heather took the Personality Profile Test she came out Melancholy/Sanguine. The score seemed normal to her as she fluctuated between wanting to have fun and disciplining herself to be perfect. As she read *Freeing Your Mind* she saw that the Melancholy/Sanguine combination often meant there had been some sexual abuse in childhood. As she prayed for recall the Lord showed her that her brother had molested her and that a date had tried to rape her. Everything to do with sex had been considered nasty in her home and Heather was not allowed to talk about any of the abuses that had happened to her. She was threatened that if she told, she'd be abused more severely.

As Heather analyzed her childhood situation she saw that her brother had been beaten each time he misbehaved and that he had no memories before he was twelve, indicating that he was probably sexually abused as well. Her sister was at least verbally abused and was called "everything that meant stupid or ugly."

Heather didn't want to be beaten or called stupid so she put on a Melancholy mask of perfection. Her Sanguine nature shut down; life was no fun. Her Choleric desires were wiped out; there was no chance of control here. Instead she put on a Melancholy mask for her own survival. "I became a perfect girl, a perfect student. I had a perfect room so I would please my parents and get love from them."

When Heather took the Personality Profile two years after her initial testing she came out evenly divided between Sanguine and Choleric. Her true personality had emerged at the age of twenty-nine. What a shame that Heather went so many years without any tool to help her uncover and deal with her abuse so she could function in her real personality. Heather concludes:

"Now that I understand some of the side effects of childhood abuse, I realize my mother was likely abused in some way. The pattern repeats itself; however, I see that God is giving me the opportunity to break the pattern before He blesses my husband and me with children. The *last* thing I would want to happen to my children is for them to have some of the burdens I had. Another task that remains to break the pattern is to discuss this all with my brother. He has two children and I don't want him to hurt them.

The memory of being beaten black and blue as a child still must be with him. I ask God to give me the courage to talk with him."

As you can see from Heather's experiences, there is hope. You can take off your mask. We suggest that you prayerfully consider whether any of these problems have been manifest in your life, so you can get a life without the strife.

PART TWO

---◆---

A Problem in the Present

2

What Are My Emotional Needs?

Each one of us is born with a personality that determines our desires, goals, and social skills and also our emotional needs, our causes of depression, and our energy levels. By taking the evaluations in this chapter you will achieve two things: You will verify your personality and you will assess your own emotional needs. We all know we have some, but we don't seem to put our finger on what they are or even understand why we get upset over things that don't bother others.

Check the following statements that sound like you. Some of these ideas may be phrases you have said many times.

PERSONALITY AND EMOTIONS EVALUATION FORM

Emotional Needs

_____ 1. I love attention.

_____ 2. I like people who are sensitive to my needs.

_____ 3. I get edgy if I'm out of control.

_____ 4. I don't function well under stress.

_____ 5. I want someone to lift me up gently when I'm down.

    _____   6. I want loyalty from the troops.

    _____   7. I need a lot of affection.

    _____   8. I have a need to be in charge.

    _____   9. I wish someone would respect me for who I am.

    _____ 10. I want praise when I look good.

    _____ 11. I desire appreciation for my good works.

    _____ 12. I never feel I'm worth much.

    _____ 13. I crave some quiet time alone.

    _____ 14. I do more for others than they do for me.

    _____ 15. I really want some peace and quiet.

    _____ 16. I hope someday I'll be accepted as I am.

    _____ 17. I always look for the most comfortable chair.

    _____ 18. I wish people appreciated art and music as I do.

    _____ 19. I get nervous when my things get messed up.

    _____ 20. I love money and wish I had an endless supply.

DEPRESSION EVALUATION FORM

PART 1

I tend to get depressed when:

    _____   1. Life isn't perfect.

    _____   2. Life is no fun.

    _____   3. Life is out of control.

    _____   4. Life is in chaos.

    _____   5. I have to confront issues and don't want to.

    _____   6. I am sick, helpless, or broke.

    _____   7. I feel my emotional pain is too much.

    _____   8. I see no hope for a brighter future.

DEPRESSION EVALUATION FORM

PART 2

When I get depressed I tend to:

_____   1. Withdraw from people.

_____   2. Tune out and build a wall around myself.

_____   3. Work harder than ever.

_____   4. Go shopping.

_____   5. Read, study, or meditate.

_____   6. Exercise even more.

_____   7. Party with friends and try to forget.

_____   8. Take to my bed and hide away.

_____   9. Stay away from things I can't control.

_____   10. Eat to cheer myself up.

_____   11. Turn on the TV.

_____   12. Eat, sleep, and ignore others.

ENERGY-LEVEL EVALUATION FORM

_____   1. I get energized by people who like me.

_____   2. I have just enough energy to make it through the day.

_____   3. I'd take a nap each day if I could.

_____   4. I run around all the time.

_____   5. I get excited over people who agree with me.

_____   6. I achieve more than most people.

_____   7. I get drained by people.

_____   8. I hardly ever need rest.

_____   9. I seem to need more rest than others.

_____   10. Sometimes I just crash.

_____   11. I have the highest energy level of all my friends.

_____ 12. I get tired at normal times.

_____ 13. I go from laughter to tears in a second.

_____ 14. I really need some quiet time to myself.

_____ 15. I like to go to my room and listen to classical music.

_____ 16. I really don't feel energy is my strength.

_____ 17. Some people call me frenetic.

_____ 18. I get exhausted watching energetic people.

_____ 19. If I'm with noisy people too long I have to leave.

_____ 20. I could keep going forever.

After you have completed the Emotional Needs, Depression, and Energy-Level evaluation forms, put a circle around each number on the scoring form that corresponds to what you checked on the evaluation forms. (Note that the numbers are scattered around the scoring forms under the different personality headings.) For example, if you checked numbers 1 and 3 on the Emotional Needs Evaluation Form, you would circle the number 1 (under Popular-Sanguine) and number 3 (under Powerful-Choleric) on the Emotional Needs Scoring Form. Count the number of circles under each personality heading and write that number in the Total column. When you have completed the scoring forms, we will direct you to add the personality totals from all three forms to reveal your dominant emotional personality.

EMOTIONAL NEEDS SCORING FORM

	Total Responses
Popular Sanguine Personality 1, 7, 10, 16, 20	_____
Powerful Choleric Personality 3, 6, 8, 11, 14	_____
Perfect Melancholy Personality 2, 5, 13, 18, 19	_____
Peaceful Phlegmatic Personality 4, 9, 12, 15, 17	_____

DEPRESSION SCORING FORM

PART 1

	Total Responses
Popular Sanguine Personality 2, 8	_____
Powerful Choleric Personality 3, 6	_____
Perfect Melancholy Personality 1, 7	_____
Peaceful Phlegmatic Personality 4, 5	_____

DEPRESSION SCORING FORM

PART 2

	Total Responses
Popular Sanguine Personality 4, 7, 10	_____
Powerful Choleric Personality 3, 6, 9	_____
Perfect Melancholy Personality 1, 5, 8	_____
Peaceful Phlegmatic Personality 2, 11, 12	_____

ENERGY-LEVEL SCORING FORM

	Total Responses
Popular Sanguine Personality 1, 4, 10, 13, 17	_____
Powerful Choleric Personality 5, 6, 8, 11, 20	_____

Perfect Melancholy Personality
2, 12, 14, 15, 19 _____

Peaceful Phlegmatic Personality
3, 7, 9, 16, 18 _____

Now add the totals for the different personality types from all three scoring forms:

Total Sanguine _____

Total Choleric _____

Total Melancholy _____

Total Phlegmatic _____

What have you learned from this exercise? First, you probably have found you have emotional needs that are not often met. Second, you've probably seen that most of them fall along the lines of your predominant personality. If you come out with your needs, depressions, and energies scattered over all the personalities, you might assume that your emotions are so consuming you that they overwhelm your birth personality. If you have more than ten checks on any one list, you will need to pay special attention to the chapter on rejection and probably the one on childhood emotional issues as well.

Normal scoring would be ten checks on one personality on one evaluation form or ten checks divided between two personalities on one form (such as ten Sanguines, or seven Sanguines with three Cholerics). You may also gain insight from the Emotional Needs and Fears table, which shows other needs—as well as typical methods of control and fears—that are commonly associated with personality types.

Emotional Needs and Fears

		Sexual Desires	Reasons Given for Supposed Need for Drugs or Alcohol	Method of Control	Fear
P O P U L A R	**S A N G U I N E**	So desperate for love and excitement, may find it in the wrong place	Looking for fun Needs boost to be life of the party Wants mood elevated	Controls by charm and wit "You'll just love what I have in mind."	Being alone and unpopular Getting old and lonely Running out of money
P E R F E C T	**M E L A N C H O L Y**	Longs for deep meaningful relationship Likes romance, candles, and music	Tends to be closet drinker Wants to blot out imperfections and failures Wants creativity lifted	Controls by moods "I'll probably get depressed if . " "Oh, not that again."	Making a mistake Having to compromise standards Being a failure
P O W E R F U L	**C H O L E R I C**	Likes the chase and conquest more than commitment Needs to be in control of relationship	When control is slipping and he or she needs a boost of nerve When he or she wants to feel strong and in control again	Controls by threat of anger "You remember what happened the last time you did that!"	Losing control Being sick Becoming weak
P E A C E F U L	**P H L E G M A T I C**	Wants someone who makes him or her feel worthwhile and won't ridicule, one who doesn't demand too much action	Needs to blot out reality and conflict, blur the problems Wants power to tell off bossy people	Controls by procrastination "If I wait long enough, someone else will do it."	Being pressured Being left holding the bag Facing conflict

What a blessing it is for us to see our own emotional needs clearly in front of us. Even when some of those needs can cause trouble it is to our advantage to be aware of those tendencies. So few people can articulate what it is they're looking for to be happy. Once we see our needs, we can do several things about them.

• We can share these needs with those close to us so they can know what we're after.

A Phlegmatic man told us with enthusiasm, "My choleric wife came home from your seminar and told me she needed me to appreciate all of her great work around the house and to let her know I was on her side. I'd been wondering what was wrong with her and why she was slamming things around. Once she had told me, it was simple. Now I make sure I praise her progress, and if I hear her getting upset I volunteer to help since she is so overworked. She usually doesn't let me help, but it cheers her right up when I offer. If I'd known how little it would take to keep her happy, I'd have been praising her before, instead of taking her for granted. Keep telling people how to share their needs with their mates. We'd be willing to meet them if we only knew what they were."

• We can bring our needs to the Lord Jesus in written prayer.

We can put these needs on paper and let the Lord know these are gaps in our emotional health. We can ask Him to fill these voids with His love and give us the maturity to accept our situation as it is. The peace the Lord will give us when we ask specifically is amazing, but few of us sincerely come to Him in prayer, expecting results.

• Go to a counselor or pastor.

If you sense that you need help, explain that you seem to have some emotional problems that stem from your never having your needs met. Let this person know that you didn't understand the nature of your problems before, but now that you see the source you are ready to get down to business.

• You can now see the needs of others and begin to meet them in a way you never understood before.

Instead of groping through life, waiting for others to guess your desires, you can lift their spirits. All you do is estimate their type of personality, remember the emotional needs for the appropriate type, and bless them with appropriate comments such as:

For Sanguines:	"You always look so adorable and you are so much fun. I can't take my eyes off you!"
	"Where do you buy your clothes? They're sensational!"
For Melancholies:	"I've always admired your depth, your talent, and your intellect. I appreciate your quiet strength and the real person of character inside."
For Cholerics:	"I can't believe how much you accomplish in a given day and I am in awe of your ability to take quick action when needed. I'm with you!"
For Phlegmatics:	"You are one of the finest people I've ever met and I respect you deeply. You bring balance to every situation, and while others are all upset you cut through and solve the problem."

We receive many letters after we teach about the emotional needs. "Finally," people say, "we know what to do with these individuals who are nothing like us." One of these notes was from Andrea, who wrote: "I am a Sanguine/Choleric and my mother-in-law is a Melancholy/Phlegmatic. After studying the personalities, I now know why she never commented about the numerous activities I wanted to share with her. . . . They exhausted her!

"I came home with your statement written on my brain, 'Are you willing to meet her needs?' Now that I know her needs, I am writing the question on my heart because I sincerely want to do that. So many times before, when I would go for a visit I was trying to meet *my* needs, and now I'm turning the picture around to meet *her* needs."

Finding out where your problems come from is a giant step on your path to wholeness. It will help you get a new life without the strife.

3

How Do I Communicate?

One of the great barriers to communication is the platitude, "We tried it before and it didn't work." In response to this answer, we decide to just listen, nod our heads, and then go about our business; but sooner or later the strain of suppressing our feelings comes out in nervousness, headaches, or sudden outbursts that surprise and devastate those around us. In this chapter we'll look at some of the communication characteristics of the different personalities, and we'll suggest ways to deal with problems inherent to those traits.

THE SANGUINE

The Popular Sanguine loves to talk but doesn't enjoy listening and often interrupts what the other person is saying. The Sanguine hates bad news and will quickly change the subject and derail the entire sentence before it even gets on track if he or she senses some critical words in the speaker's mind. If a negative thought does leak out, the Sanguine will make a joke of it, leaving the other person, often a serious-minded spouse, in a depression. *There's no point in ever trying to discuss anything of importance,* the spouse thinks. This pattern of behavior is a natural cover-up for the Sanguine's refusal to get involved in problem situations. The Sanguine doesn't mind being thought stupid as long as he or she is smart enough to avoid responsibility and criticism.

The best way to communicate serious truth to the Sanguine is to make an appointment: "Tomorrow night after dinner we need to discuss our overdrawn bank account." The thought of facing stark reality will so frighten the Sanguine that his or her defenses will be down by tomorrow night. (It also gives this person time to return unnecessary purchases and find money left in coat pockets or used as bookmarks in several novels!) Don't allow Sanguines to sidetrack you or make light of the situation. They have short memories, are easily distracted, and hate accountability, but understanding their weaknesses will change a hopelessly frustrating experience into a positive one.

If you are Sanguine, with a desire to have fun and a tendency to run from bad news, realize that it's time to grow up, face the truth, and actually listen to what others have to say. As Fred says, "When you're talking, you're not learning anything. You already know what you're saying." So listen and learn!

THE MELANCHOLY

The Perfect Melancholy is the opposite of the Sanguine. Sanguines talk whether or not they have any great truth to share; Melancholies keep quiet, even when they have the correct answer! Their thoughts are so deep their partners have to reach way down inside and pull them out. Fred used to say, "If you really loved me, you would know what I'm thinking." This statement puts an unfair burden on the other person, who has no clue as to what the Melancholy person is thinking. This game proceeds like a TV talk show:

> Sanguine: What's the matter with you?
> Melancholy: Nothing. (This is always the answer.)
> Sanguine: There is something wrong!
> Melancholy: There is nothing wrong with me.
> Sanguine: Yes, there is! Tell me! You're driving me crazy!

(Sanguines can't stand suspense.)

Melancholy: If I tell you, you'll laugh at me.

Sanguine: No, I won't laugh.

Melancholy: Yes, you will. You always do.

Sanguine: No, I promise I won't laugh. Tell me.

Melancholy: I was hurt when you said I don't have a sense of humor in front of the pastor.

Sanguine: That's the funniest thing I've ever heard. How could you be upset at the truth?

Melancholy: I'll never tell you anything ever again.

Does any of this sound familiar to you? Both parties have to repair this communications breakdown:

• The Sanguine has to listen and not scoff or laugh.

• The Melancholy has to say what's bothering him or her early on without torturing the listener.

• The Sanguine has to apologize for his or her thoughtlessness.

With these parameters in mind, let's replay that conversation:

Sanguine: What's wrong with you?

Melancholy: I was just brooding over the comment you made in front of the pastor.

Sanguine: What did I say?

Melancholy: That I have no sense of humor.

Sanguine: I realized afterward that I shouldn't have said that. I'm really sorry.

Melancholy: Thank you for saying you're sorry.

How much simpler it is when each person communicates clearly and courteously.

THE CHOLERIC

The Powerful Cholerics are the most difficult to communicate with because they are always right. They see little reason to discuss various approaches to the situation when there is obviously only one way to handle this thing: their way. "If you'd just do what I tell you to do, when I tell you to do it, we'd get along just fine." That's true if we are living with a group of robots. Press a button and off they go, preprogrammed to do it your way. But what if a Choleric is living with real people who are intelligent and who feel their way is worth a listen?

If you live under the domain of a Choleric, you might use this approach:

"I'm so glad to live with someone who is always right and who is always fair. Because you are a just person, I want to tell you something, insignificant though it may be, and see what you think about it. I don't want an answer right now. Mull it over and I'll check with you on Monday."

This approach appeals to the Choleric's strength of being right and fair. Not needing an answer now keeps the Choleric from an instant cut-and-dried solution that ends any further communication. Instead, this gives him or her time to process the information and evaluate your opinion.

If you are the Choleric, realize that even though you are usually right you need to allow others to express opinions without making them feel stupid. If you are courageous, you will ask your family, "When I talk to you do you feel I'm putting you down?" Watch the look of panic as they evaluate whether they dare to speak the truth and risk reprisal. Encourage them to talk to you even if you don't feel you need their opinion. Because one of your weaknesses is being too impulsive and acting before thinking things through, you will be doing yourself a favor to let people finish their sentences. Other people will respect you more when you have paid attention to their opinions. It's much better to have people do it your way because they want to, not because you've intimidated them. And remember, it's hard to love someone you're afraid of.

THE PHLEGMATIC

The Peaceful Phlegmatic is the easiest person to get along with because he or she wants to have peace and avoid conflict. Phlegmatics are the best listeners, they don't interrupt, and they have balanced opinions. Things don't have to go their way. These traits are essential in a marriage where the other partner is Choleric! The problem comes when the Choleric has been the sole deciding force in the relationship for so long that the Phlegmatic wouldn't dream of uttering a word. One of two things happens: Either the Phlegmatic feels worthless and retreats into a cavern of silence, or the Choleric says, "What do I need this person for anyway? My spouse hasn't had a decent opinion in years!" Either way this marriage can deteriorate into meaningless phrases like "pass the salt."

To avoid this ultimate boredom the Phlegmatic has to risk giving an opinion, even if it breaks the peace for a few minutes, and the Choleric has to listen and realize that the Phlegmatic might have a credible thought.

If you are the Phlegmatic, realize that if you answer "I don't care" whenever you are asked whether you want coffee or tea, after a while no one will ask. You'll just be handed a cup and told to "Drink it." If you are the one relating to the Peaceful Phlegmatics, push them a little to force them into making a decision and then respect their wishes. If you don't, they will become nothing more than robots.

One other element in dealing with Phlegmatics is to realize they have an underlying will of iron; while they may say "Yes" on the surface they may be saying "That'll be the day" underneath. The Phlegmatics' subtle way of control is procrastination. They think, *If I wait long enough, someone else will do it.* Again the solution takes two. The Choleric has to discuss what should be done instead of giving orders that make the Phlegmatic quietly rebellious, and the Phlegmatic has to move into action instead of postponing the inevitable and angering the Choleric.

Here are some additional quick communications tips for each of the four personalities:

Popular Sanguine:	Learn to listen, don't interrupt, don't laugh everything off. Accept the fact that life is full of strife. Grow up, face reality, and don't expect others to protect you forever.

Perfect Melancholy: Don't take everything personally. Don't make your partner play Twenty Questions to get an answer. Realize life may not be quite as bad as it seems at the moment.

Powerful Choleric: Don't expect everyone to want to do it your way. Don't assume you know everything. Let people offer opinions without cutting them off or putting them down. Don't get angry if others disagree. They might be right.

Peaceful Phlegmatic: Speak up, make decisions, move into action, say what you mean. Don't procrastinate and expect others to do your work. Be willing to take a risk. You probably have the best idea of all.

No matter what your personality is you can now recognize where other people have communication difficulties and help them out. It takes more than one person to have an intelligent two-way conversation. With this in mind, we'll devote the rest of this chapter to communication with the person who is probably closest to you: your spouse.

COMMUNICATION IN MARRIAGE SURVEY

Part 1

How well do you and your partner communicate? Communicating is not just talking. Most couples are able to talk without ever sharing their deepest feelings with each other. They hesitate to express their hurts and their pains and their discouragements because they fear they will either trigger an avalanche of rebuttal or be made to feel stupid. Some partners fear sharing their joys and achievements lest they tap into their mates' feelings of low self-worth and end up feeling guilty that they are happy.

Communication in marriage is the ability or freedom to express feelings, thoughts, or ideas to one another with the confidence that they will be openly received. In a healthy marriage an exchange of positions can be offered without any fear of rejection or retribution.

To see how well you understand each other's feelings and accept the need to share, start by answering the twenty-five questions that follow. The wife should only answer the questions for wives, and the husband the questions for husbands. Fill out your own answers without looking to see how your partner responded.

COMMUNICATION SURVEY: PART 1 FOR WIVES

Remember: Change is inevitable. Growth is intentional.

Directions: Each statement should be scored 0–4 according to this scale:

The statement applies:

         0–Almost never
         1–Seldom
         2–Sometimes
         3–Much of the time
         4–Almost always

1. My husband is generally available to listen to me when I want to talk.   _____

2. I am generally available to listen when my husband wants to talk.   _____

3. My husband is sympathetic and understanding when I want to share some deeper feelings with him.   _____

4. I am sympathetic and understanding when my husband wants to share some deeper feelings with me.   _____

5. My husband does not generally have to weigh his words carefully to keep me from getting angry or upset.   _____

6. I do not generally have to weigh my words carefully to keep my husband from getting angry or upset.   _____

7. My husband and I usually have interesting things to talk about with each other.   _____

8. I am generally satisfied with my husband's
efforts to please me sexually.   _____

9. My husband is generally satisfied with my efforts
to please him sexually.   _____

10. We are generally able to discuss our feelings about
sex quite openly.   _____

11. My husband is my best friend. I feel free to
share my hurts and frustrations with him.   _____

12. I feel free to share my feelings with my husband
even when they don't agree with his.   _____

13. We generally do not interrupt each other.   _____

14. My husband rarely belittles me or puts me down
in front of other people.   _____

15. I rarely belittle my husband or put him down
in front of other people.   _____

16. My husband generally does not criticize or
correct me.   _____

17. I generally do not criticize or correct my
husband.   _____

18. I help my husband feel good about himself,
and I let him know he is valuable and
important to me.   _____

19. My husband helps me to feel good about myself
and lets me know I am valuable and important
to him.   _____

20. We generally discuss family problems and
questions together and then reach decisions on which
we both can agree.   _____

21. My husband understands and respects my desire
for occasional privacy and times to be alone.   _____

22. My husband is generally quick to apologize
when he has offended me.   _____

23. I am generally quick to apologize when I
have offended my husband.   _____

24. We are generally able to discuss our spiritual walk with the Lord with each other. _____

25. I feel I understand fairly well what my husband desires from me emotionally. _____

Total _____

Today's date: _____

COMMUNICATION SURVEY: PART 1 FOR HUSBANDS

Remember: Change is inevitable. Growth is intentional.

Directions: Each statement should be scored 0–4 according to this scale:

The statement applies:
- 0–Almost never
- 1–Seldom
- 2–Sometimes
- 3–Much of the time
- 4–Almost always

1. I am generally available when my wife wants to talk. _____

2. My wife is generally available to listen to me when I want to talk. _____

3. I am sympathetic and understanding when my wife wants to share some deeper feelings with me. _____

4. My wife is sympathetic and understanding when I want to share some deeper feelings with her. _____

5. I do not generally have to weigh my words carefully to keep my wife from getting angry or upset. _____

6. My wife does not generally have to weigh her words carefully to keep me from getting angry or upset. _____

7. My wife and I usually have interesting things to talk about with each other. _____

8. My wife is generally satisfied with my efforts to please her sexually. _____

9. I am generally satisfied with my wife's effort to please me sexually. _____

10. We are generally able to discuss our feelings about sex quite openly. _____

11. My wife is my best friend. I feel free to share my hurts and frustrations with her. _____

12. My wife feels free to share her feelings with me even when they don't agree with mine. _____

13. We generally do not interrupt each other. _____

14. I rarely belittle or put my wife down in front of other people. _____

15. My wife rarely belittles me or puts me down in front of other people. _____

16. I generally do not criticize or correct my wife. _____

17. My wife generally does not criticize or correct me. _____

18. My wife helps me feel good about myself and lets me know I am valuable and important to her. _____

19. I help my wife feel good about herself, and I let her know she is valuable and important to me. _____

20. We generally discuss family problems and questions together and then reach decisions on which we both can agree. _____

21. My wife understands and respects my desire for occasional privacy and times to be alone. _____

22. I am generally quick to apologize when I have offended my wife. _____

23. My wife is generally quick to apologize when she has offended me. _____

24. We are generally able to discuss our spiritual walk with the Lord with each other. _____

25. I feel I understand fairly well what my wife desires from me emotionally. _____

Total _____

Today's date: _____

Instructions: Compare your scores individually on each of the questions you have just answered. If each of your totals equals 100, you understand each other well. Anything less means you have something to talk about! Any difference of two or more points should be discussed as soon as possible. A discussion means listening to what your partner is saying and feeling. There are no rights or wrongs to feelings, therefore *you must allow your partner to express his or her feelings, without interrupting, without correcting, without criticizing, and without disagreeing.* Anything less will stifle meaningful communication.

If you are not able to discuss these statements with each other due to anger, disagreement, or unwillingness you both may benefit from the help of an effective and objective counselor.

Important Note: Before proceeding with your line-by-line discussion, read the following important guidelines from Philippians 2:

Verse 3: "Let nothing be done through selfish ambition . . . but . . . let each esteem others better than himself."

Verse 5: "Let this mind be in you which was also in Christ Jesus [who] . . ."

Verse 7: "Made Himself of no reputation, taking the form of a bondservant."

And read through the following two rules of communication.

THE TWO RULES OF COMMUNICATION

Rule one: You must allow your partner to express his feelings, without interrupting, without correcting, without criticizing, and without disagreeing. Anything less will stifle meaningful communication.

Rule two: Never make "you statements": "You said . . ." or "You glared at me," or "You got angry," or "You made me feel stupid." Instead, make "I feel statements": "I felt hurt," or "I feel I'm not worth anything to you," or "I feel stupid." Everyone has feelings. Some people (such as Fred at one time) have so deeply suppressed their past hurts, they appear to have no emotions at all. They sit stone-faced, responding to nothing. Their natural feelings are dead.

If this sounds familiar be sure to read Chapter 7 on emotions and experiences.

Everyone has a right to have feelings and emotions. Even Jesus had deep feelings; Scripture frequently describes His expressed emotions. (For an interesting study on Jesus' emotions, start with these verses: Matthew 26:37–39, John 11:35 and 38, 12:27, 13:21, and Hebrews 5:7.)

It is neither spiritual nor wise to hide or suppress your real feelings. However, it is also neither wise nor spiritual to dump them on someone else in an explosion of anger or rage. Emotions must be appropriately expressed without bringing pain or hurt to someone else. Going patiently and caringly through the communications exercises in this book and following the two simple rules:

1. No interrupting

2. No "you statements"

will enable each of you to express your feelings appropriately and in a healthy manner.

Virtually every couple struggles with being able to express honest concerns and hurts to each other without erecting block walls that shut off all sharing. You are no different in your marriage relationship. The difference is how soon you *learn*. We struggled for years until we *learned*, first the two basic rules, then how to listen to each other, and then how to "hear" how the other felt. Finally we got to a point where it was safe to express our own feelings without fear of retribution, and we eventually *learned* how to encourage and edify each other (see Eph. 4:29). Now we are actually able to express anything we wish to each other. (We still consider the time and emotions of the moment so we don't dump thoughtless words that will hurt.) After forty years of marriage, we have *learned* how to enjoy each other, how to have fun with each other, how to be in love! One of the most profound steps forward came when we *learned* to communicate.

Paul said in Philippians 4:11, "I have learned in whatever state I am, to be content." Even Paul had to work at it. He had to *learn;*

and it didn't come easily or naturally. Learning to communicate may take a long time, especially if you have spent years establishing unhealthy patterns. Do not expect an overnight miracle, but begin working at it. The habit patterns that were established years ago are not quickly broken. The hurts that have been inflicted over the years are not instantly released and healed. Healing is not an event; it is a process.

The communications survey you completed earlier in this chapter will enable you to discover those areas of your relationship in which walls have been erected. The pages will do the talking, rather than your throwing emotions at each other. A differential of two or more points will clearly show you both that you have very different viewpoints of the same issue. Take time to find out why. Begin by accepting the possibility that some of the differential may be due to the way you have acted, or reacted, in the past. You, as well as your partner, may have been responsible for slamming the door shut and blocking all healthy communication.

Agree together now to reopen that door. Look at each other from a new perspective. Think to yourself, *What have I done to you that has caused you to shut me off? What can I do to make you feel safe in expressing your real feelings to me? Can I also express my innermost needs to you without fear of having the door slammed again in my face?*

This survey is a valuable tool if you will use it. It will help in building your marriage to the level of intimacy God intended for it to be. Now you are ready for Part 2 of the Communication in Marriage Survey.

COMMUNICATION IN MARRIAGE SURVEY

PART 2

Once again there are separate surveys for husbands and for wives. Complete your own list without "spying" on your partner's answers; if you prefer, write your answers on a separate piece of paper.

When you have each finished your pages, being sure you complete all five sections to the best of your ability, make an appointment with your mate. Take time to share with each other what you have written and what you feel. The same two basic rules still apply: Don't interrupt, and don't give "you messages."

COMMUNICATION SURVEY: PART 2 FOR WIVES

A. The two personality weaknesses in my husband that I would most like to see strengthened are:

    1. _____

    2. _____

B. The two personality weaknesses in me that my husband would like to see strengthened are:

    1. _____

    2. _____

C. The three major emotional needs that I want my husband to meet for me are:

    1. _____

    2. _____

    3. _____

D. The three major emotional needs that my husband wants me to meet for him are:

    1. _____

    2. _____

    3. _____

E. Three things in our marriage that I do not feel my husband and I can discuss are:

    1. _____

    2. _____

    3. _____

COMMUNICATION SURVEY: PART 2 FOR HUSBANDS

A. The two personality weaknesses in my wife that I would most like to see strengthened are:

    1. _____

    2. _____

B. The two personality weaknesses in me that my wife would like to see strengthened are:

    1. _____

    2. _____

C. The three major emotional needs that I want my wife to meet for me are:

    1. _____

    2. _____

    3. _____

D. The three major emotional needs that my wife wants me to meet for her are:

    1. _____

    2. _____

    3. _____

E. Three things in our marriage that I do not feel my wife and I can discuss are:

    1. _____

    2. _____

    3. _____

To maintain the progress you have made, resolve now to redo the survey in three months: Right now, set aside a night on your calendar. Protect that date. It's important to both of you. Don't let any other less essential activity steal away your "progress report." You may be thrilled with how much better you are doing, and you will probably see some areas that still need improvement. Redirect your attention and effort on those areas. You will be so glad you did!

CHANGING YOURSELF

When couples seek marriage counseling they must both be willing to listen, change, and resist placing the blame on the other person. We have met with couples after seminars who wanted to prove to us that the fault was the other person's. Occasionally, they try outshouting each other in a desperate attempt to win. When this happens in front of an innocent person who is trying to help, imagine what they are like at home! When each one is trying to win, they both lose.

In his book *Feeling Good: The New Mood Therapy*, Philadelphia psychiatrist David Burns says that frequently in marriage problems one member of the couple is "resistant to change...very angry, perceiving him or herself as a victim and blind to his own role in the problem.... The price of intimacy is giving up anger and hostility."

Although Dr. Burns doesn't say so, we know that without the power of the Holy Spirit in our lives, giving up anger and hostility is difficult. Yet we agree with his statement that we will never achieve intimacy in our marriage relationships until we give up anger and hostility. There is little hope that we can communicate effectively and lovingly when we are angry. Often our hostility comes from childhood issues and is not the fault of our mates. If this idea triggers any related thoughts in you, you will benefit from the additional suggestions described in the chapters of this book focusing on childhood issues.

Remember Betty, the aerobics instructor at the Mount Shasta Women's Retreat? She was the Choleric who knew she could be happy if only she had a different husband. As she told us, "Even the pastor admits Joe is boring." After the retreat we never expected to hear from Betty again, but a letter came expressing how enlightening it was to read *Personality Plus* and find out there were other people like Joe and her.

"Now that I see Joe is a genuine Phlegmatic, a balanced and low-key person, I've started to look at him differently," she wrote. "I didn't realize that two of me might be too much for one marriage. When I told Joe that I found out what kind of personality he had and that it was all right, he almost fell off the couch!

"'I didn't think you felt I had any personality,' he said.

"I told him that I didn't used to think so but I'd begun to realize that different isn't wrong. A big smile came over his face and he's been beaming ever since. He even sent me flowers at the studio and signed the card *Personality Plus!* Can you believe it?"

We *can* believe it because we get letters every day telling how lives have been changed by understanding the personality differences.

We got another letter from Betty later telling us that she and her husband had done the communication surveys. She told us that two months before she would not have even tried to do anything with him where he had to talk.

"Now that I understand my personality, I realize that I never gave Joe a chance," she said. "As soon as he'd start a sentence I'd jump in and finish it. No wonder he didn't say much.

"When I read your first rule on communication and found out that I should let my partner express his feelings without interrupting or correcting, I realized I had *never* done that. I was so impatient to get to my words that I cut his off. He had learned to sit quietly and say nothing. It was easier than trying to buck me. I took it that he had nothing to say and was boring.

"Now that I'm biting my tongue, I've found out he has still got the dry Phlegmatic sense of humor that I loved when we were dating. He's really not all that dull. There may be other women out there like me. Please tell them to encourage their husbands and let them talk. By nighttime some of these men are too tired to fight. Joe is so happy with what the communication surveys taught us that he's giving them out to people at work. (I called your office and ordered some.) He's become somewhat of a counselor on his own. Will miracles never cease!"

Isn't it amazing to see what a simple little exercise can do to change a marriage? The secret is in doing it. So few people will take the time to sit down and exchange ideas in a positive setting. They'll watch TV, go shopping, do aerobics (as Betty did), visit friends, and chauffeur children, but they will not face their marriage issues. They use that old excuse, "We've tried it before and it didn't work."

Take the time to understand your personality and exchange feelings by using the communication survey. Who knows? This could be a major milestone in your marriage.

As Betty said, "I've read a lot of books but I always used them to straighten out other people. Now I'm beginning to work on myself, and Joe is delighted."

PARENT-TEEN COMMUNICATIONS

Our daughter Marita had a teenage friend who dutifully answered her mother's questions with the correct responses, even though they were usually not the truth. One day Marita asked her, "Why do you always lie to your mother?"

The girl answered, "Because she doesn't want to know the truth."

Many parents don't want to know the truth. They would rather be deluded into thinking that all is well. "If my parents knew what was really going on," one boy told us, "they wouldn't let me out of the house." But isn't it better to know what teenagers are thinking than to postpone reality until truth calls us on the phone and shocks us with the facts?

The following communication survey for parents is not to test whether or not your child is on drugs but to find out if you are on the same wavelength with each other. Sometimes Mother may understand Child A and Father, Child B. Or all the children think Mother is tuned in to them and Father doesn't have a clue as to what's going on. If your children feel free to be honest with you without threat of being made to feel wrong or stupid, you may open up a two-way communication you never dreamed possible before.

COMMUNICATION SURVEY FOR PARENTS AND TEENAGERS

This exercise is designed to help you and your teenage children better understand how to communicate with each other. Separate surveys are provided for parents and for the teenagers. Circle the Yes column when the question can be answered as happening most of the time. Circle the No column when the question can be answered as seldom or never. (Suggestion: Fathers might circle in blue, mothers in red.)

COMMUNICATION SURVEY FOR PARENTS

1. Do you wait until your children are through talking before answering them?   Yes   No

2. Does your family do things together?   Yes   No

3. Do you talk things over as a family?   Yes   No

4. Does your child think that you respect his or her opinion?   Child A   Yes   No   Child B   Yes   No

5. Does your child think that you lecture or preach too much?   Child A   Yes   No   Child B   Yes   No

6. Does your child feel free to discuss personal problems with you?   Child A   Yes   No   Child B   Yes   No

7. Do you feel your child is mature enough for his or her years?   Child A   Yes   No   Child B   Yes   No

8. Do you show real interest in the activities and hobbies of your children?   Yes   No

9. Do you feel free to discuss matters of sex with your children?   Yes   No

10. Does your child think you trust him or her?   Child A   Yes   No   Child B   Yes   No

11. Do you make it a point to listen to what your children have to say?   Yes   No

12. Do your children know you have confidence in them?   Yes   No

13. Does your child feel free to   Child A   Yes   No
    disagree with you?   Child B   Yes   No

14. Do your children feel free to make
    requests of you?   Yes   No

15. Do your children feel that you would be
    "for them" in a matter outside the family?   Yes   No

16. Do you discuss things with your children
    before making a decision that affects them?   Yes   No

17. Would your children say you try to make them
    feel better when they are down-in-the-dumps?   Yes   No

18. Do you explain to your children why
    you are making a negative decision?   Yes   No

At the same time you take the parents' survey, ask your teen to complete his or her own survey.

COMMUNICATION SURVEY FOR TEENAGERS

This survey is an exercise designed to help you and your parents better understand how you communicate with each other. There are no right or wrong answers. Circle Yes when you believe this situation happens most of the time. Circle No when the situation seldom or never happens. Circle the answers that relate to your father in the first column and the answers that relate to your mother in the second column.

	Father	Mother
1. Do your parents wait until you are through talking before "having their say"?	Yes No	Yes No
2. Does your family do things together?	Yes No	Yes No
3. Does your family talk things over with each other?	Yes No	Yes No
4. Do your parents seem to respect your opinion?	Yes No	Yes No
5. Do your parents tend to lecture and preach too much?	Yes No	Yes No

6. Do you discuss personal problems
   with either of your parents?   Yes No   Yes No

7. Do your parents tend to talk to you
   as if you were much younger?   Yes No   Yes No

8. Do they show an interest in your
   activities and hobbies?   Yes No   Yes No

9. Do you discuss matters of sex with
   either of your parents?   Yes No   Yes No

10. Do your parents trust you?   Yes No   Yes No

11. Do you find it hard to say what you
    feel at home?   Yes No   Yes No

12. Do your parents have confidence in
    your abilities?   Yes No   Yes No

13. Do you hesitate to disagree with
    either of them?   Yes No   Yes No

14. Do you fail to ask your parents for
    things because you feel they'll deny
    your requests?   Yes No   Yes No

15. Do they really try to see your side
    of things?   Yes No   Yes No

16. Do your parents consider your opinion
    in making decisions that concern you?   Yes No   Yes No

17. Do they try to make you feel better
    when you're down in the dumps?   Yes No   Yes No

18. Do your parents explain their reason
    for not letting you do something?   Yes No   Yes No

Now that you have both filled out your answers, establish a quiet time when you can sit down together and discuss your feelings. Don't do it while your teen's friends are waiting at the door or when you have to run off to choir rehearsal. Provide a pleasant setting and make the meeting a discussion, not an inquisition.

In the twenty years we have been providing these communication surveys for parents and teenagers, we have received amazing feedback. The one major problem is with those people who never quite find the time to do it. Only you can decide what is important in your life and then act on it. Remember the words of our Lord in John 13:17: "If you know these things, blessed are you if you do them."

4

How Can I Check My Maturity?

There's an old saying: "Too soon old and too late smart." It's true that our physical bodies are getting older every day and that we never do know everything we'd like to know. But what about our emotions? Is it possible to be grown up on the outside, mature in our minds, and yet emotionally a child?

One of the biggest problems counselors have is assuming that they are dealing with a mature, responsible adult only to find the person doesn't follow through on instructions and needs to be handled as a first-grader: "If you're a good girl I'll put a gold star on your chart."

Check yes or no to the questions on the maturity index below:

MATURITY INDEX

Check Yes or No after each question:

	Yes	No
1. Do you tend to blame other people when things go wrong?	____	____
2. Do you make excuses for your failures? (I had a headache. It was raining. I shouldn't have even tried to do it.)	____	____

3. Do you prefer to ignore difficulties and
   hope they'll go away on their own?   ____ ____

4. Do you sometimes blame your poor background
   for why you've never fulfilled your
   potential?   ____ ____

5. Do you tell a little white lie if it will
   get you off the hook?   ____ ____

6. Do people sometimes say, "When are you ever
   going to grow up?"   ____ ____

7. Do you avoid responsibility if possible?
   (Let someone else do it.)   ____ ____

8. Do you find it difficult to adjust to new
   situations?   ____ ____

9. Do you wonder if you'll ever get all of
   your life together at one time?   ____ ____

10. Do you often think—or tell others—
    next year will be different, better, a
    success?   ____ ____

11. Are you usually able to talk your way out
    of most anything?   ____ ____

12. Do you feel you never get the breaks you
    deserve?   ____ ____

13. When you're caught at something you
    shouldn't have done is your first thought
    to lie or make excuses?   ____ ____

14. Do you feel if you had a bigger or better
    house you'd be happy?   ____ ____

15. Do you sometimes instruct a child answering
    the phone, "Tell them I'm not home"?   ____ ____

As you checked off this list you probably noticed that all of these questions focused on taking responsibility for your own life and not blaming people or circumstances for your failures. If you checked No to every question and you were telling the truth (immature people tend to lie) you are probably a mature person who has made the best you could out of your circumstances and who can adjust to changes without falling apart or getting hysterical. The more Yes answers you checked the less mature you probably are, and if you have all fifteen answers in the Yes column you quite likely have never grown up emotionally, even if you appear to be an adult.

If you are really immature, you may have already gone back and reread the questions, rationalizing that you were too hard on yourself. Changing some of your answers doesn't change the truth. If you came close to answering all questions Yes, you can see that for some reason you have stayed a little child inside when others around you were growing up.

Children are appealing, with wide-eyed innocent smiles, lack of worry and tension, and freedom from restraints and time pressures. All these qualities are engaging to other people who are under tremendous stress. In the same way, immature people are attractive at first and they can always find friends who will babysit them for a while; but when one person has to do all the work and bear all the responsibility, the relationship wears thin. If you know in your heart that you make excuses and avoid responsibility, then you need to find out why. Why do you run from responsibility? Why do you rationalize failures? Why do you blame other people? Why do you have difficulty in maintaining meaningful relationships?

Perhaps looking at someone else's case history would help you see yourself more honestly.

"My husband is like a little boy driving around in a big man's body!" Nicole, a strikingly attractive woman, told Fred. "He hasn't had a steady job in the twenty years we've been married, and I don't have much hope that he's about to change." Nicole's husband, Tom, was standing across the room and as she pointed him out to Fred, he saw a tall man, movie-star handsome, with a group of women standing around him, hanging on his every word.

"See?" Nicole said. "He's always got women around him. They love him! I used to love him but I'm sick of supporting him. He's like another child."

We made arrangements to meet later after the personality seminar was over. "Watch out for him!" Nicole worried. "He'll con you just the way he's done all the other counselors."

When we got together we found Tom to be a delight. He had twinkling eyes, an adorable smile, and a quick sense of humor. We could see why he attracted women wherever he went. As we sat down he winked at Florence. "I'm really not as bad as she says I am," he declared. "She always gets to the counselors first and turns them against me."

"I just tell them the truth," Nicole stated coldly.

"How many counselors have you been to?" we asked.

They both gave answers simultaneously. She said "Five," while he sighed, "A whole bunch."

"What have you learned from the counseling?" Fred asked.

"They tell him to get a steady job and stop playing around," Nicole replied.

"But they all like me. One even told Nicole (here Tom chuckled) that if she had a husband this good-looking she'd be glad to support him." Tom smiled and winked again, pleased with himself.

"I wouldn't mind so much if he was at least faithful, but he's got some new girlfriend every week," Nicole said. "He's hardly ever home."

"It's no fun to come home," Tom said.

Does this conversation sound familiar? Can you see the pattern? Can you guess their personalities?

In working with this couple we found a typical Sanguine/Phlegmatic immature man married to a Melancholy/Choleric controlling woman. She had come from an alcoholic family with an abusive father and had assumed the role of little mother when she was very young.

Tom had been pampered by his mother, who tried to keep him a baby forever to make up for her lack of love from her husband. She had told him he was "God's gift to women" and had once said, "With your looks you'll never have to go to work. You'll always find some woman to support you."

Doesn't this sound like a marriage made in heaven? Tom needs a woman to take care of him and Nicole needs someone to care for. But somehow it didn't work out right. Nicole got more and more depressed and Tom pulled further away because she was no longer any fun.

When Fred asked what the five counselors had said, Tom and Nicole answered together. The first one told the couple there was sin in their lives and they should go to church more. The second one took Nicole's side and told Tom not to come back until he had a steady job.

"The next two he conned," Nicole reported in disgust. "Tom agreed with everything they said but he didn't change a bit. I was made to look like an ogre."

Tom flashed his winning smile.

The last counselor told them they were the healthiest couple he'd seen in a long time, and then he reviewed some of the really bad cases he was working with and sent them on their way with the words, "Thank God for what you do have and stop looking for trouble."

"He let us know we were wasting his time on minor issues," Nicole said with a sigh, "but I don't think our marriage is a minor issue."

"It's sure the biggest problem I've got," added Tom.

We all could give this couple advice. Tom needs to get a job and stop fooling around, and Nicole needs to be warm and loving so he'll want to come home. In spite of their different memories of the various counselors, each counselor had suggested "behavior modification," but none had helped them to see where their problem had come from in the first place. Until people see why they are reacting a certain way, it is almost impossible for them to shift gears and change their ways.

When Tom went over the Maturity Index he could see he was still a child. This shocked him because he considered himself to be a macho hero. He began to see why he couldn't maintain a mature relationship: He just played childish games with people and only the unstable and emotionally needy stayed around. Mature and secure people saw through him and left. He'd never looked at the fact that most of his friends were, in his term, "basket cases" who were so much worse than he was that he felt like their counselor.

Tom had an office and did some consulting on personnel problems at local factories so he thought he worked, but he had few calls and often didn't bill those he serviced. Much of his time in the office was spent in "counseling" distraught women he'd met at his last account. Barely enough money came in to pay the rent and utilities.

It took us several reviews of this situation to get him to see he was not really working. Instead he was playing. As he conned others, he had also conned himself into thinking he was a personnel consultant who was hoping next year would be better.

"I really hate to think of myself as a child," Tom reflected, "but I guess that's what I am." For the first time Tom took a clear look at himself. He saw that his mother had needed him to need her and had happily supported him financially and emotionally with unrealistic and overstated compliments. He had married his mother all over again and was hurt when Nicole no longer succumbed to his charm.

The necessary changes didn't come overnight but at least Tom and Nicole had found the sources of their individual faulty behavior patterns; they were willing to work on themselves, instead of always seeing the faults in each other. They found a Christian male counselor who didn't fall prey to Tom's charms and who understood women. They went to him with their personality scores and with the results of the Maturity Index in hand.

If you scored poorly on emotional maturity, you can find out where your problems began by looking over the following list and prayerfully reflecting on the possibilities.

ROOTS OF ADULT IMMATURITY

Place a check beside the statements that apply to you.

1. _____ You were the youngest child and everyone thought you were adorable.

2. _____ You had a parent who needed you to need him or her.

3. _____ You had a parent whose own immature behavior made him or her keep you as a child.

4. _____ You were never taught responsibility.

5. _____ When you were told to do things no one ever checked up.

6. _____ You were never taught to manage money.

7. _____ You never learned experientially that all actions bring about consequences.

8. _____ One parent slipped you money when the other wasn't around.

9. _____ You could always con at least one parent and get what you wanted.

10. _____ One parent taught you not to cross the other one.

11. _____ You learned to cover up, or lie, if it would keep you out of trouble.

12. _____ One parent doted on you and the other didn't seem to want you around.

13. _____ The opposite-sex parent made you his or her little confidant.

14. _____ There was some sexual touching that you hadn't considered to be all that bad.

15. _____ You took showers or baths with the opposite-sex parent frequently as a child.

16. _____ You were the "happiness pill" for one parent.

17. _____ You learned if you cried you could get almost anything you wanted.

18. _____ One parent fixed up your problems in school and took your side against the teacher.

19. _____ If you started a job and didn't like it, you learned it was all right to quit.

20. _____ You found you could play one parent against the other to your own benefit.

21. _____ You never liked facing the big world out there without a parent beside you.

22. _____ Your personality is a combination of Sanguine/Phlegmatic: Let's have fun and not worry about the consequences.

23. _____ You expected that you'd get married and live happily ever after.

Now that you are aware of your areas of immaturity and have figured out where they come from, you are halfway there.

Scripture tells us to grow up in Christ, who is our head, and no longer be children. When we don't grow up in Christ we continue to make the same mistakes over and over, we have unfruitful and short-lived relationships, and we never reach our potential.

How do we grow up? First we become aware of our needs as we did in Chapter 3. Then we study Paul's description of a mature Christian in the book of Ephesians. We begin to use these standards as measuring sticks for our lives. We start writing to the Lord about our weaknesses, elaborating on one weakness each day until we run out of them. We stop ourselves each time we make excuses, rationalize, or blame others.

We start taking responsibility for our own mistakes. We see what part of our faulty behavior comes from our parents' treatment of us and we realize they probably did the best they could at the time. We resolve now to take responsibility for our own actions and decisions and not blame our parents. We make a choice to forgive them for what they did. We check to see if we are doing the same things to our children. If we are, we work at changing and apologize for the hurts we've put upon them. We find someone who will keep us accountable and stop us lovingly each time we lie or blame others. And we check ourselves constantly to see if we're making progress.

If some of your reasons for lacking maturity are sexually related, pay special attention to Chapter 11, which focuses on victimization, even if you don't remember any of your childhood experiences. Emotional growth often stops at a moment of abuse and doesn't begin to grow again until the source of the problem is uncovered.

Now that you have examined your personality strengths and weaknesses, assessed your communication skills, and measured your maturity, it's time to look at your home situation. Do you have an immature mate who refuses to consider himself or herself as part of the home problem? Perhaps you need to ask yourself if it's time to confront him or her.

5

Do I Need to Confront My Mate?

Is it possible that you are living in a situation that desperately needs some changes? Some women think that if they are submissive enough their mate will stop abusing them. They don't realize that the victimization has little to do with their behavior and much to do with the abuser's past. Because of his inner turmoil he has a compulsion to take it out on someone else—and that someone happens to be you. It's not a sign of spirituality to accept abuse from your mate. No matter who tells you, "This is your cross to bear," you are not required to be beaten up or verbally abused to get into heaven.

God's plan for marriage is mutual respect and love. If neither of these is in your home right now, perhaps it is time to confront. Don't say, "If you don't shape up I'm out of here." Instead express clearly, "We can't live like this any longer." Consider the questions below in deciding whether you need to confront and if the time for it is now:

ASSESSING THE NEED TO CONFRONT

Check each line to which you would answer Yes.

1. _____ Has your situation become unbearable?

2. _____ Is there a relationship that's out of control?

91

3. ____ When you look ten years down the line does it depress you?

4. ____ Is this relationship one-sided?

Do friends ask:

5. ____ What is the matter with you?

6. ____ When are you going to wake up?

7. ____ Can't you see what he or she is doing to you?

8. ____ Why aren't you fun anymore?

Ask yourself:

9. ____ Do you feel physically ill when trying to deal with a certain person?

10. ____ Do you feel exhausted much of the time?

11. ____ Do you feel as if there is no hope?

12. ____ Has your mate had affairs?

13. ____ Is he or she always looking at or commenting on the opposite sex?

14. ____ Do you feel submission means being a doormat?

15. ____ Are you being verbally or emotionally abused?

16. ____ Does your mate (or children) put you down?

17. ____ Has your mate hit you or threatened you?

18. ____ Are you in a financial bind?

19. ____ Is your mate irresponsible with money?

20. ____ Do you fear being alone or on your own?

21. ____ Do you rationalize, *This is my cross to bear*?

22. ____ Do you soothe yourself with the thought, *Oh well, everyone has problems.*

If you checked five or more statements, you are not happy with your current situation. If you checked ten or more, you need to consider options for future action. If you have checked fifteen or more, you need to confront this person or situation as quickly as possible.

No one has the desire to confront touchy or abusive situations head-on. We would all rather look the other way and hope the problem disappears. Not all marriage problems involve abuse or affairs; some stem from chronic emotional problems or repeat business failures.

Florence remembers, "One of the hardest things I ever had to do was to tell Fred that I could not handle any more financial problems and that I didn't wish to live under the threat of his anger that I felt loomed over me. I knew it would be hard for him to understand since he had always kept us in better-than-average houses and really never exploded or yelled at us. He was always a gentleman and I knew he meant well."

Some of you might ask Florence, "What did you have to complain about?" We understand that your situation may be far worse than Florence's ever was, but she wanted the best marriage possible and she was willing to take a chance.

As Florence did, you may need to examine your own life and your situation. Don't wait until there's no love left between you. Perhaps you and your spouse need to seek counsel. If there is resistance or if he thinks you are the whole problem there may need to be some personal confrontation. We suggest a few guidelines based on what we did.

1. Determine if there is a need to confront. Is the behavior of the individual in question threatening the emotional health of at least one family member? Is any physical abuse occurring? Is there an addiction—drugs, alcohol, gambling, pornography—that shows no signs of stopping? Are there continued business failures or other patterns that are damaging to the family? Is there a fear of blow-ups, temper tantrums, fits of rage?

If any of these types of problems exist now and are getting worse and not better, there may be a need for confrontation. We have talked with women who have been beaten and abused by their husbands who felt that if they were submissive enough their husbands would stop the abuse—tomorrow. In our experience, women who tolerate this treatment in a marriage over a long period of time do so because they were abused as children. They have learned to "take it." Be sure to check your own emotional stability before attempting to confront someone else.

2. Seek the Lord's direction. Do not hastily jump into a confrontation or you may end up defeated. Write to the Lord in daily prayer, asking His guidance in the situation. Make sure you are spiritually ready and divinely inspired. Don't confront just to get your own way.

3. Read at least one book on confrontation. This can better prepare you for what may happen. The victimizer may not agree to what you have in mind, so it's helpful to have studied all the background available to you.

4. Find an independent, outside person. He or she should be someone who is willing to stand with you as a mediator, not an attacker. Explain the situation as objectively as possible and have this individual ready to do the confronting if necessary. This person can be a professional counselor, a pastor, or a friend who is known to be fair by the one being confronted. Florence asked a counselor/friend.

5. Enlist family support. It's almost impossible to implement family change if your family members are not with you. If they all feel you are off balance, you will need some family counseling first. It would be devastating to go into this risky situation only to have the entire family turn against you and support your mate.

6. Develop a plan for possible solutions. Before Florence expressed to Fred that she felt he would benefit from counseling, she had talked with a therapist about the situation and knew when the counselor had a block of time available. Don't go into any confrontation until you have looked into possible solutions and have the phone numbers of professional help in hand. This meeting is not to cause trouble but to lay out a plan for a better future. Be sure to have one!

7. Be willing to hang tough. No confrontation is easy and the person may turn on you and try to browbeat or reason you into changing your mind. He or she has probably already done that many times in spontaneous confrontations you've had in the past. You must be ready and willing to hang tough because if you don't enforce what you agree upon, your mate will never take you seriously again.

8. Be prepared for the worst. You don't want to approach this meeting with a negative attitude, but you must be alert to the possibility that the person might pack up and leave. Consider what is the worst that can happen. Will you be out of money or out on the street? Do you have a Plan B?

9. Set an appropriate time. No time is perfect for a confrontation, but make sure you choose a time when the person to be confronted will be under the least amount of stress and when he or she is not under a time pressure to leave. Florence chose a vacation time where there was no excuse for running off to work.

10. Approach with love. Don't make the confrontation an attack. It is shocking enough for the person to find himself or herself in a position where everyone seems to have suddenly turned against him or her. Continue to say, "We love you. We want the best for you, but we need some changes made." Be willing to modify your own behavior and compromise in minor areas as long as the confronted person is willing to take major steps. Set timetables for changes and hold your mate and yourself accountable to a third person.

Our time of facing reality was not easy, but it was necessary and the changes over these many years have been remarkable. Because we were both willing to adjust and Fred was willing to find the root of his problems, God has blessed our ministry and given us a new depth and understanding. We can both say in unison, "We are more in love today than we have ever been before." We have a new life with a lot less strife!

6

How Can I Know My Children's Personalities?

"The four hours we spent in family discussion after your personality seminar changed our lives." So wrote LouAnn, a pastor's wife from Alabama.

She explained that she and her daughter are Sanguine; her husband, Choleric; and one son, an easygoing Phlegmatic. Another son, Doug, twenty-one, Phi Beta Kappa with a 3.95 average in pre-med, is a brilliant Melancholy. Because the family hadn't understood the personalities they had always looked at Doug as different. "He has walked his own path with great difficulty—always the outsider who was never really in contact with the rest of the family."

Because Doug "didn't fit," they had sent him for counseling—which only confirmed that he wasn't like the others. Ultimately, they all read *Personality Plus* and lights began to go on! When we came to their area to speak about personalities, they all attended, Doug with some reluctance. After they went home that night, they sat up until 3:30 in the morning and talked honestly. For the first time Doug admitted that he didn't want to be a doctor but felt they had programmed him to be one and he didn't want to disappoint them. He shared his newfound perception of each family member's personality and how unhappy he had been over the years because of his family's lack of understanding. As they talked and listened, Doug began to feel that his parents were open to hear what he had to say. His parents had meant well, but without an understanding of personalities they had unknowingly pushed a child into a direction that didn't fit him. Doug is now studying to get his masters in chemical engineering. He has always liked experimenting in a lab and now that he's doing what he enjoys his relationships with the family have improved.

In writing to thank us for the clear teaching on the personalities, LouAnn expresses, "Our motives were pure, but we weep at the fact we did not know the personalities until it was almost too late."

Is it almost too late for your family? Do you have one child who doesn't seem to fit? Do you get along better with one child and your mate with a different one? Do you think all children in a family should be treated the same?

The sooner we can use the knowledge about personalities with our children, the better we will understand their strengths so that we can encourage them individually in the direction that will fit them. Also we will become aware that each child has some weaknesses, and he or she is not "out to get us."

Personality differences that are not understood cause clashes in home and school, according to a study done by Australian psychologist Alan Chittenden. "Very often there is nothing wrong with the child aside from the fact they have a personality which doesn't agree with that of the parent. But if the parent understands their child's personality and how that child sees the world, then they understand why the child does what it does to annoy them. Personality can be influenced by environment at an early age although a lot appears to be hereditary."[1]

WHAT DO WE INHERIT?

Scripture tells us we reproduce after our own kind, and we all know children who look just like their parents—same eye color, same hair texture, same body structure. Yet until the last twenty years few people thought we inherited our personalities as well as our physical characteristics.

The perspective of how and what we inherit changed due to a widely reported study conducted by the University of Minnesota, which analyzed 358 sets of twins adopted at birth and reared apart. Of the 44 sets of identical twins who were brought up in different environments, the experts found they all had extremely similar personalities. Both Pennsylvania State University and Harvard have also published reports on how we inherit our personalities and social behavior. This area of psychological research has been labeled "nature versus nurture," or in simple terms, what we inherit versus what we learn from our circumstances. Conclusions show that we all come into this world with a pattern of temperament traits, including the following characteristics:

Shyness

In his lab at Harvard, Jerome Kagan video-taped hundreds of infants and concluded that the seeds of extreme shyness and caution are already sown at birth and probably lie within the genes. Kagan estimates that 20 percent of middle-class white American children—the only category he has studied—are born temperamentally shy.[2]

Type-A Personality (Choleric) Traits

According to a study done at Boston City Hospital and Clemson University and reported in *Pediatrics* in March 1993, Type-A people are impatient, competitive, hard-driving, and involved (Choleric) while Type-B people are more low key (Phlegmatic). The babies tested and compared to their mothers showed that some personality qualities are inherited. Dr. T. Berry Brazelton, founder of the Child Development Unit at Boston Children's Hospital, said the study "points out that there is a genetic component to temperament."[3]

Difficult Children

"Difficult" children are not spoiled brats, and they aren't out to get their parents. They do have difficult traits, but their behavior is a result of their temperament, which they can't help. Some people are just born with different personalities, and parents can't change a child's basic nature.[4]

After years of assuming that if you moved a hurting child from one environment to a better one you could change his personality and direction, social scientists have changed their minds. In general, they now agree that we inherit our personalities and that environment influences our behavior for bad or good.

Our inheritance also includes other traits, such as weight, behavior patterns, gender, differences, and learning disabilities. Here are a few examples of what has been concluded about these traits in the last ten years.

Fat or Thin

A team from the University of Pennsylvania found that weights of 540 adults, adopted as young children, closely paralleled the weights of their biological parents, not their adopted ones. "Genetic influences have an important role in determining human fatness in adults whereas the family environment alone has no apparent effect," wrote Dr. Albert Stunkard for the *New England Journal of Medicine*.[5]

Behavior Patterns

The concept of temperament was also defined by doctors Alexander Thomas, Stella Chess, and Herbert Birch in their landmark New York University longitudinal study in which they traced 133 people from infancy to young adulthood. They found these individuals had inborn natural behavior patterns that stayed consistent.[6]

Gender Differences

During the seventies, the decade of the feminist revolution, talk of inborn differences of men and women was taboo. But studies since then have shown innate sexual differences. "When I was younger, I believed that 100 percent of sex differences were due to environment," says Jerre Levy, professor of psychology at the University of Chicago. But after twenty years of studying the brain she concludes, "I'm sure there are biologically based differences in our behavior."[7]

Attention Deficit Disorder

New studies by investigators at the National Institute of Mental Health in Bethesda, Maryland, show that hyperactivity is not a psychological problem but rather a specific neurological problem that often is inherited. About 4 percent of all school-age children, and about twice as many boys as girls, have A.D.D.[8]

If we can't change a child's basic nature, what influence do we have upon him or her? Since we have an adopted son, we can explain the difference between his nature versus his nurture from our own personal study. Little Fred was already quiet and serious when we received him at age three months. He lay in his crib and seemed to be quietly analyzing all who passed by. He didn't like loud noises, he seemed shy, and he pulled away from unfamiliar faces. He manifested Melancholy traits right from the beginning, and thirty years later he is consistently deep, thoughtful, organized, and introspective. As adoptive parents, we had no genetic responsibility for his nature. But what about his nurture? What could we give him?

- We could understand his inborn personality and work with it, not against it. In these thirty years, we have nurtured his nature.

- We could influence his early sense of security and give him love.

- We could teach him manners and moral standards.

- We could bring him up in a Christian home and lead him to the Lord at an early age.

- We could help him set goals and choose his occupation.

When we were in Australia we met George, a high-school career counselor. He told us how he began to use the Personality Profile Test to teach his pupils about themselves and then show them career possibilities that fit their natures. George made four columns on the blackboard and titled each one. Then he chose one student of each personality to go to the board and list the strengths and weaknesses of his type. The Melancholy went up first, took one look at the way George had written the title, erased it, and rewrote it more neatly. She numbered each trait and when all the traits wouldn't fit in the space, she erased all the words and rewrote them smaller. She also divided the strengths and weaknesses and labeled them, even though he had not instructed her to do so.

Next the Sanguine got up and began to write in large, dramatic letters with a circle over each *i* instead of a dot. As she saw she was going to run out of room, she kept making the letters smaller. Even then, she couldn't get in all the words so she wrote up the side of the column, giggling all the way. She found room for a heart, which she filled with the initials of her and her boyfriend. As a finishing touch she added a daisy in the corner of her column. She was quite pleased with herself, but the Melancholy was disgusted and let out a noticeable sigh.

Next came a Choleric boy who only wanted to write strengths because none of the weaknesses applied to him. He pressed down so hard on the chalk that it broke in his hand. He wrote in large letters and his words went over the line into the Phlegmatic column. When George mentioned this the boy replied, "I needed the space."

When the Phlegmatic got up she wrote all around the words the Choleric had put in her territory without complaint.

George sent us this example and added, "I hope you can use this material. My wife and I are direct opposites and *Personality Plus* has done more for our marriage than anything else ever!"

HOW CAN WE RECOGNIZE OUR CHILDREN'S PERSONALITIES?

On the following pages we divide the basic attributes of each personality into behavior as a baby, a child, and a teen. Check the traits that apply to each child so that you will have a Personality Profile of each one. (Use different color checks for each child or put initials by each characteristic to identify the specific child.)

SANGUINE
THE POPULAR PERSONALITY

FOR CHILDREN: BRIGHT YELLOW LIKE THE SUN

The Extrovert   **The Talker**   **The Optimist**

Desires Fun

Strengths   **Weaknesses**

In Babies

Strengths	Weaknesses
_____ Bright and wide-eyed	_____ Screams for attention
_____ Amusing and adorable	_____ Knows he or she is cute
_____ Gurgles and coos	_____ Needs constant company
_____ Shows off	_____ Gets into trouble
_____ Responsive to people	_____ Self-centered

In Children

Strengths	Weaknesses
_____ Engaging personality	_____ No follow through
_____ Daring and eager	_____ Disorganized
_____ Innocent-appearing	_____ Easily distracted
_____ Cheerful and enthusiastic	_____ Short interest span
_____ Fun-loving	_____ Emotional ups and downs
_____ Chatters constantly	_____ Wants credit
_____ Bounces back quickly	_____ Forgetful and flighty
_____ Energized by people	_____ Exaggerates

In Teens

Strengths	Weaknesses
_____ Cheerleader type	_____ Deceptive
_____ Charms others	_____ Creative excuses
_____ Gets daring	_____ Easily led astray
_____ Joins clubs	_____ Craves attention
_____ Popular	_____ Needs peer approval
_____ Life of the party	_____ Con-artist potential
_____ Creative and colorful	_____ Finds studying dull
_____ Wants to please	_____ Immature
_____ Apologizes quickly	_____ No sense of money
_____ **Total strengths**	_____ **Total weaknesses**

Sanguine grand total _____

CHOLERIC
THE POWERFUL PERSONALITY

FOR CHILDREN: HOT RED LIKE A FIRE

The Extrovert   **The Leader**   **The Optimist**

Desires Control

Strengths   **Weaknesses**

In Babies

_____ Determined look	_____ Strong-willed
_____ Adventuresome	_____ Demanding
_____ Energetic	_____ Loud and shrill
_____ Outgoing	_____ Throws things
_____ Precocious	_____ Not sleepy

In Children

_____ Born leader	_____ Controls parents
_____ Daring and eager	_____ Manipulative
_____ Productive worker	_____ Temper tantrums
_____ Sees the goal	_____ Constantly moving
_____ Moves quickly	_____ Insists on own way
_____ Self-sufficient	_____ Tests control
_____ Competitive	_____ Argumentative
_____ Assertive	_____ Stubborn
_____ Trustworthy	_____ Defiant

In Teens

_____ Aggressive	_____ Too bossy
_____ Competent	_____ Controls friends
_____ Organizes quickly	_____ Knows everything
_____ Assumes leadership	_____ Looks down on dummies
_____ Problem solver	_____ Unpopular at times
_____ Self-confident	_____ Decides for all
_____ Stimulates others	_____ Insulting
_____ Excels in emergencies	_____ Judgmental
_____ Great potential	_____ Unrepentant
_____ Responsible	_____ Blames others

_____ **Total strengths**   _____ **Total weaknesses**

Choleric grand total _____

MELANCHOLY
THE PERFECT PERSONALITY

FOR CHILDREN: DEEP BLUE LIKE THE OCEAN

The Introvert   **The Thinker**   **The Pessimist**

Desires Perfection

Strengths   **Weaknesses**

In Babies

_____ Wants to please   _____ Dislikes strangers

_____ Serious and quiet   _____ Looks sad

_____ Well-behaved   _____ Cries easily

_____ Likes a schedule   _____ Clings to parents

In Children

_____ Thinks deeply   _____ Moody

_____ Talented   _____ Whines and fusses

_____ Musical or artistic   _____ Self-conscious

_____ Daydreams   _____ Too sensitive

_____ True friend   _____ Hears negatives

_____ Perfectionist   _____ Withdraws

_____ Intense   _____ Sees problems

_____ Dutiful and responsible _____ Won't communicate

In Teens

_____ Good student   _____ Too perfectionistic

_____ Creative—likes research _____ Depressed and critical

_____ Organized and purposeful _____ Inferiority complex

_____ High standards   _____ Suspicious of people

_____ Conscientious and on time _____ Poor self-image

_____ Neat and orderly   _____ Revengeful

_____ Sensitive to others   _____ Lives through friends

_____ Sweet spirit   _____ Needs to be uplifted

_____ **Total strengths**   _____ **Total weaknesses**

Melancholy grand total _____

PHLEGMATIC
THE PEACEFUL PERSONALITY

FOR CHILDREN: COOL GREEN LIKE THE GRASS

The Introvert   **The Follower**   **The Pessimist**

Desires Peace

Strengths   **Weaknesses**

In Babies

_____ Easy-going   _____ Slow
_____ Undemanding   _____ Shy and withdrawn
_____ Happy   _____ Indifferent
_____ Adjustable   _____ Unresponsive

In Children

_____ Watches others   _____ Selfish
_____ Easily amused   _____ Indecisive
_____ Little trouble   _____ Avoids work
_____ Dependable   _____ Fearful
_____ Lovable   _____ Quietly stubborn
_____ Agreeable   _____ Lazy and sleepy
_____ Relaxed   _____ Retreats to TV

In Teens

_____ Pleasing personality   _____ Indecisive
_____ Witty humor   _____ Unenthusiastic
_____ Good listener   _____ Too compromising
_____ Mediates problems   _____ Unmotivated
_____ Hides emotions   _____ Sarcastic
_____ Leads when pushed   _____ Uninvolved
_____ Casual attitude   _____ Procrastinates

_____ **Total strengths**   _____ **Total weaknesses**

Phlegmatic grand total _____

Once you have totaled the scores for each child you will have a
family Personality Profile that will explain some of the conflicts you
have been facing. If your children are old enough to talk about their

strengths and weaknesses, these scores will provide a place to start. If the terms are too cumbersome, use the descriptive colors indicated under each heading. For instance, tell the Melancholy, "You are deep blue like the ocean." Children enjoy any kind of self-analysis if you make it seem like a game and don't lecture them at the same time.

Now that you see each one's strengths and weaknesses, how can you learn to use this information to improve your skills as a parent? How can you understand each personality and meet the emotional needs of each child? The following pages will give you examples.

HOW TO USE YOUR NEW INFORMATION TO IMPROVE PARENT/CHILD RELATIONSHIPS

The Sanguine Child

If you have a Sanguine child, rejoice! This one is happy-go-lucky and the life of the party; he or she loves fun, people, activity, and life itself. With the bubble and bounce come a few traits that may bother you a bit. Sanguine children forget where they are going, what time it is, how long they've been gone, and what they went after. They are easily distracted by other children, the dog, or a falling leaf. Any minor event can turn their attention to something new and wipe out their memory as easily as lifting the cellophane on a magic slate.

These children don't mean to be bad; they just can't remember how to be good. Any kind of fun dangled before them acts as a powerful magnet, pulling them away from responsibility.

Once you understand the natures of these adorable children, you can enjoy their humor and help them become somewhat disciplined. Don't try to make them into Melancholy perfectionists or you will deflate their bubble and be left with depressed children who don't think life will ever be fun again. Remember that these children dislike dull or routine tasks, boring people, criticism, endless details, or goals too lofty to reach without a ladder.

The Sanguine child needs more eye-to-eye attention than any of the other personalities. He or she also needs constant approval and praise for any minor achievement. This child is desperate for affection, hugs, and kisses, and wants to be accepted as he or she is and not compared with a smarter, more serious sibling. The Sanguine youngster loves people and can easily charm others into doing things his or her way. As a teen the Sanguine will be the most popular, involved in everything that comes along, and voted most likely to succeed.

This pursuit of pleasure can be carried to an extreme if the teen becomes a "party animal." The parents need to teach discipline without wiping out the joyful spirit. If the parents can make home a fun place, give plenty of attention, compliment constantly without making negative comparisons, and praise every positive act, the child will blossom into a delightful adult and reign as homecoming king or queen forever.

If the parents look at this child as a frivolous flake or if they don't look at this child at all, the Sanguine may give up, put on a Melancholy mask, or get involved in teen sex, drugs, or alcohol to cheer himself or herself, as Terry Jo did.

Terry Jo had the typical emotional needs of the Sanguine, with a touch of Phlegmatic. Neither one of her parents, both Christian leaders, seemed able to supply even a small amount of what she craved as a child.

"I so wanted the attention and approval of my father but he was incapable of giving it," she said. "He was Sanguine too, and he was so emotionally needy that he had no thought of giving, only of receiving. We were both alike, both crying out in our mutual needs, and neither one of us knew how to help the other. I also craved approval from my Melancholy mother, but because nothing I did was perfect, I never got my desired praise and affirmation. I tried so hard to please her. When I was seven years old, I cleaned my brother's room without being asked. I waited for praise and was spanked because I had not hung up the pants with the crease folded perfectly.

"One time I had a friend visiting. We decided to surprise my mother and fix dinner before she came home from work. When she walked in she blew up and gave me a tongue-lashing in front of my friend for using the hamburger she was saving for the next day. After many events like this I gave up expecting my emotional needs to be met, put on a Melancholy mask of pain and perfection, and tried never to feel or care again.

"Through your book, *Your Personality Tree,* the Lord has helped me solve many of the emotional puzzles in my life. Now I know what God created me to be (Sanguine/ Phlegmatic). There is relief and joy that comes with the realization that I am a unique creation and that God doesn't expect me to be just like my mother or brother or husband. With His help I can develop my strengths and diminish my weaknesses."

The Choleric Child

If you have a Choleric child, be grateful because he or she can do much of your work. From the time little Cholerics can toddle, they are looking for jobs to do that will bring words of praise from their parents. They have the highest energy level of all personalities. If you keep them busy and appreciate all they can do for you, they will be your handy helpers. If you don't, they will get into trouble for they can't just sit around. They need to know you are their loyal friend, their co-laborer, their cheerleader. They want to hear you brag about their achievements and see you hang up their blue ribbons and make a display case for their trophies.

Choleric children are born leaders and have an innate drive to control situations and people. Help them develop their leadership skills and show them how to value the opinions of others, even when they don't agree. Let them know they will never be the leaders they could be if they are too bossy and push people around.

Recognize their need to be in control of something and give them opportunities to participate in family decisions. They usually have judgment beyond their years and love to contribute opinions. They can be fierce competitors and they need to be taught that an occasional loss doesn't mean they are failures. They tend to feel that the end justifies the means and that cheating is acceptable if it will produce a victory. Watch for this attitude and teach them the value of honesty over manipulation. This feat will be difficult if they perceive you to be above the law yourself. If you tell them to lie on the phone for you or watch for the cops when you're speeding, you may find them discounting your discourse on honesty.

With exemplary modeling on your part and with enough appreciation of work well done, you could produce a president. Without meeting this child's emotional needs, however, you could turn out a workaholic who strives for recognition but never quite lives up to his or her potential, as Carol did.

Carol grew up in a family she calls "abusive in every area." She was never encouraged so she carried her Choleric nature to an extreme, hoping she would receive credit for her good works. In her adult life she began to deal with her multiple abuse and realized she had become a compulsive worker, still trying to get the appreciation she needed and had never received. As she saw her pattern, she was able to prayerfully change her pace. She told us, "After hearing you speak I am placing my running shoes on the shelf and walking in the Shepherd's green fields with bare feet, taking time to smell the roses."

The Melancholy Child

If you have a Melancholy child, you may have produced a genius, but this little flower needs the most tender care of all the personalities. The Melancholies are serious from the start; they desire order and organization, and don't like to be jollied up by a giddy Sanguine parent. Even as children, Melancholies take their pleasure in quiet moments of meditation and are offended by noisy siblings who try to cajole them into foolhardy frivolities. They are easily hurt and take a Sanguine's flip comments and vain humor as personal affronts. Melancholy children desperately need a parent to sit down with them in an unhurried, peaceful atmosphere and discuss their inner thoughts. At first they won't expose their feelings. They are testing you. How long will you try to reach their hearts? Will you become impatient and give up as a Choleric parent would? Will you toss off a hurtful attempt at humor as the Sanguine parent would? Will you doze off while waiting for the Melancholy child to start talking as the Phlegmatic parent would? Or are you willing to wait?

The Melancholy child tends to have a feeling of insecurity, and when not handled with patience and sensitivity he or she withdraws, clams up, and refuses to participate in family activities. Telling these Melancholies they are no fun or depressing pushes them further into the pit of despair. They need quiet appreciation for their depth and abilities. They also need a place they can call their own where no one can touch their things. If possible, give Melancholy children a room of their own; but above all don't make them share space with a Sanguine sibling who steals pencils and litters the room with soiled socks. Remember, Melancholy children need security, stability, separation, support, and silence. They don't want to hear, "Cheer up and be happy." They wait for the words, "I believe in you." Irene never heard those words from her parents, and she grew up not feeling she was of any value.

"There was no joy in my life," she told us. "I had an extremely hard childhood, no love, no encouragement, and no silver boxes. When I became a Christian I never knew why I was so picky, organized, and strong-willed—thinking my way is the right way and my time is the only time.

"After I married the wrong man because of my low self-esteem, the Lord brought a counselor into my life who introduced me to your book, *Personality Plus*. When I learned I was a Melancholy/Choleric, that explained my personality. Understanding the truth renewed my mind and set me free from a lot of pain and damaged emotions."

The Phlegmatic Child

If you have a Phlegmatic child you can relax, for you have the easiest child of all to raise. By nature the Phlegmatic's desire is to please others and cause no trouble for anyone. From the time they are babies, they are happy to lie around wherever you put them and eat whenever and whatever the parent desires. This Phlegmatic child is the direct opposite of the demanding Choleric and can be totally overwhelmed by bossy siblings of any age. He or she doesn't fight back, so the parent has to watch that the Phlegmatic child doesn't get picked on or made the target of pranks. Phlegmatics are easily intimidated and don't like to complain because if they tattle they will get into more trouble.

Phlegmatic children are passively appealing with a dry, low-key sense of humor. They won't buck the Sanguine show-biz sister, but they will come up with a funny line if anyone is listening. Phlegmatic children tend to fall through the family cracks because they don't demand attention as the others do. They aren't the life-of-the-party children like the Sanguines, they aren't the super-achievers like the Cholerics, and they aren't the geniuses like the Melancholies.

Because of the Phlegmatic's peaceful nature, the parents must be sure to pay attention to this quiet child so that he or she won't feel completely worthless. The parent needs to build a relationship that says, "I love you for your sweet disposition. You always make me feel so good." The parent's tendency is to say, "When are you going to get up and become something?" This challenge immobilizes the Phlegmatic and causes him or her to cease functioning at all.

Since Phlegmatics have low motivation anyway, it is the parent's job to gently help them find direction. Phlegmatics tend to have single-minded interests, so it's like taking them to a cafeteria of opportunity and quietly explaining each menu item until you find one that whets their appetite. This approach may be frustrating, especially to Choleric parents who make instant decisions and can't bear people who vacillate, but it's better than facing life with this child on the couch watching TV. Remember that the Phlegmatic has a low energy level, avoids decisions and responsibility, and hates tension, quarrels, and conflict. Give him or her loving attention and keep this child out of the eye of the storm. In return your Phleg-matic child will be your best friend for life, bring peace to your spirit, and stay in balance when all around are losing their heads. Remember the Scripture, "Blessed are the peacemakers, / For they shall be called sons of God" (Matt. 5:9).

Elaine, a Phlegmatic who spent her life thinking she was strange, finally realized, "I'm a Phlegmatic and it's okay. I'm not peculiar after all." Elaine loved being alone in her room, away from all the noisy members of the family.

"However," Elaine wrote, "I lived in an Italian neighborhood where everyone talked loudly, laughed loudly, and used excessive body language. They were exceedingly demonstrative! All of those things hurt my ears and embarrassed me. The neighbors thought I was peculiar.

"My mother, who I now know was a Sanguine, was a constant source of embarrassment to me. She loved everyone—whether she knew them or not! She would talk to strangers as if they were old friends. And worst of all, she *hugged* anyone who would let her. All those things mortified me.

"I remember one evening after some company had left, she asked me, 'Don't you love Uncle Dave?'

"I said, 'Of course, I love Uncle Dave.'

"She said, 'Uncle Dave thinks you don't love him because you didn't hug him.'

"When I was twenty-one years old, my mother became terminally ill. I took a leave of absence from work and spent the last six months of her life hugging her, loving her, and taking care of her—trying to make up for all the times I had been unable to demonstrate my love to her.

"A beautiful healing took place in my heart when I came to know Christ as my personal Savior. Having His love within me enabled me to be more open and affectionate toward those close to me.

"But the final phase of healing took place when I attended CLASS and learned by taking the Personality Profile Test that I am a Phlegmatic. All the traits that made me feel I was peculiar are normal after all. And best of all, the Lord created me that way. Jeremiah 29:11 is directed to the Jews in Exile, 'I know the thoughts that I think toward you, says the LORD, thoughts of peace and not of evil, to give you a future and a hope.' In the same way, the Lord assures me He has a good plan for my life. He is going to help me nurture my strengths and conquer my weaknesses. And as I become more comfortable with who I am I will be able to better understand and love others who are Sanguines, Cholerics, or Melancholies without feeling peculiar!"

Understanding your child's personality traits can have a tremendous impact on achieving harmony in your home. Some of these traits are summarized in the Emotional Ups and Downs chart. Although the table was created with adults in mind, you may notice many of these characteristics in your children.

Emotional Ups and Downs

		Emotional Needs	Causes of Depression	Stress Relief	Energy Level
POPULAR	**SANGUINE**	Attention from all Affection, touching Approval of every deed Acceptance as is	Life is no fun No hope for the future Feeling unloved	Go shopping Party with friends Eat to cheer up	Energized by people High frenetic pace Has exhaustion spells
PERFECT	**MELANCHOLY**	Sensitive and understanding Support when down Space to be alone Silence, no people	Life isn't perfect Emotional pain unbearable Lack of understanding	Withdraw from people Read, study, meditate, pray Go to bed	Moderate energy Drained by people Needs peace and quiet
POWERFUL	**CHOLERIC**	Loyalty from troops Sense of control Appreciation Credit for good works	Life is out of control Problems with money, job, mate, children, or health	Work harder Exercise more Stay away from unyielding situations	Highest energy Needs little rest Thrives on people to control
PEACEFUL	**PHLEGMATIC**	Peace and quiet Feeling of worth Lack of stress Respect for who he is	Life is in chaos Should confront issues Pressure to produce	Tune out on life Turn on the TV Eat and sleep	Lowest energy Needs much rest Drained by people

What a blessing it is when we can understand ourselves, accept other people (especially our children) as they are, and know how to meet their emotional needs.

PART THREE

◆

A Problem in the Past

7

Where Do My Feelings of Rejection Originate?

During the question and answer session at a recent retreat, a young woman raised her hand and asked, "Can you feel your parents rejected you, even if they were nice people?"

"Most people don't mean to reject their children," Fred answered. "Tell us what made you feel rejected."

"Well, my parents were very social and highly respected in the community. They went out a lot and when I'd run to say good-bye, my mother would stop me and say, 'Don't touch me. You might get a spot on my dress.' As I got older I just said good-bye from across the room. Mother seemed more comfortable with that. I realize now that I always felt she liked her clothes better than she liked me!"

This girl was in extremely casual clothes, quite under-dressed compared with the other women. In contrast another woman stood up who was perfectly groomed. She had glossy black hair, fair skin, and dark eyes. She turned to the first lady and said, "I bet you wear T-shirts so you don't have to worry about spots and so your kids will know you love them." This comment hit the first woman wrong, and she burst into tears.

The second woman, an obvious Choleric personality, had little sympathy and added her personal story. "I bet you all think I'm well dressed and confident," she said.

The ladies nodded, half-watching the first woman, who was still sniveling.

"It's only a front. My father told me when I was a child that he had hoped I would be a blue-eyed blonde. 'Men always like blondes better,' he said. Once I even bleached my hair but still couldn't please him because he said I looked worse. 'You should stay dark as long as that was how you were born,' he said. You can imagine how I felt. So I've tried to be stylish and wear designer clothes in hopes people would accept me with dark hair."

Having said her piece, she sat down, and another woman, a tiny lady with mops of fluffed-out brown hair and earrings that hung down to her shoulders stood up. We had observed her as out of place at the Christian women's retreat because of her tight-fitting mini-dress with a plunging neckline. She had already confided in us that she had been engaged several times but each time she would panic when it was close to the wedding and break it off.

This woman stood before the group, looking as if she'd just received a revelation from the Lord. "Now it all makes sense. My father told me that I should try to grow tall because only tall women had sex appeal. I couldn't get over five feet and so I've worn clothes like this to attract men. But the minute they get serious, I get scared because I know I'm not what I appear to be." The women applauded her honesty and new understanding.

These three women had all suffered from the results of rejection. They all had decent parents who didn't set out to hurt them but who let them know they were not acceptable as they were. All of their rejections showed up in their clothing. The first wore sloppy clothes so her children could touch her and not feel rejected as she had felt. The second wore expensive clothes so she would be fashionable even without blonde hair. The third wore sexy clothes so she could attract men even though she was not tall and statuesque.

It is better to find out why we feel the way we do, why we dress and act the way we do, than to try to change the outward symptoms. Each of the three women could have changed their style of dress or hair color. This would never, however, change the way they felt about themselves.

Let's face our issues head on. Let's find out why we feel the way we do and when it was we first started thinking we were not good enough to please the important people in our lives. Carefully answer the questions that follow by circling yes or no. You may be surprised at what you learn about yourself.

UNDERSTANDING THE ROOTS OF REJECTION

Childhood feelings

1. As a child did you feel that your brothers and sisters got more attention and privileges than you did?   Yes   No

2. As a child, did you sometimes feel that you were not loved?   Yes   No

3. Do you remember crying yourself to sleep at night?   Yes   No

4. Did you feel that your parents didn't come to your special events, plays, recitals, performances as much as the other children's parents did?   Yes   No

5. In childhood photos or snapshots do you often look sad?   Yes   No

6. Did you sometimes hug yourself in bed because you simply needed to be hugged?   Yes   No

7. Did you sometimes wonder why you were ever born?   Yes   No

8. Did you know as early as you can remember that you were not wanted or that your parents really wanted a boy (or girl)?   Yes   No

9. Did your mother ever say, "If it weren't for you kids, I could have been..."?   Yes   No

10. Did you have difficulty answering these questions because you can't remember much, if any, of your childhood?   Yes   No

Subtotal of childhood questions to which you answered Yes: _____

Note: A Yes answer to question 10 is a clear indication that the adult rejection issues you may be struggling with are related to your childhood.

Teenage memories

11. Do you look back on your teenage years and wonder why no one spent time to help you with:

   a. Making career choices, education, and training?   Yes   No

   b. Getting along with the opposite sex?   Yes   No

   c. Preparing for a job interview?   Yes   No

12. Did you have any dreams that you never pursued because no one encouraged you?   Yes   No

   What were those unfulfilled dreams?

   a. _____

   b. _____

   c. _____

13. Did you sometimes stand outside a group of kids because you felt you were not as popular as the others?   Yes   No

14. Did you do things as a teenager that you now wish you hadn't done?   Yes   No

   Did you do these things only to attract attention?   Yes   No

   What were some of these things you did to attract attention?

a. _____

b. _____

c. _____

15. If you were sexually active as a teenager was the real reason, because

    (a) As a girl, you just needed someone to hold you close and make you feel loved?   Yes   No
    Or
    (b) As a boy, it made you feel you were really a man, that you were worth something?   Yes   No

16. Did you sometimes think of running away because no one really cared about you?   Yes   No

17. Did you hesitate to call a friend for a date or to do something with you because you were afraid he or she would say no?   Yes   No

18. Did you have some physical feature or characteristic that made you feel unattractive?   Yes   No

19. When you walked into a room, did you feel the others were talking about you because you didn't look good enough?   Yes   No

20. Did you sometimes hope or wish you would be chosen as captain or president, but knew you never would be?   Yes   No

21. Was your life as a teenager sometimes so disappointing or hurtful that you wondered if there were any reason at all to continue?   Yes   No

Subtotal of teenage questions to which you answered Yes: _____

Adult emotions

22. As a woman, when you arrive at a function, do you often feel you are wearing the wrong outfit?   Yes   No

    As a man, do you wish you had not come to the event?   Yes   No

23. Did you feel that in marriage you would have someone you could depend on to love you and hold you?   Yes   No

24. Do you sometimes have dreams in which you're "flying" and you can look down and see everyone else?   Yes   No

25. Do you sometimes feel God loves others but He could never really love you?   Yes   No

26. Have you been in counseling for depression, or have thought you should be?   Yes   No

27. Do you have any knowledge, or even a suspicion, that you may have been sexually violated or interfered with as a child?   Yes   No

Subtotal of marriage questions to which you answered Yes: _____

In marriage
28. Is it very important that your partner frequently says, "I love you"?   Yes   No

29. When you communicate a desire for intimacy to your mate and he or she doesn't respond do you tend to pout, feel hurt, or withdraw emotionally?   Yes   No

30. When your partner makes a suggestion that sounds critical to you do you sometimes feel that means he or she really doesn't love you?   Yes   No

31. If your partner were to make a positive comment or get excited over someone of the opposite sex, would that make you feel that you're not acceptable?   Yes   No

32. If your partner wants to go somewhere or do something without you does that tend to make you feel depressed?   Yes   No

Subtotal of marriage questions to which you answered Yes: _____

Grand total of Yes answers: _____.

If you circled Yes even two or three times in any of the sections (childhood, teenage, adult, marriage), you may be struggling with rejection issues and not even be aware of it. Your responses also give you a clear picture of how rejection feelings may be affecting your adult life. Feelings of being unloved, unworthy, unaccepted, or abandoned will always drain your natural energy. They will cause you to function at levels of achievement far below your potential.

Fred states, "As a child I always knew I didn't feel loved. I had what many would consider an ideal childhood: plenty of money, big house, and educated parents, but they were so busy I never felt they cared about me. I often thought if I could be good enough, if I could be perfect, maybe someone would love me and appreciate all I had done. Maybe if I were better, people would stop picking on me or making fun of me; maybe my friends would like me better. I never had more than one or two friends at a time, and I always felt a little jealous of those who had lots of friends. Why didn't the other kids call me to do things with them? Why did I always hope I would be invited to go along and then feel depressed when I stayed home alone?"

Negative feelings, like the ones Fred expressed, become characteristics that tend to push other people away rather than draw them in. It becomes a self-defeating cycle. Because the child with hurt feelings is not fun to be with, other children do not seek to play with or even be around him or her. The child senses this and once again feels rejected. This lonely child tends to have a few select friends who are also ones with similar feelings of emotional deprivation. Even children tend to be attracted to others on a similar level of emotional pain or health.

Your Yes answers to the questions in the section on childhood feelings will help you see how early such feelings began to impact your life. As you continue through the questions on your teenage and adult years, you can clearly see if rejection has been an issue for you. And you can begin to get a sense of how it may now be causing related problems in your marriage, in your work, in your church, and in social relationships. Even the decisions we make in life are often based on how we feel about ourselves or what underlying needs are unfulfilled.

Fred recalls, "In my years of being in business, I can see many decisions I made that were not carefully thought out, that were not tested before being implemented. I hoped these decisions would bring about a quick and significant success, thereby making me feel good about myself. And, yes, people would notice me because of my success. I then could feel good about myself. Underneath, without ever even verbalizing it to myself, I could show my parents that I could make it.

"I remember in my early thirties finding a portable, multiple electrical outlet that had some special features. I thought I could market it successfully by mail order to create additional income. This would supplement the food service management business I had started. In my youthful naivete I thought there was no limit to time or ability; if this venture became successful then I would run not one, but two, growing companies. Wouldn't that be fine! Look at what I had accomplished! Rejection-based feelings are never a healthy foundation on which to start a new business.

"I contacted the manufacturer and they agreed to put my label on the product. I called it 'Tempo Timer.' It was designed to be used for stereo component systems—a good name too.

"I created my own advertising agency in order to save, or earn, the normal 15 percent agency commission for creating and placing the ads. With my limitless self-confidence I designed the ads and paid about ten major monthly periodicals to run my mail-order ads for Tempo Timers. Wasn't I proud to see those magazines come out with my handsome little ads? My, they did look good. Now I just had to sit back and wait for the mailman to bring me sacks of envelopes with checks all made out to me! Oh, I was on the way.

"I would come home each day from my food service business, eager to see the growing pile of orders. Then they started. Just a few orders at first, then a few more. After two or three weeks the orders started to dry up, and pretty soon the anticipated windfall had become a mere trickle. The orders continued for about a year at the astounding rate of one or two a month. For a ten-dollar retail cost, this was not big business!

"With all my impulsiveness I did make at least one healthy

decision. Even though I had to place a rather inexpensive minimum order of seven hundred Tempo Timer labels, I only ordered the units in lots of fifty as I needed them. Fortunately, I only ended up with two or three unsold units and a modest loss compared to what it might have been.

"Why did I start with ten magazines at once? Why didn't I test market this idea first? Because I so desperately needed to be a success. Because of my deep emotional hurts and feelings of rejection I needed a victory. And not just a little one, but a major success! Unfortunately (or perhaps fortunately), the Tempo Timer business died aborning, a victim of my immature impulsiveness.

"At this time in my life I had no idea that the trauma of my childhood had put the development of my emotions on hold. It would be twenty-five years later before those early rejection feelings would be taken out of the hold mode and allowed to grow to equal stature with my mind and body. I wish I could say that this was the only time I made what could now be labeled as an emotion-based decision, but there were many, many others in the years that followed. Each mistake carried a cost that eventually would have to be paid. The mistakes continued until I came to the point of being willing first to accept that I had a problem, and second to find the cause, or root, of that problem. I had no concept of how deeply the rejection feelings were affecting every area of my adult life—my marriage, my business, my sense of self-worth, and my relationship with my Lord."

Oswald Chambers wrote, "Impulse is all right in a child, but it is disastrous in a man or woman . . . every project born of impulse put into action immediately, instead of being imprisoned and disciplined to obey Christ, will probably fail."[1]

"I did not even know Christ, or how to obey Him when I was having these problems," Fred said. "I simply functioned on the basis of those impulsive emotions that were locked into everlasting immaturity."

Jesus said, "I have come [a] that they may have life [eternal life], and [b] that they may have it more abundantly [inner peace here on earth]" (John 10:10).

The first step is to acknowledge or admit: "I have a problem." "I am not as happy as I want to be." "I do not have the sense of peace that I want to have." "I am not content with my life as it is."

The tendency of most of us when we have recognized that we have a problem is to blame other people or our circumstances. If only they would change; if only he or she would be more understanding; if only I had more money, fewer children, fewer responsibilities, more help. What else can you think of that would make your life better?

How easy it is to focus on the externals when we really need to look at ourselves, to see what it is that is robbing us of the peace and joy that Jesus promised to us. "Peace I give to you; not as the world gives do I give to you. . . . that My joy may remain in you, and that your joy may be full . . ." (John 14:27, 15:11). "Your joy no one will take from you" (John 16:22).

These verses clearly tell us that His joy and peace are a gift, and we are entitled to experience them. Are rejection feelings robbing you of the gift of joy and peace that is rightfully yours?

Let's go back to the Roots of Rejection questionnaire and identify those issues, those emotions, that have let you feel unappreciated, unrecognized. In the spaces that follow, list, one by one, every question to which you answered Yes. Then briefly summarize your feelings. Counteract that feeling by writing in the truth that God wants you to accept and believe as an adult.

Two sample suggestions are given to get you started. There are no rights or wrongs in your feelings, so write the truth. If you wish to use this exercise as a Bible study, look up key words in a concordance and find verses that amplify the truth.

Counteracting Rejection Feelings with Truth

Question No.   **My Feeling**

   1   *I always felt neglected.*

Truth: *Even though I felt that way as a child, as an adult I will not allow those feelings to keep me in bondage.*

2   *No one said, "I love you."*
Truth: *Father God, take away that childhood feeling,
for I know now that You love me, always have, and always
will.*

Now it's your turn. List the questions to which you answered
Yes. Then summarize your feelings, and write in the "truth." (Do
not skip this self-help exercise.)

Question No.   **Feeling**

1. ____ _____

Truth: _____

_____

2. ____ _____

Truth: _____

_____

3. ____ _____

Truth: _____

_____

4. ____ _____

Truth: _____

_____

5. ____ _____

Truth: _____

_____

6. ____ _____

Truth: _____

_____

7. ____ _____

Truth: _____

_____

8. ____ _____

Truth: _____

_____

9. ____ _____

Truth: _____

_____

10. ____ _____

Truth: _____

_____

11. ____ _____

Truth: _____

_____

12. ____ _____

Truth: _____

_____

13. ____ _____

Truth: _____

_____

14. ____ _____

Truth: _____

_____

15. ____ _____

Truth: _____

_____

One of the traits we have noticed over and over again is that
people are reluctant to do the *work* that is necessary to achieve
freedom and healing. Instead they would like to take a pill that
would wash away all their pain, all their hurts and struggles. Why
else would so many Christians be taking mood-elevating drugs to

lift them out of their depression? Why else would so many Christians prefer to go weekly to therapists and pay fees ranging from fifty to a hundred dollars or more an hour to find help but rarely freedom? Why are these same Christians unwilling to go to the Counselor (see Isa. 9:6) for one hour a day to find the freedom and healing that He alone can give?

If you are weary and loaded down from all your emotional burdens, His promise is that He will give you rest. However, this is a conditional promise. There is something you must do. You must come to Him. You must come to Him daily.

What is the best way you know to come to Him? Is it not in prayer? If you are willing to take drugs to cope with your dilemma, if you are willing to pay a professional therapist, why would you not be willing to come to Jesus for one hour a day in prayer? He asked, "Could you not watch with Me one hour? Watch and pray, lest you enter into temptation. The spirit indeed is willing, but the flesh is weak" (Matt. 26:40–41).

If you have now identified that some, if not many, of your adult emotional frustrations can be traced to feelings of rejection, you have a decision to make. Are you willing to do the work of healing? Over the past several years of our restoration ministry we have seen a clear pattern emerge: *Those who are willing to make the most effort make the most progress in the shortest time.*

Have you completed the section titled "Counteracting Rejection Feelings with Truth"? Most people who skip over "workbook" sections rarely return to them, and therefore lose the benefit they would get in taking the time to do the work. If you have completed this section, or are now willing to go back and work on those pages, you are serious about your intent to reach for the best God has for you.

Two things now remain for you to win over the feelings of rejection.

The First Step is to:

A. Identify the source of rejection. Go back to your Yes answers in the Roots of Rejection questionnaire. In the spaces below list the person who may have been involved in several of your Yes answers (it is only necessary to write that person's name down one time).

I Was Hurt or Felt Rejected

	By (Name)	At about (my age)	What he or she did or said to me
1.			
2.			
3.			
4.			
5.			

And,

B. Cleanse away the hurt. You now do the work of cleansing by being obedient to the Lord as you prayerfully forgive each person you have named. This will be most effective if you read the following prayer of forgiveness aloud to a trusted friend, prayer partner, or compassionate spouse. You may be amazed at all the locked-away damaging emotions you will release when you do this aloud in the company of another person. It will melt away all the pride barriers. When we do this exercise in a "Promise..." workshop we pair up the participants and have them read over the list. Often they become emotional as they feel the depth of hurts they have experienced. Some cry, but all state later that they have never had such a cleansing experience.

Feel free to modify this suggested prayer as you pray it to fit the situation or the feelings you have.

STEP ONE:
A PRAYER OF FORGIVENESS

Dear Lord Jesus, I thank You that on that cruel cross You made provision for all my sins and trespasses, and that when I surrendered my life to You, You forgave me of my sins and trespasses and washed my slate clean in Your eyes.

*I now confess, Lord Jesus, that I have held _____
(anger, bitterness, resentment, etc.) against _____
for what he or she did or said to me. I ask You now to forgive me, Lord, for holding those feelings, and now I, at the same time, release and forgive _____ for that sin and hurt that was done to me.*

I thank You, Lord, that in Your Name I am cleansed of this hurt, which I have held onto for so long. I praise You for the freeing power of forgiveness. Amen.

Did you have more than five names on your list? Continue until you have individually forgiven each person who offended you, abused you, or simply hurt you by not seeming to care.

Were you praying and truly forgiving? Or, were you just "mouthing" the suggested prayer? Some hurts may be so deep and painful that forgiveness does not even seem possible at this time. If you feel that way, tell the Lord how you feel in Step Two, which follows. He will understand your feelings and He will not judge or condemn you. Ask Him to give you His ability to forgive that person. Ask Him—and keep asking Him—until you know in your heart, "Now I can forgive."

STEP TWO:
DAILY PRAYER

The second step is to fill that huge gaping hole in your heart. Fred writes, "The deep chasm that I had within my soul has been totally filled and covered over. Its location has been so well landscaped that the original pit will never again be found."

This is done by coming daily to the Lord in prayer. Spend time with Him. Get to know Him. Learn to trust Him. Glorify and praise Him. Confess to Him. Ask Him to guide you. He promised you that if you would come to Him daily, He would give you rest for your weary soul. We strongly recommend written prayer, especially if prayer has been difficult for you or if you find it hard to discipline yourself to set aside a daily time with the Lord.

In August 1987, Fred began writing his prayers each day. Written prayer is simply writing a daily letter to the Lord, a letter of adoration, confession, thanksgiving, and supplication. As you spiritually commune with Him at a regular time you will learn to sense His presence, to hear His voice, to know His leading, to accept His unconditional love for you. His love will gradually, day by day, fill that huge chasm. (For further help, read Chapter 15 on how to plug in to God's power through prayer.)

Fred says, "I have sometimes heard the same kinds of words coming out of Florence's mouth that would have formerly devastated me and reactivated those old, deep feelings that she didn't really love me. Now there is no reaction. What does that tell me? Two things: First, my former reactions were due to what was inside of me, not to what she said. Second, I have become secure in the Lord's love for me. I no longer need Florence's constant attention to satisfy this rapacious appetite. The Lord has filled the hole in my heart with His love as I come to Him daily!"

If we told you that you would see some changes in three months, significant improvement in six months, and complete release and healing in one year if you would come to Him daily, would you do it? If you manage to come to Him only twice a week, plan on three and a half years. If you come to Him once a week, plan on seven years. No, on the other hand, since it's hard to build an intimate relationship on a once-a-week meeting, better double it. Plan on about fourteen years!

Are you willing to do the work? Jesus said, "Come to me . . . I will give you rest!"

8

Why Am I Under All This Stress?

Stress became a byword in the eighties and has now firmly settled into the vocabulary of the nineties. Some stress is good. Some is bad. And often we don't know the difference. Picture a large rubberband lying on your desk, limp and useless. It doesn't become functional until it is stretched and put around some loose objects. But if we test it too far the band will break. There's only so much pressure it can handle.

Now look at our lives. To be totally without stress, we would have to lounge in bed all day and have servants wait on us because the minute we arise we put stress on ourselves. If we get up late, we put on more stress. If we run out of gas on the way to work, our patience is really stretched. A certain amount of stress is motivating and some of it is positive, but as with the rubberband, we can never be sure how much stretch we can take before we break. Once the snap comes, it's too late for prevention.

"Stress becomes a problem when it is no longer manageable," wrote Dallas psychiatrist Dr. Doyle Carson. "As problems increase and are not resolved, a person can develop telltale symptoms, including anxiety, irritability, lack of focus, difficulty in sleeping and significant changes in daily routines."[1]

As with all problems the first step is finding the source and being willing to act upon it. The following questions are to help you think about how far you are being stretched. Look at your symptoms now before it's too late. Once you have checked Yes or No on the following questions, we will show you how to evaluate your stress level. We will then divide the areas into categories so you can see what part of your life needs attention first.

STRESS TEST

Answer each question as to how it applies to your life today. *Leave blank any that do not apply.*

	Yes	No
1. Do you tend to wake up and worry during the night?	____	____
2. Is there someone at work who often makes you feel you're not worth anything?	____	____
3. Do you get nervous when you have to carpool the children home from school?	____	____
4. Do you frequently have headaches?	____	____
5. Are you afraid you may be losing your job or getting laid off soon?	____	____
6. Do you tend to get upset with your mate when he or she forgets to do something?	____	____
7. Do you tend to feel sexually frustrated in your marriage?	____	____
8. Do you tend to pick at your meals or to eat a lot of junk food during the day?	____	____
9. Has someone very close to you died within the past year?	____	____
10. Do you suffer from PMS?	____	____
11. Do you frequently have bad dreams?	____	____
12. Do you tend to miss work due to illness more than your coworkers?	____	____
13. In high school or college, did you usually "cram" at the last minute for tests or term papers?	____	____

14. Are you afraid to ask for a raise even though you know you deserve one?   ____ ____

15. Are you still grieving over someone who died several years ago?   ____ ____

16. Would your children say that you get angry a lot?   ____ ____

17. Do you tend to take on more tasks than you should?   ____ ____

18. Do you find it difficult to forgive people who have been insensitive to your needs?   ____ ____

19. Are you accused of usually being late?   ____ ____

20. Do you have a friend who makes you feel guilty if you don't do what he or she wants you to do?   ____ ____

21. Do you feel that your mate is constantly criticizing you?   ____ ____

22. Do you sometimes feel, *What does it matter, nobody cares about me anyway*?   ____ ____

23. Do you often go to bed exhausted, even though you only finished part of what you needed to do for the day?   ____ ____

24. Do you have an impulse to "get even" when someone cuts you off on the road?   ____ ____

25. Do you complain (or often feel) that your mate doesn't do his or her share of the housework?   ____ ____

26. Are you apt to get panicky or tense when you are in an enclosed or unfamiliar place?   ____ ____

27. Would others describe you as a depressed or downcast person?   ____ ____

28. Have you gotten violently angry at any time in the past two months?   ____ ____

29. Are you presently on any medication for mood elevation or insomnia?   ____ ____

30. Have you ever been told you're a workaholic?   ____ ____

31. Are you struggling with any compulsions
    or addictions?   ____ ____

32. Are you and your mate apt to have
    arguments over finances or purchases?   ____ ____

33. Do you tend to have dandruff?   ____ ____

34. Do you grind your teeth, or have you
    been told you have TMJ?   ____ ____

35. Are you a fingernail biter?   ____ ____

36. When the family is going somewhere, are
    you usually the last one to get in the
    car?   ____ ____

37. Are you apt to use the words
    "I hate..."?   ____ ____

38. When you prepare a meal, is it often
    an emergency, or done in a sense of
    urgency?   ____ ____

39. Are you a "chocoholic"?   ____ ____

40. Do you tend to avoid intimate relationships
    with your mate, and then feel guilty later?   ____ ____

41. Are you frequently tired and have less
    energy than others around you?   ____ ____

42. Does any kind of fear tend to control
    your life?   ____ ____

43. Do you have any type of eating disorder?   ____ ____

44. Have you been in counseling or therapy,
    or thought you needed to be?   ____ ____

45. Have you ever had dreams of snakes or
    spiders?   ____ ____

46. Do your credit cards tend to be "maxed out"?   ____ ____

47. Do you tend to go shopping when you
    feel depressed?   ____ ____

48. Are you a popular Sanguine married to
    a controlling Melancholy-Choleric?   ____ ____

49. Are you afraid your mate may be having
    an affair?   ____ ____

50. Do you often feel defeated when at the
    end of the month there are still bills
    to pay but not enough money in the account?   _____ _____

                              Total number of Yes answers checked: _____

Calculating your stress level:

Number of Yes answers you checked _____ multiplied by 2 = _____%

Evaluate your stress level according to the following scores:

0–20 percent, Minor Stress Level

Congratulations! This score indicates your life is probably in balance. You haven't been stretched too far. If you have answered the questions honestly there may not be much to be concerned about. However, by reviewing your Yes answers you may see some areas where you can quickly and easily make some positive changes. Move on to the "Source-of-Stress Analysis." It will help you focus on those specific areas that are contributing to what minimal stress you have.

20–40 percent, Moderate Stress Level

You are above average, but there is probably more stress in your life than you would like to have. Though most stress issues may not be deeply troubling, enough of them warrant digging at the source to bring about some changes and some healing. The "Source-of-Stress Analysis" will enable you to focus on some specific areas.

40–60 percent, Major Stress Level

Your score in this range indicates that significant issues in your life need to be eliminated. Remember, virtually everyone is subject to stress at some time, but your levels indicate you've been stretched too far. Don't be upset, but move on to the "Source-of-Stress Analysis." It will show you some areas where you can begin to improve immediately.

60–80 percent, Unhealthy Stress Level

If your score falls in this range, be very glad you took the time to do this stress test. You already know you've been pulled in too many directions for too long. What you may not have known is that there is hope, and there can be changes in your life, if—and it's a big *if*—you are willing to admit there are problems and if you are willing to put in the effort to bring about changes. The "Source-of-Stress Analysis" will be important for you.

80–100 percent, Traumatic Stress Level

As with the rubberband, you are overstretched, overworked, and overextended. You need relief from your tension. The "Source-of-Stress Analysis" will be important for you.

Your levels of stress are extremely high and you may need the help of an objective and insightful person. Perhaps you should call your pastor, a friend, or a counselor. The sources of some of your present-day stress probably result from unresolved childhood trauma or pain. This possibility is increasingly valid if you have few or limited memories of your childhood years. The tests provided in later chapters of this book will be very important for you to consider carefully.

If you think your life is in shambles and you often feel depressed, remember that Jesus said, "He has sent Me to heal the brokenhearted, . . . To set at liberty those who are oppressed" (Luke 4:18; see also Isa. 61:1). There is hope for you; help is available. Our Lord can and will heal you . . . if you come to Him! This is not a quick fix but a long-range promise.

SOURCE-OF-STRESS ANALYSIS

To help you determine the sources of some of your stress, go back to the stress test. For every number that you checked Yes, circle that number wherever it appears below. (For example, if you answered Yes to number 5, put a circle around number 5 wherever it appears on the lines that follow. Some numbers will appear more than once.)

A. Poor Scheduling or Planning: 13, 17, 19, 23, 25, 30, 36, 38

B. Physical Problems: 8, 12, 23, 41

C. Financial Difficulty: 5, 32, 46, 47, 50

D. Marital Stress: 6, 16, 21, 25, 40, 48, 49

E. Low Self-Worth: 2, 14, 17, 22, 27, 30, 44

F. Work-Related Stress: 2, 5, 12, 14

G. General Tension: 1, 3, 4, 5, 9, 10, 29, 33, 34, 35, 37

H. Depression: 27, 29, 47

I. Rejection: 7, 16, 20, 22, 39

J. Childhood Victimization: 4, 10, 11, 15, 16, 18, 20, 24, 26, 28, 31, 34, 40, 42, 43, 45

You have now separated the sources of your stress into ten categories. (These sources are often interrelated; that's why they may appear on two or more lines.) It is particularly significant when you have circled *several*, or *most*, of the numbers on any given line.

These ten categories can now be seen as falling into three groups. The first three (A, B, and C), are indications of poor scheduling or planning, physical problems, or financial difficulties; they are sources you may be able to change simply by understanding their nature and determining to do something about them yourself, or by getting someone to help you.

A. Poor Scheduling or Planning

You may be causing much of your stress simply because you don't take time to plan in advance what you can do and what is too much. This is typical of the Popular Sanguine personalities who are impulsive and spontaneous. Their lack of planning will frequently cause unnecessary pressures as they bite off more than they can chew. Some people take on more activity or responsibility than they should to help them overcome feelings of low self-worth and to make sure people like them.

B. Physical Problems

Yes answers in this category also may be relatively easy to deal with. Positive changes in diet, eating habits, nutrition, vitamins, or hormones can be implemented quickly. Checking into the possibilities of hypoglycemia and chronic fatigue syndrome may indicate sources of stress.

C. Financial Difficulties

Financial problems are among the most frequent sources of stress. Ask yourself if you are in trouble because you buy impulsively without thought of how you can pay the bills. Whatever the cause, you cannot afford to sit there and hope the Good-News Bears will arrive tomorrow with bags of money. Constant borrowing with high interest rates is not a long-term solution either. Sit down immediately with your checkbook, bank statements, and bills and take an objective look at your situation. If it is too much to face, enlist a Melancholy mate or friend to help. Sanguines hate the thought of budgets but they need restraint and responsibility. One Sanguine man who was in severe financial trouble gave the bookkeeper of his company the authority to deposit his paycheck and pay his bills. He didn't even see the money and for two years he lived on a five-dollar weekly allowance. He didn't like it at the time, but he now is out of debt. It's amazing what we can do when we care enough to make changes. The book *When Spending Takes the Place of Feeling*, by Karen O'Connor (Nashville: Thomas Nelson) can help you find the source of your financial problems.

D. Marital Stress

This category begins the second and deeper level of stress sources. These issues are usually the result of long-standing relationships that have gradually gone downhill. Like a huge ocean liner at sea, changing direction requires strong hands on the rudder and plenty of time to swing around. Some root causes, such as personality differences, an overly dominant mate, immature emotions, and unrealistic expectations, can be changed quickly. Deeper issues that will take longer are those born from rejection, sexual frustration, childhood victimization, denial, unwillingness to face real issues, self-righteousness, and rebellious attitudes. We will talk more about what to do in the rest of Part Two and in Part Three of this book.

E. Low Self-Worth

Many of us do things to compensate for feelings of insecurity, inadequacy, and lack of self-esteem. When these efforts fail or fall short, we are very apt to have financial problems, thereby adding marital stress, and emotional strain. Picture a wife who feels left out socially. Without her husband's agreement she throws a big, expensive party, inviting the people she perceives as keys to social acceptance. After the party, there is no flood of reciprocal invitations, only bills for the party, tension between husband and wife, and added feelings of worthlessness.

Since low self-worth is not a God-given characteristic, it must be the result of something we have learned, something that was put upon us or done to us. The source of much of the stress we bring upon ourselves is the effort made to compensate for our feelings of low self-worth. We need to find the root cause, which we will help you do in the next chapters. When the root is removed, or healed, self-esteem is transformed and the stress will be history.

F. Work-Related Stress

Some people bring job-related stress home with them, creating new strains, while others have learned to "leave it at the office." Isn't it interesting that two different people on the job can be subject to the very same stress but handle it in totally opposite ways? Invariably it is because of what is inside them, and because of other issues in their lives. Generally, people who are emotionally healthy have a far higher stress-acceptance factor than those with unresolved deeper issues. Which one are you? If most of your stress is work-related, take steps to cure or change your situation. It may be that easy. If you have high levels of stress in several categories, your difficulties are likely to be related to other sources. Resolving those other issues may go a long way in curing on-the-job stress.

As Christians our gift from the Lord is peace—inner-peace that handles stress, not freedom from strain and tribulation (see John 14:27 and 16:33).

G. General Tension

The eleven questions of the Stress Test that fall within this category will help you identify stress and tension within you. The number of responses you have circled may surprise you, but every single one represents a symptom of inner stress. These are all of a general nature, and the resolution of the roots of the problems may bring surprising changes. You may have wondered about question 33, "Do you tend to have dandruff?" Not long ago, when Fred was telling a young couple in Australia about the changes in his life since his healing from childhood sexual victimization, he added, "Oh, and I used to have bad dandruff, but I don't anymore. It's gone!" The wife, who was a nurse, said to him, "Dandruff is caused by stress. That's a well-known fact."

We had never heard that before, but it does make sense. Since that time numerous other people have confirmed that fact to us.

Find the source or the cause of the tension, deal with it effectively, and you'll be delighted with the changes.

H. Depression

Depression is considered to be the major unsolved mental illness of our time. Even though only three of the questions on the test are directed to depression, many of the others are related to it. Depression often renders a person unable to function normally, and high levels of stress are apt to surface at work or in the home. The growing pile of uncompleted obligations or daily responsibilities adds to the pressure until there seems to be no hope.

Treating depression with medication only deals with the symptom, not with the cause. There are three basic interrelated causes that form a continuing cycle. The first and most prevalent is childhood sexual victimization. The second is rejection, often beginning in childhood. Virtually every victim of sexual abuse, or sexual interference, also suffers from rejection. The third cause is unrelenting stress and a corresponding inability to cope, which brings on depression. This is very common in men and women who have been sexually violated and who therefore suffer feelings of rejection, abandonment, and unworthiness. Each of these feelings is apt to feed the others, and the depression becomes all-consuming. Once again, the attention must be on discovering the roots of the problem. Later chapters will deal with these issues, which are more common than generally recognized.

I. Rejection

No one was reared by perfect parents. The healthier our parents were emotionally the better the chance we had to grow up to be balanced, productive adults. If we had to fight, protect, and hide to survive, we may have missed the nurturing we should have received from childhood. The feelings of rejection are deep and should not be ignored. We cannot leave well enough alone. Others of us were healthy as young adults but entered into a marriage with a person who was deeply hurting inside. In his or her search for self-worth this person unintentionally put expectations on us that we couldn't and shouldn't be expected to fulfill. This spouse pulled us down to his or her level. After a number of years of marriage we feel rejection, unworthiness, and loss of confidence.

Feelings of rejection are so common among Christian adults that unmanageable times of stress inevitably result. Whether the rejection feelings develop during childhood or adulthood, they can be readily healed over time as we learn to replace the inordinate craving to fill the void that we unrealistically expect of others with the certainty of the Savior's love for us.

Rereading the preceding chapter will help you identify the possible results and the sources of rejection issues in your life. Getting to the real and root problems quickly will enable you to get a life without the strife.

J. Childhood Victimization

Last and deepest of our ten categories is childhood victimization, which can be either emotional, physical, or sexual. Sixteen of the questions relating to stress are symptoms of this childhood trauma. While all three forms of victimization are highly prevalent, childhood sexual violation has the most significant adult manifestations. It is the cause of much anguish, stress, and dysfunction.

According to a recent comprehensive survey, 75 percent of all women in the church today and 60 percent of all men have either clear knowledge or clear symptoms of childhood sexual victimization. Of those men and women 50 percent have no conscious knowledge of such trauma. Only 25 percent of women and 10 percent of men are aware of what was done to them as children.[2]

Of the men and women who have asked us for help over the past several years, fully 98 percent have shown clear symptoms of sexual violation. Their stress levels are frequently overwhelming. Often they have tried in vain to do everything they can think of to seek relief. Childhood physical sexual violation is pervasive, so common that it is the single most significant cause of stress in adult life. Chapter 11 is devoted to helping you identify if this is a factor in your search for wholeness. You may be surprised at what you learn about yourself as you work through those pages.

Through the daily discipline of putting certain specific truths of Scripture into practice, thousands like you are finding not only relief but healing from the sins that were committed against them as little boys and girls. Dealing with the emotional damage caused by these violations is the focus of that chapter.

9

Have I Dealt with My Past Grief?

Don and Debi had been married for several tumultuous years before Barry, Don's son by a former marriage, was killed by a drunk driver. Don went through the stages of grief, shock, denial ("It can't be true"), and anger ("I'll kill the man who did it") without moving on to acceptance and resolution. One year later Don was just as livid as he had been when the tragedy first struck. His anger so consumed his energy that he could hardly go to work. He was constantly exhausted and many days he slept sixteen hours in a row. When he would open his eyes the reality of death stared down at him and he'd go back to sleep.

Debi came to us, desperate for help. "If he doesn't stop moaning and sleeping I'm going to go crazy or divorce him." She had already given Don an ultimatum, and her heartless statement threw him into a renewed depression. He hadn't spoken to her in days.

When Don agreed to talk with us, he started with a hopeless sigh. "There's no point talking about this because you can't bring my son back, and that's all that will cheer me up." We explained that we had lost two sons so we could understand, but he would have to do what we did: face the fact that his son was gone, that it was not his fault, and that he had to consciously decide to move on with his life.

"But it *is* my fault. It *is* my fault!" Don said, bursting into tears. As we talked to him, we found a man guilt-ridden over the failure of his first marriage. Don had an affair with Debi while married to Jean, a faithful woman who had been a consistent parent to their three children while Don had played around from the beginning. Jean had forgiven him his roving eye and even his first fling with Debi.

Don recounted the day that he had left for good, thinking that the sexual attraction to Debi was more important than maintaining his family responsibilities. "When I said good-bye at the front door, Barry cried and begged me not to leave. I told him he had a nice mother and they'd get along just fine. For the next few months I didn't go see the children. I kept telling myself I was free and having fun, but I know now I felt so guilty I couldn't face the kids. Once I got divorced, at Debi's insistence, and then married her, I had to take over being a father to her children. There were days when I'd look at them and say to myself, *Why aren't you taking care of your own?*"

Don put his head in his hands and cried. "Now Barry is dead and it's my fault."

As we talked to Don we had to go back to his childhood, to his philandering father who had shown him, by example, that being macho was being unfaithful. Don had to confess that what his father's example had taught him was erroneous. He felt he should apologize to his mother for not being supportive of her when his father was involved with other women.

Don had not grieved over his parting with Barry as an emotional death. He had rationalized that it was not his fault and lived on the principle "Out of sight, out of mind." He was stuck at the point of anger, not just at the drunk driver but at his father and at himself.

Don had to grieve that he had ended a marriage that should have been continued. Then he had to ask the Lord to forgive him for his unfaithfulness to Jean and to remove the constant memory of his son pleading with him not to leave. By coming to the Lord daily in written prayer Don poured out his grief on paper and got in touch with his long-hidden pain so that he could move on to emotional health.

When family and friends don't treat grief in a serious manner and tend to move people quickly through their pain before they are emotionally ready, they push the grieving ones into not dealing with their pain fully at the right time. As a result the person suffering the loss may walk around the rest of his or her life with a continual shadow over his or her daily activities.

The death of a spouse or child is always number one on every emotional stress test, with divorce close behind. Each one is the end of life as it was and a cause of grief. We've never met anyone who said, "I had such a wonderful divorce. Let me tell you about it." Often when the ramifications of divorce are not dealt with as the death of a dream, the injured parties suppress their real feelings, deny their pain, and move on—only to be shocked when some event brings out an overreaction or a prolonged depression.

There is no timetable for overcoming grief, but you might ask yourself these questions.

1. What deaths can you remember from your childhood?

   _____   _____
   _____   _____

2. Does any one of these give you an emotional tug at this point? Which one?

   _____

3. Write down what you were told about death when you were a child.

   _____
   _____

4. Write down what you think about death now.

   _____

5. What does the Bible say about death?

   _____
   _____
   _____
   _____
   _____

6. What traumatic experiences have you suffered as an adult?

_____

_____

_____

_____

7. Do you feel in your heart that you have thoroughly dealt with each of these issues? If not, which ones are still a problem?

_____

_____

_____

8. What do you still feel guilty about?

_____

_____

_____

9. What bad counsel have you received about grief situations?

_____

_____

_____

10. What do you still need to work through in order to be free?

_____

_____

_____

Whether your grief is from death, divorce, or emotional pain, it's time, to face it, pray through it, and put it to rest.

Claire lost a baby boy in a miscarriage. The doctor removed the baby quickly, Claire never saw him, and the attitude of family and physicians was equal to what sympathy Claire might have received from having a tooth pulled. Cheerful comments were made by those standing around her bed. "You didn't see the baby so you didn't get attached to him." "You're young. You can have another." "You've got one child so you won't miss this one." "God must have needed him more than you did."

With these words of quick dismissal, Claire didn't allow herself to cry. "They must be right. It's not really a big deal. I'll get over it." Claire got involved in redecorating part of her house and told herself she was happy.

Claire never had another child and she tried not to think of the one she'd lost. When she was in her mid-forties, Claire learned that her husband had terminal cancer. She dropped into a depression far worse than his. During the quick advance of the illness, Claire was in shock. She did her daily duties somewhat like a robot; she didn't want to feel the pain. When her husband died, Claire didn't cry. At the funeral everyone told her how brave she was. One lady even told her that grieving became her and she looked good in black.

Life was mechanical from that day on—until Claire fell apart three months later. She couldn't seem to get hold of herself. First she went to her pastor, who told her it was time to get over her grief and move on: "Draw a line in front of the past, step over it, forget it all, and move on. Never look back, buy some new clothes, and find a new husband. That will give you something to look forward to. Now let's pray."

Claire was not in the mood for a new husband even if one had been presented to her. She was stunned at the pastor's cavalier attitude toward her pain and she went next to "a fine Christian counselor." He told her she was suffering from what he labeled "delayed grief." He told her he had created this term for people like her, who thought they were too spiritual to cry and then reacted later, showing that they really weren't spiritual at all. He chuckled over his analysis and said, "Most Christians are phonies when it comes to death. What you need to do is forget your faith for a while, cry like a real person, and then read my book. If you'd done this in the first place you'd be over this by now."

Claire paid for the book and the visit, but she went home feeling defeated. As the grief continued and she could hardly get up each day, she went to her doctor who took one look at her and decided to increase her medication: "We'll double your dosage and see if this cheers you up." It didn't; instead she was so groggy she couldn't get out of bed.

At the insistence of a concerned friend Claire went to a noted psychiatrist who saw she was on the verge of a nervous breakdown.

Claire agreed to go into the mental health unit of the hospital and there, with the gentle prodding of a therapist, she recalled the loss of her baby. She realized she had repressed her feelings at that time and she was now in a state of double grief. None of the three helpers she had gone to had even asked her questions about her past experiences or feelings. Instead their advice had been, in essence: "Draw a line, read a book, take a pill. If this doesn't work there's something wrong with you."

As Claire found the source of her "delayed grief" she started to deal with the past in the present. She named her dead child and had a funeral for him all by herself. She laid him to rest for the first time and then moved on to the death of her husband. She now realizes she would never have been healed of her current grief if she had not taken care of the past.

10

Will My Childhood Pictures Help?

A few years ago *Time* magazine had a cover article titled "Through the Eyes of Children." On the cover was a pretty young girl with sad eyes. The article told the difficulty of growing up in America today, and the pictures of each child gave a cross section of emotional highs and lows. The reader could look first at the pictures, make a calculated evaluation, and then read the biography to check the accuracy.

A few months later the cover of *Life* magazine featured Lisa Marie Presley and her mother, Priscilla Presley. The contrast in their eyes was so remarkable that even an unobserving person would have noticed it. Priscilla's eyes were bright, clear, and controlling while Elvis's daughter had eyes that seemed half-shut, hurting, and tuned out on life.

On the cover of *Newsweek* magazine in February 1992 the eyes of serial killer Jeffrey Dahmer seemed to penetrate and even frighten the viewer.

We can see pain in the eyes of others, but we can also read our own eyes if we look at our childhood pictures. Whether we are working on self-analysis or preparing to go to a counselor, examining childhood pictures can be most revealing. Usually our parents have taken pictures of us, the firstborn being the most photographed, with decreasing shots of the others. Yearly school pictures are among the best. Line them up on a long table and look at yourself. There may be a marked difference in one year: Sadness in the eyes, no smile, looking down. This change is often an indication that something traumatic happened at that time.

To help in discerning childhood hurts, cover the face in the picture, leaving only the eyes revealed, and look for pain, anger, apathy, or fear. Practice by reading the guidelines for self-analysis of pictures included later in this chapter and then observing pictures in magazines and newspapers.

As each of us thinks about the significance of the eyes in pictures and practices on ourselves and others, we will become discerning and be able to use this skill in helping to uncover some of our childhood's hidden hurts.

To collect childhood pictures ask around the family, starting with parents, grandparents, aunts, and cousins. Don't mention that you are trying to uncover pains of the past or you may never get a single snapshot. Families are rarely cooperative if they sense they are under investigation. If they feel, however, that you are showing a positive interest in family history and putting together a scrapbook that would be available for the relatives to enjoy, they may enthusiastically search the attic. If they will only lend and not give you pictures, be grateful and have copies made.

We remember when we were gathering pictures for a family tree to be displayed on a wall in our home. The Chapman side (Florence's) contributed a collection, but the Littauers gave nothing of value. We painted a tree on the wall, had the pictures framed in gold ovals, hung them on the branches like apples, and produced an eye-catching but somewhat lopsided tree—until Mother Littauer saw that it was loaded with Chapmans. Within days we were presented with photos of ancestors we'd not even heard about—and with childhood pictures of Fred that first gave us the clue he had suffered some childhood trauma.

In our book *Your Personality Tree* we give steps to building a family-tree album, and those who have written us with their results said they were thrilled at how much they were able to collect once they let the relatives know of the legacy they were attempting to preserve.

One woman, for instance, had a family party with each member bringing a childhood photo. She numbered the pictures and laid them down without names, then had each person write his or her guesses about the pictures. Then they went around the room. Each person picked up his or her own picture and told all he or she could remember about the clothes, the background, the situation, and childhood feelings that were part of the photo when it was taken. The whole family agreed they had learned more about each other in that one evening than in the preceding years.

Once you have your photographs lined up in front of you, consider the following questions:

ANALYSIS OF INDIVIDUAL PHOTOS

1. Cover the face, exposing only the eyes. Do you see:

   Anger _____   Sparkle _____

   Fear _____   Fun _____

   Pain _____   Tenderness _____

   Intensity _____   Joy _____

   Sadness _____   Life _____

   Apathy _____   Excitement _____

   Is this child hurt _____ or happy? _____

2. Look at your clothes.

   Did you like that outfit? _____

   Did your mother make you wear it? _____

   Does the picture bring back memories?

   Good ones? _____ Negative ones? _____

3. Ask your mother (or other family members) if there were family problems at the time of the picture.

   Divorce _____ Damaged relationships _____

   Death _____ School difficulties _____

   Moving _____ Abusive treatment _____

4. Ask your parents about any problems you had as a child that you might not remember. Parents with nothing to hide will give you an

episode or two, but be alert to a parent who insists you had a perfect childhood and says you should not even think of reviewing it. This may be an indication of a cover-up or something to hide.

Now consider group pictures.

ANALYSIS OF GROUP PHOTOS

As individual pictures in a series can pinpoint traumatic changes in a life so group pictures can give indications of family dysfunction. After you have collected whatever group pictures you can find, look at them with a discerning eye. Florence comments on a posed picture of her grandparents with their children: "Even though we had seen this picture before we had not examined it closely. Grandpa sat rigid and authoritarian, leaning away from Grandma, who was cuddling the youngest girl at her knee. The three older girls were behind their mother, away from their father. My mother was at the far side, apart from the others. No one looked happy, some looked fearful. The brother stood behind the father, and the only one the father was touching was the collie dog at his feet.

"In discussing this grouping with my mother, she told me how frightened they were of their father's discipline and how she sometimes took the blame for her brother's pranks so he wouldn't get beaten. When I asked about the dog my mother told me he was her father's best friend and when he died her father wrote a poem, 'On the Death of Noble.'"

What to Look for in Group Pictures

Place: Who is in the center? Who is the focal point? Do the children seem to be arranged in any order?

Position: Look at each person's hands: Are they folded, tense, loose, clutching a toy or person?
   Look at the arms: Are they outstretched, around a child or parent, or behind the back?

Look at the body: Is it facing front, turned away from the group, standing too straight, slumping, cuddled up?

Look at the head: Is it looking toward the camera, another person, the ceiling, the side, or the floor?

Proximity: Are the people standing apart from each other or are they gathered together? Are the parents touching each other or any of the children? Do the children seem evenly distributed or grouped on one side? Are the girls and boys together or divided?

Pride: Is there a sense of self-worth in each individual or a feeling of insignificance? Do the parents appear proud of their children or indifferent? Is there one person who wants to be noticed more than the rest?

Poverty: Is the background a house with peeling paint or broken shutters? A parched field or cracked driveway? Are the clothes simple, tattered, without style? Is there a feeling of poverty about the people and the setting?

Pain: Look at the eyes of each individual. Is there pain, fear, or boredom? Joy, sparkle, excitement? Does one person seem gloomy, aloof, close to tears? Does this look like a happy family or is it a depressive group? Is there a feeling of warmth and love or just a sense of duty?

Personality: Can you spot the probable personality of each person? Is there an obvious Sanguine who is making faces, smiling broadly, hamming it up? Is there a controlling Choleric who seems to be in charge, looks stern, is pushing someone else? Is there a Melancholy who is positioned perfectly, is dressed neatly, and is taking this whole procedure seriously? Is there a Phlegmatic who is leaning, resting, looking off into space, not caring one way or another about this picture taking?

Physical appearance: Do these people look healthy, robust, in good shape? Or are they sickly, frowning, joyless?

Protection: Is one child holding, protecting, or mothering another?

Does one seem to be more watchful of the others than the parents are? Does the mother seem tired or remote?

We all know we cannot sum up the emotional state of the family by analyzing one old picture, but we can begin to get a feeling of our own family background. Therapists often use pictures to help find the source of a client's problems, and we can save valuable and costly time if we do this first ourselves.

Now put a few pictures of your childhood in front of you in chronological order, including at least one family grouping. Pretend a counselor is asking you the following questions about the pictures. Write in your answers, remembering that the purpose is to help you get in touch with your childhood emotions and experiences so that you can find the source of the struggles in your adult life.

1. When you examine your childhood pictures what words come to your mind about yourself?

   _____

   _____

2. How does looking at yourself as a child make you feel?

   _____

   _____

3. How would you describe the family in these pictures? More happy than sad, or more troubled than peaceful?

   _____

   _____

4. If you see changes in your demeanor at what age did this change take place?

   _____

   _____

5. From your pictures what personality did you appear to be? _____ Are you still like that today? _____ If not why not?

6. What feelings do you have about this place or about the day it was taken?

_____

_____

7. Who are all these people and what are their relationships to you?

_____

_____

8. What do you feel was your worth to the group? How did your parents value you?

_____

_____

9. Where are you standing in the group, is this position of any significance, and is anyone touching you in a loving way?

_____

_____

10. Who appears to be in charge of the group or protective of the others?_____

11. What do you see in yourself that you hadn't seen before?

_____

_____

Continue to gather pictures, analyze your position in the family, and keep notes of your emotional responses. If you have a strange feeling when you see a certain person, there may be a logical and valid explanation. Your emotions remember what your mind has forgotten.

Ask the Lord to give you fresh memories and new insight, as He did for Fred, so that the picture of your life might be made whole.

Fred says, "Even though I had many symptoms of childhood interference (deeply buried anger, low self-worth for which I generally overcompensated, and strong sexual curiosity that I never did act upon), I would never have attributed them to childhood trauma. Like most people, I just didn't know. I simply didn't understand.

"But that has all changed. My eyes have been opened. I have seen lives devastated by childhood interference and rejection. I have also seen lives transformed by the cleansing and healing power of the Lord Jesus Christ. Mine is one of them."[1]

Oswald Chambers said, "Do not be morbidly introspective, looking forward with dread, but keep alert. Keep your memory bright before God.... Never be afraid when God brings back the past; let memory have its way. It is a minister of God."[2]

11

How Can I Know If I Was Sexually Violated as a Child?

Before reading this chapter, please take the following survey. Simply read over the list. If the statement applies to you or has applied to you at any time in your life—childhood, adolescence, teenage, or young-adult years—put a check on the appropriate line. If it applied when you were a child but no longer does, you still put a mark on the line. Leave the line blank if it does not or never did apply. In thousands of applications this simple test has proven to be better than 99 percent accurate when answered honestly.

Some of you may prefer to have someone else—your spouse or a close friend—read the survey aloud to you as you mark your answers. The results may be surprising. You should take the appropriate survey (for men or women) before reading the explanations that follow the list.

SURVEY OF EMOTIONS AND EXPERIENCES
FOR WOMEN

Check each line that applies or *ever has* to you. Leave blank any that do not apply or you are not sure of.

	Clear	Strong	Possible	Group
1. Abusive spouse			___	
2. Afraid of big or black dogs				___
3. Alcoholic parent		___		
4. Anorexia/bulimia or other eating disorders		___		
5. Being chased in dreams	___			
6. Brother or sister molested as a child		___		
7. Candles in dreams				___
8. Childhood "bad houses" or "bad rooms"	___			
9. Childhood depression			___	
10. Date rape	___			
11. Dislike roses, or their smell				___
12. Don't like full moon				___
13. Downcast looks as a child		___		
14. Dreams of snakes	___			
15. Early-childhood anger	___			
16. Early-childhood masturbation (before age ten)	___			
17. Emotionally abused as child			___	
18. Emotions suppressed in childhood			___	
19. Fear of being alone		___		
20. Fear of knives				___
21. Fear of losing weight		___		
22. Fear of rape	___			
23. Feel unworthy of God's love	___			
24. Feeling dirty	___			
25. Fits of rage	___			

	Clear	Strong	Possible	Group
26. Guilt feelings			_____	
27. Hate Halloween				_____
28. Hate men	_____			
29. Hear chanting or laughing in dreams				_____
30. Hide real feelings			_____	
31. Lack of trust		_____		
32. Low self-worth		_____		
33. Marital sexual disinterest			_____	
34. Memory gaps in childhood	_____			
35. Migraine headaches		_____		
36. Panic attacks	_____			
37. People wearing hoods or robes in dreams				_____
38. PMS (called PMT in some countries)		_____		
39. Poor teenage relationships with boys			_____	
40. Recurring bad dreams		_____		
41. Rejection feelings			_____	
42. Same sex attraction	_____			
43. Scared by bells, chimes, or gongs				_____
44. Self-hatred	_____			
45. Sexually abused or molested as a child	_____			
46. Sexual compulsions	_____			
47. Sometimes hear voices				_____
48. Spiders in dreams	_____			
49. Strange feelings about "the cross"				_____
50. Suicidal feelings			_____	
51. Teenage promiscuity			_____	
52. TMJ (a jaw problem)		_____		

	Clear	Strong	Possible	Group
53. Temptation to touch children sexually	___			
54. Uncomfortable with nudity in marriage	___			
55. Uncontrollable anger		___		
56. Uncontrollable crying		___		
57. Undiagnosed pains and aches		___		
58. Unexplained fear of darkness				___
Your totals:	___	___	___	___
Possible:	(21)	(14)	(11)	(12)
Grand total (add all four column totals): ___				

Survey adapted from Fred Littauer's *The Promise of Restoration/Healing** (Nashville: Thomas Nelson Publishers, 1994). All rights reserved. This form may be reproduced. (*Note: In 1994, Thomas Nelson Publishers changed the name of the book from *The Promise of Restoration*, originally published by Here's Life Publishers to *The Promise of Healing*.)

SURVEY OF EMOTIONS AND EXPERIENCES FOR MEN

Check each line that applies or *ever has applied* to you. Leave blank any that do not apply or you are not sure of.

	Clear	Strong	Possible	Group
1. Affairs during marriage			___	
2. Afraid of big or black dogs				___
3. Alcoholic parent		___		
4. Being chased in dreams	___			
5. Brother or sister molested as a child		___		
6. Candles in dreams				___
7. Childhood "bad houses" or "bad rooms"	___			
8. Childhood depression			___	

	Clear	Strong	Possible	Group
9. Downcast looks as a child	_____			
10. Dreams of snakes	_____			
11. Early-childhood anger	_____			
12. Early-childhood masturbation (before age ten)	_____			
13. Emotionally abused as child			_____	
14. Emotions suppressed in childhood			_____	
15. Fear of being alone	_____			
16. Fear of knives				_____
17. Feel unworthy of God's love	_____			
18. Feeling "dirty"	_____			
19. Fits of rage	_____			
20. "Flashbacks" of sexual nature	_____			
21. Frequent teenage masturbation	_____			
22. Guilt feelings			_____	
23. Hate Halloween				_____
24. Hate homosexuals	_____			
25. Hear chanting or laughing in dreams				_____
26. Hide real feelings			_____	
27. Lack of trust		_____		
28. Low self-worth	_____			
29. Marital sexual disinterest			_____	
30. Memory gaps in childhood	_____			
31. Migraine headaches	_____			
32. Obsessive focus on breasts or vagina	_____			
33. Panic attacks	_____			
34. People wearing hoods or robes in dreams				_____
35. Physically abused as child			_____	
36. Poor teenage relationships with girls			_____	

	Clear	Strong	Possible	Group
37. Recurring bad dreams		_____		
38. Rejection feelings			_____	
39. Same sex attraction	_____			
40. Scared by bells, chimes, or gongs				_____
41. Self-hatred	_____			
42. Sexually abused or molested as a child	_____			
43. Sexual compulsions, magazines, videos	_____			
44. Sometimes hear voices				_____
45. Spiders in dreams	_____			
46. Strange feelings about "the cross"				_____
47. Struggle with holiness		_____		
48. Suicidal feelings			_____	
49. Teenage promiscuity			_____	
50. Teenage sexual touching with boys	_____			
51. Temptation to touch children sexually	_____			
52. Tendency to overreact			_____	
53. Tendency to look at others' penises	_____			
54. Uncomfortable with nudity in marriage	_____			
55. Uncontrollable anger		_____		
56. Uncontrollable crying	_____			
57. Undiagnosed pains and aches	_____			
58. Unexplained fear of darkness				_____
Your totals	_____	_____	_____	_____
Possible	(24)	(11)	(13)	(10)
Grand total (add all four column totals): _____				

SCORING THE SURVEY

Add up your responses in each of the four columns and enter your score on the Totals lines (the numbers under each Totals line indicate the possible number for that column). Then add up your four column totals to get your Grand Total of responses.

Before interpreting your score, let's look at some others who have taken the test.

Anne, the woman from the retreat who had spent thirty thousand dollars on therapy and was no better, had no memories before the age of twelve. Because she couldn't find the source of her pain, she had shown little improvement in spite of diligent effort, years of counseling, and an assortment of medications. What could Anne do next? And Joy, whose husband had walked out on her, had no money for counselors and was so bogged down as a single mom that she had given up on finding anyone who could even understand her.

One Sunday after the Mount Shasta Women's Retreat, both Anne and Joy came to see us. Even though they had not been friends before the retreat the time we had spent around the table had shown them they had some mutual concerns: They were both depressed and each one had memory gaps about her childhood. Anne had been to many kinds of counselors and still owed the last one money but she had never gotten to the heart of her problems. "It's been one big band-aid," she sighed. She had taken all kinds of prescription drugs and the latest had turned her hostile; she felt like killing anyone who crossed her, and this was not consistent with her Melancholy nature. Anne had studied alternative medicine and read books on depression, but nothing seemed to work for her. Her former husband called her a hypochondriac and said he needed a woman who was cheerful.

Joy was even more depressed; she could have worn a sign around her neck that said "Victim." Her eyes were so full of pain it hurt to look at her. Her clothes were old and without any sense of style; in fact, Anne had already offered to give her a few dresses she no longer wore. Anne and Joy were on different levels financially and socially but they were new friends, drawn together by their mutual pain. They had gone over their personalities together. Anne was totally Melancholy and Joy was Phlegmatic. "I used to have a sense of humor," Joy told us. "But my life sure isn't funny anymore."

As they filled us in on their backgrounds and feelings of hopelessness, we handed them the Survey of Emotions and Experiences. They both started checking off the items on the list that applied to them.

Anne had ten responses in the first column, indicating the emotion or experience clearly applied to her; eight responses in the second column, indicating that these situations strongly applied; and six responses in the third column, showing those emotions and experiences as well for her. She had no checks in the fourth column.

Since this survey has proven accurate in our use with thousands of people, we explained that there was strong evidence that she had probably experienced some sexual interference in her childhood. Since she had no memory before the age of twelve, this score gave her a tangible reason for her suppression. "Is that what's been wrong with me all these years?" she asked. "Wouldn't I remember if I'd been molested?"

We explained that when children are abused they frequently shut out the pain, and this blanks their memories. They repress memories for four reasons: One, their young minds can't understand what's being done to them. Two, the perpetrator is loving to them and says, "You are so special to me. This is our little secret. Don't tell anyone and I'll keep giving you presents that I don't give to anyone else."

When we got to this point in our explanation Anne stopped us. "That's it! The man by the playground. He told me I was special and he bought me ice cream. I'm sure he did something to me, but I can't remember what."

Joy asked, "What are the other reasons?"

We explained, "Third, the abuse is so bad that the child has to block it out in order to exist, and the last reason is that God allows us to put our abuse away until we're old enough to deal with it."

"Well, I'm old enough," Joy added. "It's time I found out where my problems came from."

"I want to find out now," Anne stated firmly, banging her fist on the table.

"There must be a little Choleric in you!" Joy said. She smiled a bit as she added, "You really hit the table with a vengeance."

"That's because I'm mad! If that creep touched me and that's why I'm a mess I could kill him."

We got her calmed down and asked if she would like to pray for her lost memories.

"But I can't remember any of them."

"You don't have to remember. You just have to ask the Lord to show you what He wants you to see to be set free."

We prayed with Anne that Jesus would take her where He wanted her to go, and immediately she was in the living room of a house across from her school. We asked her questions:

> What is the room like?
> Are you alone?
> How old are you?
> What are you wearing?
> How are you feeling right now?
> Is someone in the room?
> Who is it?
> What is he wearing?
> What is he doing to you?
> What is he saying?

From these questions we learned that Anne was four years old, wearing a red shirt and denim shorts. Her babysitter had let her stay after nursery school and play on the swings. The sitter was in a car with her boyfriend when the man came by and asked Anne if she wanted ice cream. He took her to his house, took off her shorts and panties, played with her, had her give him oral sex, gave her a Coke to wash out her mouth, handed her a popsicle, and took her back to the playground. The sitter was unaware she'd been gone.

"Did this seem like a one-time experience?" we asked.

Anne sighed, "It must have happened before because I knew what he was going to make me do."

"How do you feel after going through this memory?" we asked.

"It sounds strange," Anne said, "but I feel relieved. It wasn't fun, but I know it's true. That's why I've always felt dirty and why I rinse out my mouth with Coke. My husband used to tell me I was weird."

"Jesus revealed this to you," we reminded Anne. "This is what the Lord wanted you to see today."

Anne affirmed that the Lord had given her this picture of her childhood. "What do I do now?" she asked.

We referred her to our book, *Freeing Your Mind from Memories That Bind,* and suggested that she start writing her prayers to Jesus each day. "Thank Him for what He's already done for you and ask Him to show you anything else you need to see to be free."

"Should I do that too?" Joy asked. "Maybe something strange happened to me. Look, I've got a whole lot of checks on my survey too."

We looked at Joy's survey and saw she had made thirty-five checks, with several in the fourth column, indicating the possibility that she had been violated by a group, or more than one perpetrator. Joy was too fragile to work through her experience at that time so we didn't want to tell her that the fourth column refers to group abuse for fear it would be too unsettling. We referred her to *Freeing Your Mind* and *The Promise of Restoration* and suggested that she begin to write her prayers daily.

When we said good-bye to the two women, Anne was smiling and Joy said, "Maybe there's some hope for me."

Why had Anne and Joy not been successful earlier in getting to the source of their pain? Why does sincere counseling sometimes fail?

Some people have little success when they go for help because the counselor doesn't ask them the right questions or they don't give honest answers. By the time people get to counseling many of them feel so dreadful about themselves that they're desperate to find one person who will support them and tell them they're decent people. They must have this person's approval. But they think, *If you really knew me you wouldn't like me*. The extension of this common attitude is, *So I just won't tell you the truth.*

A recent letter we received chronicled the sordid life of the writer, who had been victimized from the crib on. Counselors hadn't been able to solve her problems, and she wrote us in desperation. At the end she added a victim's typical plea: "I hope you'll answer my letter and like me even when you know what a horrible life I've been through and what a bad person I really am."

Because of victims' need for someone to accept and love them, they unconsciously avoid being open and honest with the counselor. If their helper is also their pastor, the search for truth may be close to impossible. As one lady told us, "I couldn't bear to have him look down at me each Sunday and say to himself, *There's the one who had sex with her brother.* So she had minimized her childhood problems to the point that the pastor didn't know what she was trying to solve.

As we look at these two reasons for counseling failure, we can see why many people in counseling don't make any progress. They give up and resign themselves to lifelong depression.

A third reason for lack of progress is that we sometimes don't know what happened to us; our memory is blocked. The counselor could ask insightful questions, and we could respond with the truth as we know it and still not uncover the source of our pain. Some might ask, "Is it possible that something could happen to me and I wouldn't remember it?" Yes, we find that 65 percent of all women and 80 percent of men who were violated in childhood have suppressed the memory of the incidents.

Sometimes people ask, "Is it necessary to uncover these buried memories?" Our answer is, "Yes, if you wish to get rid of the symptoms." You can take medication for headaches and go to eating-disorder clinics, but if you wish to be relieved of the list of symptoms it is necessary to discover the root cause.

"The good news," Nancy, a victim of incest, wrote after she had prayed for memory retrieval, "is that the truth has set me free and now I am truly free to go on and be the person that God had originally intended me to be before my abuse. Knowing the past explained to me why I had been the way I was all of my life:

compulsive; an overeater, gaining weight; bulimic; filled with unresolved anger, bitterness, resentment, unworthiness; and feeling unlovable to anyone including God. Now, I am so excited about the future. God loves me. He has healed me and given me special work to do.

"Thank you for what you two have done for me. The blessings in my life are beyond expressions of gratitude."

Nancy is already speaking about her healing journey, teaching workshops on the real cause of eating disorders and the solution, preparing TV programs, and beginning to write a book to help others. All of this has happened within a year of the time Nancy uncovered the trauma of her childhood. Although she doesn't consider herself a writer, Nancy says, "I have a story to tell, messages to get out, and God says write it down and share it with the world. So I obey!"

Is it possible that you are like Anne? Have you been to counselors who didn't ask the right questions? Have you at times avoided the truth because it might be too painful to talk about? Or have you so little memory to go on that neither you nor a counselor could piece together your childhood? If you answered the Survey of Emotions and Experiences honestly, you will now be able to diagnose the source of your problems.

The first thing to realize in looking at your scores is that every statement on the list is a possible symptom of childhood sexual victimization or interference, with one exception: "Sexually abused or molested as a child" (No. 45 for women, No. 42 for men). It is not a symptom. It is a fact.

The survey, therefore, is simply a list of these symptoms, which lead us to the source. When you go to a medical doctor to find out why you're not feeling well, the first thing he or she does is to check for symptoms. When the symptoms are found, the diagnosis can be made and the appropriate remedy or medication prescribed. When your car is sputtering, the first thing a mechanic does is to check for the symptoms. Is there any reason to think it would not be the same with emotional problems? That is why this survey is so effective. As a list of symptoms it quickly leads us to the source of the problem.

Once we have discovered the root then we can apply the remedy. As you look at your scores (the number of symptoms you have acknowledged about yourself) you may have felt one of the typical reactions listed here. Put a check in front of the one with which you most closely identify.

    ____ 1. I've always wondered about that. Maybe now I can get to the bottom of my problems.

    ____ 2. Is this possible? I can't believe it could have happened to me.

    ____ 3. This is impossible! I was raised in a good Christian home. My father would never have done such a thing.

    ____ 4. If it's true, I don't want to know. I'm afraid I couldn't handle it.

Which one is closest to your feelings? The first response is the healthiest. It may be summarized as acceptance; the second, doubt; the third, denial; and the fourth, fear. If you had approximately twelve or more responses on the survey and your response above was number 2, 3, or 4, begin praying for God to remove your doubt, denial, or fear of the possibility.

Remember the statistics:[1]

- Three out of four women have significant symptoms of victimization.

- One out of four acknowledges or is aware of it.

- Two out of four have no knowledge of it but do have the symptoms. The violation has been suppressed into the unconscious or unknown.

- Six out of ten men have significant symptoms of childhood sexual victimization!

- Only one out of ten acknowledges or is aware of it.

- Therefore, five out of ten men have the symptoms but have no conscious awareness.

Responses in the First Column

The first of the four columns, labeled "Clear," is of special significance. This means in our judgment every statement answered in the first column is a clear symptom of childhood sexual violation. If properly and honestly answered, it can directly and clearly be attributed to no other thing. On this test most people who have in fact been violated, whether known or unknown, will indicate at least four symptoms in this column. Many, however, will mark eight, ten, fourteen, or more responses. The following discussion will explain the significance and meaning of these responses. The numbers correspond to the questions on the surveys.

SIGNIFICANCE AND MEANING OF "CLEAR" SYMPTOMS

Being chased in dreams. 5 (women), 4 (men). When a child, or even an adult, is running or trying to run in a dream, he or she is escaping from something that is bad or frightening. If you have been chased, try to remember who or what was pursuing you or what the chaser was wearing. Also, was it a single person or more than one? We have personally prayed with literally hundreds of people for retrieval of lost memories. Without exception each one who had dreams of being chased discovered instances of sexual violations.

Childhood "bad houses" or "bad rooms." 8 (women), 7 (men). When you think of your childhood homes, do you have strong negative feelings about any of them? Or was there a room in any of the houses or places in which you lived that you didn't like? These feelings are usually related to traumatic experiences in that room or house. The entire experience, perhaps even the whole house or room, may be blocked out of your memory, but the emotions remain. The saying is true, "Our emotions remember what our minds have forgotten!"

Date rape. 10 (women). Why is this symptomatic of an earlier childhood violation? When an emotionally healthy young woman (one never violated as a child) is "pressured" on a date into going further, she will resist, even fight to protect herself. Usually the overaggressive date who is decent will give up in defeat. When a child has been violated, however, the natural and inherent God-given ability to protect herself has been drastically weakened if not altogether destroyed and instinctively the aggressor senses this. The victim, when confronted again later in life, may put up some resistance, but she knows she cannot win. Her early victimization has made her vulnerable to a repetition of abuse. This does not mean that every woman who was ever raped was sexually abused as a child, but we find a high correlation.

Dreams of snakes. 14 (women), 10 (men). This is a symptom not commonly understood, even by most professionals. From our experience in working with over three thousand men and women, we have found only one cause of dreams of snakes, and therefore only one explanation. Think for a moment, what part of the male anatomy most closely resembles a snake. Without exception, every man or woman we worked with who had dreams of snakes had been orally violated by an adult-aged (approximately fourteen or older) male. It is the most common form of violation of little boys and girls.

New Zealand is described as the only major country that has no snakes at all. Nevertheless, on our trips to New Zealand we have met and prayed with several people who had never lived outside of New Zealand yet had dreams of snakes! One pastor could not understand it either until he prayed with Fred and discovered oral violation by his father.

Dreams of snakes is the single most significant symptom; it clearly identifies the nature of the victimization.

Early-childhood anger. 15 (women), 11 (men). When there was enough anger in childhood for an adult to respond to a related question on the survey, that anger must have been significant. While anger in itself is a healthy emotion, for a child to have so much anger that he or she remembers it as an adult may be clearly construed to be an aberration from the way God created us. When a child has been violated, anger is a natural result of that intrusion. In most instances the child is not "permitted" to express that anger. The abuser warns, "If you make any noise...," or "If you tell anyone...." Unexpressed anger does not go away or disappear; it is merely suppressed to erupt when triggered at other times. Significant early-childhood anger is, therefore, a clear symptom.

Early-childhood masturbation (before age ten). 16 (women), 12 (men). According to God's design for the development of a child's mind, body, and emotions, puberty is the age for the awakening of human beings' dormant sexuality. The capacity for sexual feelings is already present at birth, but it is not planned to be activated until generally twelve or thirteen. Therefore, when a child has sexual feelings before the age of ten, and well before puberty, it is inevitably a result of something that was done to him or her. It is not uncommon for adults who had clear symptoms of victimization to tell us they had very strong sexual feelings as early as they could remember, even at the age of three. This is not the same as the child who explores his or her body and soon stops because there are no special feelings. Early-childhood masturbation is evidence of inappropriate sexual contact with the child.

Fear of rape. 22 (women). The key word is *fear* versus healthy avoidance of being in a vulnerable position. This fear is a strong, consuming emotion that may prohibit normal activity, a fear to go where others easily tread. If you find yourself looking constantly over your shoulder in public places or streets, if you feel anxious when others don't, the reason may be traced to something that happened in childhood that has left you ever on guard and ill at ease in questionable places.

Feel unworthy of God's love. 23 (women), 17 (men). God created us in His image to love Him, to worship Him, to have fellowship with Him. None of us are worthy of His love. We can do nothing to deserve it. When we have intellectual understanding of the Scriptures but still don't feel good enough, or when we feel that God could love everyone else but He could never love us, there has to be a reason. These rejection "feelings" are contrary to God's purpose and design for us. It inevitably gets down to feeling, *I'm too dirty, I've done too many bad things, I'm not good enough.* God did not create us with those feelings. Someone did something to us to make us feel this way. If you checked this symptom, you may be surprised to know that it is one of the most commonly seen in people who have been victimized.

Fits of rage. 25 (women), 19 (men). Rage is an extreme form of anger, an explosive outburst, usually triggered by something relatively minor compared to the reaction. A "fit of rage" is an indication of a boiling cauldron of anger. If you have been subjected to periodic fits of such explosive anger and you later wonder, *Why did I get so upset?* you may have found the answer. It may have been in you for years and years just waiting to let go. Most childhood victimization begins between the ages of three to five, when a child is defenseless and knows only two things: trust and obey.

Flashbacks of a sexual nature. 20 (men). Flashbacks are sudden, mental images. They are usually more like photographs than motion pictures. We all experience them from time to time. It is when they are sexual in nature and relate to our childhoods that we should pay particular attention to them. It is as if God is knocking on the door of our minds. Often the normal tendency is to feel, *Oh no, that couldn't have happened, that couldn't be me,* and to push the image back down into the subconscious. It would be far healthier to permit them to develop into a conscious memory of the whole scene.

Frequent teenage masturbation. 21 (men). (Although this symptom appears only on the survey for men, it is frequently experienced by women as well.) Many men presume that because they masturbated frequently all teenage boys did so. Not so. It is not unusual for teenage boys to play with themselves sexually, but it becomes especially significant when it is often and compulsive. Some men tell us they did this once a day during teen years. Even a few times a week could be considered compulsive. Frequent teen-age masturbation is a result of sexual feelings gone out of control, far beyond what God intended.

Hate homosexuals. 24 (men). As Christians, we know that our Lord always had mercy for the sinner but hated the sin. Why then do some of us have such strong feelings about the sinner? We have found through experience that feelings of *hate*—not moral indig-nation—are rooted in childhood violation of some type, usually by an adult male.

Hate men. 28 (women). Many women never realize how deeply they hold feelings of hatred or resentment toward men until they are confronted by this line on the survey. Suddenly they realize they do have these feelings. Why? Did God create them in these women? Did He create woman to hate man? Of course not. But if some man did something bad to a little girl, wouldn't it be understandable that she might have feelings of hating men? It would be even more explainable if such incidents either happened several times or they were perpetrated by different men.

Memory gaps in childhood. 34 (women), 30 (men). Psychol-ogists have a term for this phenomenon. They call it *traumatic amnesia*. Carl Jung called suppressed memories the personal uncon-scious. Jung wrote, "The personal unconscious contains lost mem-ories, painful ideas that are repressed (i.e. forgotten on purpose) ... the negative side of the personality, the sum of all those unpleas-ant qualities we like to hide."[2] We prefer to call it memory gaps, periods of our childhood years that have become a blank. Adults who have these blocked-out years think that everybody does. They have no other standard of reference until they begin to learn that many people have very clear memories of most of their childhood years, often beginning as early as the age of two. Unless you are aware that you suffered an accident as a child, these lost years are probably due to a childhood sexual trauma.

The good news is that no matter how they were blocked out, they can be readily retrieved in detail through prayer. This is what we term memory retrieval, an amazing process that is fully explained in Fred's book, *The Promise of Healing,* published by Thomas Nelson.

Genevieve knew she had memory gaps in her childhood. She came up to us after a conference in Los Angeles and showed us her symptom list where she had checked off ten in the first column. Genevieve had been to several counselors but no one had touched on why she had no childhood memories. One counselor suggested that no one can remember their childhood, another told her to leave well enough alone. By the time Genevieve reached us, she had about given up on finding any answers for her life.

Florence spent time with Genevieve in memory-retrieval prayer, and instantly she saw herself in the house across from the local park. An older man had enticed her in with promises of treats, but once there she was molested and left naked. Shame overwhelmed Genevieve as she saw the reason for her low self-worth and guilt.

On the way home from our time of prayer, Genevieve saw two rainbows in the sky, one above the other. The one on top seemed faded. It was broken in sections with gaps and didn't touch the ground on either end. Underneath the patchy rainbow was a bright one. The ends touched the ground, there were no breaks, and the colors were strong and clear. As soon as Genevieve saw these two rainbows, she knew God was offering her a new covenant, and she pulled off the road to admire them. As she stood in awe, God began to speak to her mind. She grabbed a piece of paper from the seminar workbook and wrote God's words:

"This is my full covenant with you to make you whole like the complete rainbow, not fragmented and faded like the rainbow above, which represents your old life. But I will make you whole and full and strong and bold in color like the rainbow below. And what existed before, that faded out life, will fade away and your true colors will shine. You will be bold, bright, brilliant, and shine forth the light of the Lord. You will be on show for all to see Me in you.

Just as many admired and saw the rainbow with its true colors so will they see you with all your changes and true colors shining through. The two rainbows represent your life: the faded one, the life before, the one that had no true beginning or end, with patches here and there. Underneath that, was a complete rainbow with no breaks (no memory gaps), but a start and a finish and a bold display of color. That is what your life will be like when the Lord is through healing you."

Obsessive focus on breasts or vagina. 32 (men). This is another symptom that many men think is normal and natural; however, we are not just talking about enjoying the sight of an attractive woman. Rather, we are referring to the focus on her with sexual thoughts. As one young man said, "I undress them all in my mind." When this desire becomes an obsession it indicates a lack of control. It is an appetite that is never really satisfied, a distorted sexuality resulting from childhood trauma.

Panic attacks. 36 (women), 33 (men). Recently we were speaking in a hotel at a women's retreat. At the same time in an adjoining room was a conference on Panic Disorder and Anxiety Attacks, sponsored by the area County Mental Health Department. It was attended by some three hundred mental health professionals, including psychologists and psychiatrists. At one of the display booths sponsored by the U.S. National Institute of Mental Health, we picked up a pamphlet entitled "Panic Disorder." It stated, "The symptoms of a panic attack appear suddenly, without any apparent cause.... At least 1.6 percent of adult Americans, or 3 million people will have panic disorder at some time in their lives." And to answer the question, "What causes panic disorder?" it answers, "Scientists don't know exactly why this happens."

Once again, without exception, every single person with whom we have met, who was subject to panic attacks or disorder, had several, if not numerous, other clear symptoms of childhood sexual violation.

At a "Freeing Your Mind Conference" in Virginia, we passed out a similar but somewhat briefer form of the Survey included here. This was done to help people determine the source of the issues in their life with which they were struggling. Late Saturday afternoon, when the conference was over, a mature, deeply committed Christian pastor named Ron, approached Fred to show him his Survey form. He had only checked off seven symptoms on the whole list. But four of them were in the first column, one of which was panic attacks. Never in his life had he even suspected anything might have happened to him in his childhood, nor did he think he had any adult emotional issues.

"I looked at his survey," Fred said later, and noticed that panic attacks was checked. I asked Ron about it.

"He told me he had experienced an attack only once in his life, the previous year in Oklahoma. He was sitting in the back seat of his favorite uncle's car, and suddenly, a tremendous surge of anxiety came over him. He had to get out of that car! Why would a mature pastor have a panic attack?

"If there was anything there, Ron told me he wanted to know. Because he had traveled quite a distance to come to the conference, I agreed to meet with him for memory-retrieval prayer if he didn't mind waiting until everything was cleared up.

"About an hour later, Ron, his wife, and I found a private room where we could bring his desire to know the truth to the Lord. Within minutes of the time we both had prayed, Ron remembered little Ron, at four years of age, standing in his front yard. He saw a car in the driveway. Someone was sitting in it. It was a man. The door opened; the man got out. He came toward little Ron. It was his favorite uncle.

"As he approached, Ron saw him unbutton his pants. And then, he saw clearly. He re-experienced the complete violation.

"After the memory was over, Ron sat, surprised, but knowing he had seen the truth he had prayed for.

"Suddenly, Ron began to sob. He wept for about three minutes while his wife tenderly comforted him. Then, just as suddenly, he stopped crying and said, 'I feel so free, so released. I can't believe it.' I continued to minister to Ron's discovery and hurts, and then we closed in a prayer of thanksgiving.

"Ron and his wife had a two-and-a-half hour drive home, and he still hadn't finished his sermon preparation for Sunday morning. The next afternoon, I called Ron to see how he was handling the revelation God had given him. He said, 'Fred, I feel great! I have never experienced such freedom in a service before. I never felt such power in my preaching as I did this morning! It's amazing!'

"Ron had no apparent emotional problems, but he had been locked up somewhat by what his 'favorite uncle' had done to him some forty-five years ago. Now, he understood the one-time panic attack. The suppressed trauma had been released. There would be no more attacks."

Same-sex attraction. 42 (women), 39 (men). The rallying cry of the gay community is, "You don't understand. We were created this way." This is their attempt to justify their lifestyle or choice. This assertion does not agree with Scripture (see Gen. 1:27–31 and Lev. 18:22) or with our experience in ministering to people with homosexual or bi-sexual tendencies. Every single man or woman we encountered who has struggled with this issue had been sexually violated as a child. They didn't ask for it; they are not to blame; and most don't even remember the initial incident. God certainly did not create anyone to have attraction, fantasies, or sexual dreams about a person of the same sex. This is not only an aberration; He says it is an abomination. Even though attempts are being made to find evidence to show homosexuality is genetic, no such proof exists. Homosexuality is contrary to God's creation.

Self-hatred. 44 (women), 41 (men). In the second great commandment, the Lord Jesus said, "You shall love your neighbor as yourself" (Matt. 22:39) in the same *way* that you love yourself. Jesus told us to love ourselves, to have a healthy respect for who we are. Then how can we also hate ourselves? God would not command us to do something He didn't equip us to do. Self-hatred is therefore not from God. It must be the result of something that was done to us, in childhood, most likely, a sexual violation, most definitely.

Sexually abused or molested as a child. 45 (women), 42 (men). If you are aware of this in your childhood you are in the minority. The vast majority, two out of three women and five out of six men who have the same kinds of symptoms as you, have no idea why they are struggling. Some don't even know they're struggling. It's their families who are struggling to live with them.

If you are a known victim, but not yet a victor, it may be valuable to consider the possibility of additional and possibly earlier violations. When a person tells us of a known trauma, our next question is always, "How old were you at the time?" or "What is the earliest age you can remember this happening?"

If the earliest known age is approximately eight or even older, our next question is, "When it first happened, can you remember what you did or what your reaction was?" The most frequent answers are (1) "Nothing," (2) "I froze," or (3) "I didn't know I could do anything." On rare occasions, the answer is, "I screamed," or "I tried to make him (or her) stop."

What do answers 1, 2, or 3 mean to you? You answered correctly if you said, "It probably means that wasn't the first time." Correct, because it shows the child had no ability to protect himself or herself. But doesn't a child of eight or nine years of age have a fairly well developed sense of what is right and what is wrong? Correct again. Their God-given defense mechanism has been stolen from them, perhaps even years before.

If the healing is not taking place in your life as you think it should, maybe you need to begin shining God's laser beam to see if there are undiscovered earlier occasions. These unknown incidents may be keeping you in emotional bondage.

Sexual compulsions. 46 (women), 43 (men). Often an issue with women and very common with men, a compulsion is an irresistible impulse or drive to perform some irrational, uncontrollable act. Most frequently sexual compulsions are expressed in a drive to view magazines or videos. Men believe this is natural, thinking, *Doesn't everybody?* For men to be curious, to be interested, yes. To be compulsive, no. By definition a compulsion is not a natural urge, but irrational or uncontrollable. Therefore, virtually every compulsion must result from something that negatively impacted us at some time in our lives. Sexual compulsions always indicate some form of early trauma.

Spiders in dreams. 48 (women), 45 (men). Spiders in dreams are a common symptom, very similar to that of snakes in dreams. Many people in describing the spiders, tell of a tarantula with large hairy legs and a thick black center. Symbolically this represents pubic hair, usually male but sometimes female. Some people tell us they don't have dreams of snakes or spiders, but they "hate" them. The emotion that pours out of them as they speak the word *hate* clearly taps into some kind of suppressed traumatic feelings.

At a "Freeing Your Mind Conference" being held in a hotel, a lady came up to Fred with her symptoms survey in hand. "Could I see you for a moment?" she asked.

Since Florence was speaking at that moment, Fred and the woman went out from the meeting room and sat down in the hotel lobby. As they talked, Fred said casually, "How do you feel about snakes or spiders?"

"I hate them," she exclaimed. Moments later I noticed her swatting her skirt and legs.

"What are you doing?" I asked.

"I'm trying to get the spiders off me. They're crawling all over me."

We were not sitting on a barnyard fence but in the lobby of an elegant hotel. There were no spiders crawling over Fred, and he couldn't see any on her either. There weren't any!

The woman was having "body memories" related either to dreams or even more likely to an actual experience of a torturous type of sexual violation. She not only thought there were spiders, but in her emotions, she could feel them! Fred's simple question had tapped into the darkness of her soul and the pain hidden there.

Harrison came to us with a diagnosis of arachnophobia, a fear of spiders. The only suggestion given him to help his fear was to stay away from spiders. He was trying to content himself with the fact that he now had a lofty sounding title for all of his nervous habits and fears. He also hoped it explained why he was obsessed with women's sexual parts, although he admitted he didn't see the connection. In questioning him we found he had a whole list of symptoms and little memory of his childhood. He was anxious to find answers. So we prayed and asked the Lord to take him wherever he needed to be, in order to see whatever he needed to see, to be set free.

Instantly, Harrison could see himself in a crib in a room, in a house where he lived only until he was three months old. He could see his blue and white booties and his female cousin leaning over the crib. She picked him up, took off his diapers, played with his penis, and then removed her own panties and put his little baby face into her pubic hair. He not only relived the feeling but he had strong smell memories that went with the sense of suffocation.

Retrieving this memory in the power of the Lord, not through psychological probing, was quick, direct, and obviously real. The next day Harrison returned to our seminar with a radiant look on his face. He could hardly wait to tell us of his changes in less than twenty-four hours.

"Every morning I go to this coffee shop for breakfast. There are girls sitting at the counter and I always imagine them in a sexual way, giving them a score on a 1 – 10 bedroom scale. It's like a game I play that no one knows about. Today I sat down in my same place and instead of looking at their bodies and stripping them with my eyes, I looked at their eyes and I saw their pain. For the first time I saw them as hurting people who needed help."

Harrison's healing proceeded quickly. He came to the airport one day before we left the country to give us an update on his progress. He told us he no longer needed to cling to arachnophobia as an excuse for faulty behavior. He has found the real spider and has killed it.

Teenage sexual touching with boys. 50 (men). As boys move from adolescence into puberty and on into teenage years they become very sensitive about their bodies, much more so than girls. Suddenly they want complete privacy when they undress. Generally, they are very uncomfortable if another person is around, even another boy of the same age. Their body is growing through changes that are new to them, changes they are learning to accept. These feelings continue for several years until they become completely comfortable with their bodies.

The idea of touching another boy sexually or being touched is out of the realm of reality—unless their healthy emotions have been distorted by some earlier violation. Nevertheless, many men do respond to this statement. They freely remember such incidents and talk about them without hesitation, never realizing that all boys didn't do this.

Temptation to touch children sexually. 51 (men), 53 (women). You might be surprised at how many men and women check this symptom. As we talk about the survey in our seminars, men and women freely admit having these feelings when, for example, they might be changing their own child's diapers. Many have privately confessed to us they did, in fact, give in to the temptation with their own children or when they were babysitting. From our experience, virtually without exception, every victimizer was once a victim! (Every victim, however, does not become a victimizer.)

The act of touching a child or the thought of it is clearly an aberration from God's intention when He created man or woman. If you have had this temptation or succumbed to it, it is a clear sign that someone first victimized you.

Tendency to look at others' penises. 53 (men). This symptom on the men's survey represents an unhealthy and abnormal attention to body parts. It may be, but is not necessarily, connected to homosexual feelings.

Uncomfortable with nudity in marriage. 54 (men), 54 (women). This symptom is very common with women, but is occasionally checked by men as well. In the sanctity and privacy of the bedroom, healthy husbands and wives are very comfortable with their bodies. Those who respond to this statement will usually justify their feelings by saying, "Well, I'm too fat" or "I'm too thin" or "I have too much here" or "Not enough there." They might also say, "I just don't feel good about my body," "I think my body is ugly," or "I don't know why I feel this way; I just do."

The real truth often lies in the fact that their bodies were defiled in childhood. They have grown up ashamed or uncomfortable with their bodies and don't know why. Putting a ring on one's finger does not change those deeply entrenched and never verbalized feelings.

Uncontrollable crying. 56 (men), 56 (women). Have you ever broken out with sobs that you just couldn't seem to stop? Has anyone ever said to you, "Why are you crying so much? It's not that important"? Have you wondered yourself, *Why this torrent of tears?*

Fred remembers that he cried so much as a child that his brothers and sister called him "La-la." In family pictures and movies little Fred was frequently crying. Have you also experienced this uncontrollable crying? Crying taps into the buried pain that resulted when bad things were done to the child. Consistently, every one who has checked this symptom in the past had several other clear symptoms as well.

Even if you have checked off only one statement in the first column, do not think, *Oh, well, this doesn't apply to me.* Even as few as one response in this column means we need to be sensitive to the possibility. The few times the test has been inaccurate is when the person seeking truth or answers has failed to check things that probably did apply and therefore showed nothing in the first column. Later, through memory-retrieval prayer, a violation was usually discovered.

When Rodney took the test at one of our Promise of Healing workshops in California, he checked only one line in the first column: "dreams of snakes." During the practice sessions he said there was no point for the prayer director to pray with him. He knew he had never been violated and he could easily explain the dreams of snakes (an especially clear symptom that invariably indicates a specific type of abuse). Rodney said he had lived in the country as a child where there were many snakes and he "hated snakes." Having no proof and not wishing to argue, we responded to him, "The Holy Spirit can reveal the roots of rejection."

Suddenly Rodney said, "He's revealing something to me right now."

"What is He showing you?"

"I can see a man, he's a neighbor, walking along the side of my house by the garden. He's holding my hand, and I can see his pants are open."

"Well, then, your dreams of snakes may be significant."

"No, I'm sure that's all that happened. There is nothing more." That quickly he slipped from acceptance to denial. It's hard to conceive that an adult man would be standing with a little boy or girl, holding the child's hand, with his pants open, if he didn't have something further in mind.

"Even if that is all that did happen," we told him, "what he did to you by exposing himself is very clearly a form of sexual violation."

Rodney was willing to acknowledge that much, which was revealed to him by a flashback, but he remained insistent that nothing more could have happened. *Surely,* he thought, *I would have remembered it.* He hadn't remembered any part of the incident by the garden, but the dreams of snakes, which Rodney acknowledged having, indicated there was more. He will not "see" it until he is ready and willing to know all the truth. The Lord is gentle and compassionate (Heb. 5:2) and will never force truth upon us.

If you did not check anything in the first column and your totals in the second and third columns are very low, perhaps only five or six, then this chapter does not necessarily apply to you. You can be very thankful that as a child you apparently escaped this type of damaging defilement of your emotions and body.

You might want to continue reading this chapter, however, since the Lord may someday bring a hurting soul to you who desperately needs this insight. If you are a parent, the next chapter, which deals with violation of children, might give you some valuable information for the future.

Responses in the Second and Third Columns

Responses in the second column, labeled "Strong," mean these responses are frequently seen in people who have suffered childhood trauma, but their roots could also be attributed to other sources. They are important, but of lesser significance in getting to the bottom line quickly. The third column, identified as "Possible," shows that these symptoms are of still lesser importance. Their roots are even more apt to have come from nonsexual abuse and usually indicate rejection. However, these symptoms do give an enhanced picture of the overall issues that someone may be facing. (The fourth column, labeled "Group," will be discussed later.)

Analyzing Your First-, Second-, and Third-Column Responses

How many first-column symptoms did you check on the survey? Remember: The symptoms lead us to the general area of the truth. Through memory-retrieval prayer the Holy Spirit can reveal the exact nature of the truth. If the possibility that you may have been violated is a shock to you, if you want to disbelieve or doubt that it could have happened, then look at some of the other symptoms that you checked in the second and third columns. Why have some of these things been a problem for you? Did you check, perhaps, a total of twenty-four symptoms? You may be able to rationalize two or three of them. But can you explain away every single one of them? Remember that Jesus said, "I have come that they may have life, and that they may have it more abundantly" (John 10:10). You may have eternal life, but is your life here on earth abundant? If your answer is no, then perhaps it is time to open your mind to the fact that there must be a reason why you checked so many symptoms. Acceptance is the first step on the healing journey!

Responses in the Fourth-Column (Group Symptoms)

The fourth column on both forms of the survey is used to indicate "group symptoms." Your marks in this column may be an indication that when violation occurred, it could have been by a number of perpetrators, or a group, rather than a single violator.

If you checked several of the fourth-column symptoms, you have most likely checked many in the first three columns as well. Generally, people who have checked five or six in the fourth column will have checked ten or more in the first column. They are also apt to have a grand total of about thirty-five or more responses. The symptoms in the fourth column indicate an even more traumatic form of victimization. Chapter 13 will help you further understand and identify this type of group abuse. But a few ideas need to be discussed here about the group symptoms. Two of the statements, numbers 2 and 58 on both surveys, may not be very significant when checked in the fourth column: "Afraid of big or black dogs" and "Unexplained fear of darkness." If those two are the only ones checked in the fourth column, they are not necessarily indicators of group abuse. However if they are checked along with two or three others in the fourth column, they take on particular importance.

2 Afraid of Big or Black Dogs.

If you checked this one in the fourth column, it could mean nothing more troublesome than being chased or attacked by a big dog while you were walking home from school in the fourth grade. (That is a very valid reason to have a healthy respect for big dogs!) An important question to ask, however, is, "What age were you when the dog attacked you?" If your answer is, "I was nine; I remember because I was in the fourth grade," then you have fixed the time of the attack.

The next question is, "Were you afraid of big or black dogs before that?"

If you answer yes then clearly your fear of dogs does not originate with that fourth-grade incident.

On the survey form, when the fear of dogs statement is checked *along with several others in the fourth column,* and a significant number (eight or more) are also checked in the first column, two things become evident:

1. Childhood sexual violation is clearly indicated.

2. The fear of big or black dogs may be related to bestiality—common in certain forms of group victimization.

58 *Unexplained Fear of Darkness.*

The same criteria apply to this symptom as to fear of dogs. If this is the only symptom you checked in the fourth column and very few other statements are checked on the survey, it is not important. You may remember not liking to be alone in the dark as a child. If your fear of darkness is an adult fear *without other symptoms* it may simply be related to an adult traumatic experience.

If, however, you checked several in the first column and no others in the fourth, it would generally indicate that a traumatic (versus seductive or game-playing) form of victimization took place in the dark.

When fear of darkness is checked *as well as others* in the fourth or group column, then the inference becomes clearer of types of group violation, which invariably take place in the dark of night. These will be further discussed in Chapter 13.

Of the other symptoms in the fourth column, we would hesitate to make any conclusions if a person checked just one of those lines. We would want to ask him or her, "What did you mean when you marked that one?" "How do you really feel about that?" If our question evoked no emotion, or uncertainty as to why he or she had answered "yes," we might tend to overlook it. On the other hand, if we were to ask "What do you mean by 'fear of knives'" (numbers 20 and 16) and the person answered, "Ooh, I get shivers whenever I see a knife. I hate knives; even in my own kitchen I'm afraid of them!" we would know the question tapped into some deep, probably repressed emotion. The obvious inference is that a knife was used in the victimization. In certain types of group violation, knives are often prominent, creating very real fear in the mind and emotions of the child who was present.

If you have checked several symptoms in the fourth column, we would strongly urge you not to read Chapter 13 alone. **It should only be read and reviewed when accompanied by a mature, trusted, and emotionally stable adult.** This chapter could conceivably trigger explosive emotions that you don't even know exist, memories that are buried in the basement of your mind.

If you are a counselor or pastor, or if you minister to people who have been sexually abused, we especially urge you to carefully read and evaluate this chapter. It may contain information that will be quite new to you. The questionnaire may be especially helpful to you in understanding people who make slow, little, or no progress.

If you have come up with many symptoms while reading this chapter, you may be a little discouraged at this point, but we want to offer hope. We have seen thousands become healed when they found the roots of their problem. Your desire now is to prayerfully work to dig up the roots of your pain.

This letter from Ruth will encourage you and give you the desire to seek the truth.

"I always was the dumb one," Ruth wrote. "My mother and father both put me down and made me feel stupid and worthless. Like a lot of others, I refused to believe that anything could've possibly happened to me when I was a little girl as far as being abused. My father was a highly respected preacher. But as I was reading *Freeing Your Mind* I was taken by surprise. I told my husband that someone I didn't know wrote a book that told everything about me that I never shared with anyone! Out of the thirty-eight symptoms listed in your book . . . I marked thirty-one.

"I checked so many symptoms it was unbelievable! Once my husband and I started to understand my problems we then quit fighting each other and started pulling together."

Ruth explained that she had a memory gap before age six and through counseling and working through *Freeing Your Mind* she uncovered the abuse from her "religious father." Since he was dead she called her mother to talk about the issue. As so often happens, the mother denied the possibility and scolded Ruth in the same berating manner she had used on her as a child. This time Ruth was emotionally strong enough to hear the words, refuse to accept them, and give her mother to the Lord.

After two years of prayer, counsel, and study, Ruth took the Personality Profile Test again. She had done a "complete flip-flop," she said.

"Then I was 50–50 Melancholy/Phlegmatic. Now I am 50–50 Sanguine/Choleric. I just wanted to share with you a small bit of a long story of how God used you to free me of the bondage and garbage of my past:

1. "It feels so good to feel good and to be the real me.

2. "I don't think I'm ugly and stupid. As a matter of fact I have to pull myself away from the mirror.

3. "I can look anyone in the eyes and talk to them.

4. "I'm sharing my steps of healing with other women.

5. "Because my dad was a preacher I couldn't look up while any pastor was preaching. I felt guilty and thought they were preaching to me when it was something negative and when they preached something positive I thought they were preaching to the people around me. I was a bad one. Now I can look the preacher in the eye while he is preaching. Now, I can even play the guitar and sing solos in front of everyone.

6. "I now can pray more intimately to my heavenly Father. I lay in bed one night and I started to pray and before I knew it tears were coming when I told God how much I love Him for what He's done for me. I used to know about my God—now I want to know my God.

7. "I'm in touch with my feelings for the first time. I had to be so tough all my life I never cried, now I can cry at the least little thing."

12

How Can I Know If My Child Has Been Violated?

At the conclusion of a seminar on *Freeing Your Mind from Memories that Bind,* couples often ask us, "How can I know if my child has been sexually abused?" The simple answer would be to ask them, but they usually won't say. Chances are the molester threatened them if they dared to tell. We have heard tales of unbelievable threats: "If you tell, I will chop you up in little pieces" or "Kill your mother, little sister, puppy" or "Put you in a box and nail the cover shut" or "Bury you alive in the cemetery" or, as one was told, "under the front porch."

After you have taken the Symptoms of Childhood Victimization questionnaire if you have any possible thought that your child may have been harmed, approach him or her carefully. Do not, under any circumstances (such as your own panic, anger, or fear) frighten your child. If he or she has been molested, any strong or sudden approach from you will revictimize the child. All victims feel dirty, ashamed, and hurt, and the last thing they need is a parent who appears to be questioning them in an accusatory manner. Knowing that a child may lie because of fear of retribution, you should watch his or her eyes for reactions. Put your hand on top of the child's head and ask, "Has anyone ever patted you here?" The answer is usually truthful. Move down the body in a nonthreatening way, almost like a game. When you get to the child's private parts, watch for any frightened look, shivering, or downward or sideward glance that might indicate possibilities of abuse. If you are suspicious of a certain person ask, "Did Mr. _____ ever pat you on the head?" and then move down, not forgetting the mouth. If you feel there has been a violation but the child says no, don't force the point. Let the child know you love and will protect him or her.

People also ask us, "Don't these children make this all up?" "Can we really believe them?" It is a rare child who would get any pleasure from reporting that "Mr. _____ pulled down my pants and this is what he did." The evidence is almost totally in the other direction: They don't tell when it does happen.

We should *never* disregard the testimony of a child. Children don't make up stories of inappropriate touching or sexual contact. During memory retrieval one woman saw not only her father orally violating her in the kitchen of her childhood home, but also saw him sharpening the kitchen knives. Each time he would get one really sharp, he would show it to her and say, "If you ever tell, this is what you'll get." This repeated trauma, which occurred after each violation, so terrified her that she suppressed the memories in order to survive. As an adult, she'd always wondered why she had such a fear of knives and why she wouldn't let her husband sharpen the dull knives she had. Too many parents in their naivete scold and berate their children, even punish them, for "saying such dirty things about..." (the perpetrator, who may be a loved and respected member of the family, religious leader, or a close friend).

Until recently few child psychologists were trained and experienced in determining probable violation, and even now persons with such skills are difficult to find. Further, if the counselor has limited experience and skill, the questions may be highly traumatic for the child and he or she may be "revictimized." A pediatrician told us that when he suspected a child had been molested he had to call the sheriff's department. They then sent over a uniformed officer with a holster and gun who stood over the child while the doctor did a reexamination. This required procedure so panicked the children that it added to their fear. This doctor personally worked to change this frightening legal system and has persuaded the county to put two-way glass in the examining rooms.

As the parent, make sure that your child is not subjected to any such procedure by an authority figure. Medical doctors can make physical examinations to determine vaginal or anal penetration (the latter is less common in little girls than in little boys). There is probably no medical examination that will determine oral penetration, one of the most common forms of violation of both little girls and little boys. During one six-month period, we prayed with sixty-two women and some men who had repressed memories of violation in childhood. Fifty-eight of them, or 94 percent, received from the Holy Spirit clear memories of having been orally violated! Most had been victimized by adult males, but some by women as well.

Your answers to the following questions may give you the insight you are seeking. Place a check on the line beside every question to which you answer Yes. These questions generally apply to children under eight years of age.

SYMPTOMS OF CHILDHOOD VICTIMIZATION

*_____ 1. Have you noticed your child playing with himself or herself sexually (more than a three-year-old just exploring body parts)?

*_____ 2. Does your child tend to rub toys, sheets, blankets, or dolls between his or her legs, or rub himself or herself on the arm of a chair or sofa?

*_____ 3. Does your child like to run the faucet water in the tub directly onto his or her genitals?

_____ 4. Have you noticed a sudden mood change in your child?

_____ 5. Has your child gone from once happy and bubbly to downcast and sad?

_____ 6. Does your child, who formerly enjoyed playing with other children, want to be alone?

_____ 7. Have you ever found your child hiding in a closet or under a bed for no apparent reason?

*_____ 8. When going to sleep, does your child usually want to get close to the wall?

_____ 9. Has your child suddenly started wetting the bed?

_____ 10. Does your child want to lock the door when he or she goes into the bathroom?

_____ 11. Has your child suddenly expressed a fear or refusal of going to school?

_____ 12. Does your child cling to your leg when certain people are around or will be coming over?

*_____ 13. Does your child have dreams of being chased?

*_____ 14. Does your child have dreams of snakes or of spiders?

_____ 15. Does your child tend to break into sobbing when you are about to leave and plead, "Please don't leave me!"?

_____ 16. Does your child have a perceived aversion or even a fear of any babysitters?

*_____ 17. Does your child seem to have a compulsion to wash certain body parts or brush his or her teeth?

*_____ 18. Does your child tend to gag when taking liquid medicine, a procedure that formerly was not a problem?

_____ 19. Does your child express real fear at being alone?

*_____ 20. Has your child ever awakened screaming during the night and said there was someone in black in the room?

*_____ 21. Has your child ever told you about dreams that were surprisingly sexual in nature?

_____ 22. Has your child complained to you that his or her bottom hurt? Was there perhaps a redness, but no rash?

_____ 23. Has your child frequently come home with candy from the same person?

_____ 24. Does your child have an inordinate curiosity about things that are sexual?

*_____ 25. Have you noticed or heard about your child wanting to touch another child's genitals (even a brother or sister)?

_____ 26. Has there been a noticeable change in your child's behavior, attitude, or grades at school?

_____ 27. Have you seen flashes of raging anger in your child?

_____ 28. Does your child have a tendency to make remarks such as "I'm dirty," "I'm no good," "God couldn't love me"?

*_____ 29. Does your child have a tendency to have a gagging problem that he or she didn't have before?

_____ 30. Do you fear that your child has already been sexually violated?

_____ **Total Responses**

If you checked only one question, you might want to continue to watch for other possible symptoms. Each question reflects a symptom of sexual violation although some of these symptoms are general and could come from other sources. Several, however, are very clear symptoms. They are marked with an * at the left margin. Just one of these is significant. However, it is not likely for a child to show only one "Clear" symptom and no others.

If you have checked several or many questions, particularly those that are starred, there would be valid reason for concern. If there are some specific questions to which you don't know the answer and you think it is appropriate, ask your child. If you ask, you may be surprised at how forthright the responses are.

If you suspect or are quite sure of a violation of your child, do not be afraid to gently, lovingly ask him or her if anyone has ever touched him or her down there, or put "anything bad" in his or her mouth. If so, "Did it taste 'yucky'?" If you get affirmative answers ask, "Who was it?" Again, don't be surprised if your child answers no to everything, even though in your heart you feel sure something did happen. Remember that your child may have been threatened. Little children take such threats very seriously!

Never push the child. Never get impatient yourself. You must put your child's needs and feelings ahead of your desire to know. Failure to do so may shut down your child's ability to communicate with you forever. Even though a child does not comprehend the intensity of what may have been done to him or her, it is still a highly traumatic experience. It will inflict long-range damage and manifestations as he or she matures into adulthood.

Never make the mistake of thinking, *Oh it was minor; she'll get over it, or she'll forget all about it*. It was not minor, it will cause lasting damage! But many do "forget all about it." In our judgment, that's the worst thing that could happen. In adult life, the grown child has to deal with all the adult symptoms of childhood violation and has no idea why he or she has such struggles.

Please also bear in mind that if a violation did in fact occur, it may already have slipped into the subconscious. Your child may answer no and in fact be telling the truth because he or she has no memory of it. This is part of God's built-in escape mechanism (see 1 Cor. 10:13).

Finally, an important warning: Be prepared for any answer your child gives. Be sure that you are not guilty of any kind of overreaction, anger, or of denial! The child must feel that he or she will be believed. Most children, even at very young ages, feel guilt and shame after a violation. They sense that it was wrong, and often they feel it was their fault! Therefore, be sure *you* never put blame on the child. The average child can no more seduce an adult than the cow can jump over the moon. (The only exception is those few children who are specifically trained for this in a satanic ritual.)

Of the thousands of adult victims we have talked with, the majority didn't tell their mothers because "She never would have believed me," "She wouldn't have been able to handle it," or "She would have blamed me." Believe them and don't blame them. Many report they told their mothers, who in turn punished them for making up such bad stories.

In the Childhood Victimization questionnaire we intentionally made no effort to determine the identity of the victimizer or the nature of the violation. With little children, the most important thing is to determine the fact of the occurrence.

HOW CAN I HELP MY CHILD WHEN VIOLATION IS KNOWN OR INDICATED?

The suggestions we offer to you are based on our experience in ministering to adults who were abused as children and who either never told anyone or told and were not believed.

1. Keep the memory alive in the child's mind. When the memory slips into the unknown subconscious realm it is often lost forever unless retrieved by questionable psychological techniques or by Holy Spirit-guided memory retrieval.

When memory is accepted or "owned," your child will develop a freedom to talk about the event itself. Allow your child to express the feelings that have resulted from the abuse—watch especially for his or her perceived shame and guilt. Take steps to prevent any possible recurrences. Victimized children are often repeatedly violated because they are both vulnerable and without strong defense options.

In evaluating their childhoods many adults have been able to see how the original abuse set up a never-ending sequence of incidents common to the "victim personality." They have then understood why they married an abusive or alcoholic spouse. "Owning the memory" is an important factor in both the cessation of flashbacks and bad dreams, and in the healing process. *Extreme caution must be taken not to talk incessantly about the issue or to discuss your child's private hurts with your friends or with their friends.* Remember, keeping the memory alive does not mean making it the focal point of family life but of making sure it is not suppressed, only to be dealt with painfully in later years.

2. Remember your child has been changed. God places a normal healthy sexuality in each child in the mother's womb. By God's design this sexuality is not to be awakened until the age of puberty. When a child has been physically interfered with or violated in any way, this dormant sexuality is immediately activated. It is like a light switch, intended to be off, that has been inappropriately turned on. Therefore, in such cases it is "normal" for a child to have sexual feelings, sexual curiosity, and even sexual experiences.

In other words, do not scold your child for masturbating or for playing with himself sexually. Do not scold him for wanting to touch other children sexually but do point out that touching others sexually is unacceptable behavior because it hurts them too. These children have real feelings they don't understand and shouldn't have had to handle at their young age. They have been changed forever by one act of defilement. Instead of chastising, they need loving guidance and direction, helping them to understand what is inappropriate behavior.

3. Become fully aware of the symptoms of childhood violation. Some symptoms will appear at an early age, but others do not manifest themselves until adolescence or the teenage or adult years. When these issues do arise you will be in a healthy position to encourage, rather than berate or alarm, your child if you understand the symptoms. Read all you can on the subject of children and adults who have been victimized. All too soon your child will also become an adult and need your loving support.

4. Be alert to protect your child. Since victimized children are prone to revictimization, you must never allow them to be in a vulnerable position. If your child screams when a certain babysitter arrives, or begs you not to take him or her to Mrs. So-and-So's house, don't use that person again! Never, never allow your child to be alone with a known or suspected abuser even if he or she is a close relative. Also don't believe for one minute that because the victimizer has apologized or "confessed it to the Lord" that he or she will never do it again. It is a compulsion that the best of intentions usually can't control.

One woman told us that as a child, she told her parents what Grandpa had done to her. They immediately took her to Grandpa's to confront him. Grandpa vehemently denied any such thing. Grandpa was believed instead of the child. On the way home the child was scolded for making up such bad things. On later occasions when the parents needed convenient free babysitting, the little girl was taken to her grandparents. The violations continued and the child was doomed to the whims of the perpetrator, totally unprotected by her parents.

5. Make certain your child is indeed a Christian and knows he or she is going to heaven. You and your child must be sure of their salvation. One of the first thoughts the enemy plants in a victimized child's mind is, *You are not good enough for God to love you.* Thus abused children think they are dirty. They begin to have feelings of shame, and when we meet them as adults they check "feel unworthy of God's love" on the adult survey.

To help your child you must first be certain of his or her salvation; reinforce it often in the child's mind. Only the Lord Jesus can bring healing (see Isa. 9:6). You can't. The pastor can't. A counselor can't.

If your children do not know Jesus as their Savior, this is the starting place. Teach your children about Jesus, His virgin birth, His perfect sinless life, His death on the cross, His blood that cleanses them from all their sins, and His resurrection on the third day. Tell them He sits forever at the right hand of glory, with all power in heaven and on earth, including the power to heal them of all the bad things that were done to them. Then experience the joy of leading your own child to the saving knowledge of Jesus Christ as Savior in a prayer of salvation.

If you need help, here is a simple but effective prayer. You say the first line, then let your child pray it. Go through the prayer one line at a time, with the child repeating each line.

Dear Lord Jesus,
Thank You for dying on the cross for me.
Thank You for giving Your life for me.
Forgive me those things I've done wrong.
Heal me from bad things others have done to me.
I ask You to come into my life as my Savior and Lord.
Thank You for coming into my life.
I will love You forever. Amen.

Next you might ask your child:
"Did you ask Jesus to come into your life?
(Yes.)
"Then where is He now?
(In my life.)
"And He will never leave you, because He said, 'I will never leave you nor forsake you' (Heb. 13:5). That's His promise to you!"
Write down today's date: _____

Note to Mom and Dad: If you are not sure that you have ever prayed such a prayer, or if someone were to ask you right now, "Are you going to heaven?" and your answer is "I don't know" or "I hope so," then we urge you to pray the prayer with your child.

6. Pray daily for your child's healing. We have already witnessed and personally experienced the awesome power of God to bring healing into our lives. When we come to Him daily, asking for cleansing, for healing, for growth, and for wisdom, His promise is that He will hear and answer.

We are strong believers in the power of our risen Lord to bring healing from emotional and physical trauma. He promises if we will come to Him He will give us rest, peace, and healing.

We also strongly believe in the value of intercessory prayer. Particularly when your children are young, and their relationship with the Lord is in its infancy they may not have the spiritual maturity to pray for their own healing. They probably don't even understand the wound. Pray for them in their behalf. Come to the Lord daily for them; stand in their place. God loves it when we come to Him over and over again, day and night (see Luke 18:1, 3, 7).

7. Encourage your children to write their prayers each day. As your children learn to write, sit with them each day, and each of you spend time "talking" to the Lord in writing. Notice our emphasis on "sit with them." It will take effort on your part. They're not likely to "come to Him" if you tell them to. They are very likely to do so if you also "come to Him" on your own at the same time.

These intercessory prayers for your child will be very effective. The Lord will hear and He will respond. The major burden for healing, however, always falls on the shoulders of the one who has been wounded: "Let us cleanse ourselves from all filthiness [defilement] of the flesh [our bodies] and spirit [our emotions], perfecting holiness [our faith] in the fear of God" (2 Cor. 7:1).

Early healing of childhood sexual defilement requires coming to the only One who can do the work of healing. You model for your child the daily coming to Him in prayer. Your child's healing depends on this. You will be amazed at what He will do for your child. In the process you will be amazed at what He has also done for you!

WARNING!

The next chapter contains information and a questionnaire that could be severely traumatic to some persons. It could evoke deeply suppressed emotions that may be very painful. The questionnaire should not be used before reading Chapter 11 on identifying childhood sexual victimization, taking the survey of emotions and experiences found in that chapter, and carefully reading the section on "group symptoms."

If these symptoms apply to you, this chapter should only be read and reviewed when accompanied by a mature, trusted, and emotionally stable adult.

It is important for you, the reader, to know that we did not set out to investigate ritual or group abuse. We were as naive about it as the average Christian. We have always tried to stay away from controversial issues or those that divide believers. This subject is something we would prefer not to deal with at all, but because of the number of people we have prayed with who have found ritual abuse when none of us was looking for it, we know we must set forth the facts as the Lord has revealed them to us.

13

Is There Such a Thing as Satanic Ritual Abuse?

As hard as it may be for most Christians to comprehend, people do worship satan as the most powerful god. *(In this chapter we have intentionally avoided using capital letters regarding satan for we specifically wish to do nothing that might be construed to ascribe dignity to him.)* They gather together in small groups, called covens, with a fervor and intensity that would make the commitment of most Christians look anemic in comparison. They will do anything to please satan, to gain favor from him, which they believe will give them great power.

These covens generally meet in after-midnight rituals. The entire proceedings are kept highly secret by the blood oaths that are taken upon acceptance into the coven. Few adults escape, for the price for desertion or disobedience is death by sacrifice, dismemberment, and disappearance. The less traumatic parts of a ritual are singing, chanting, and dancing. The participants are most often clothed in black or dark robes, and they take blood communions. This blood is either drawn from a child in a most heinous manner while he or she is tied, chained, or held on an altar, or from an animal or human sacrifice.

The cross is commonly used in the most despicable manner imagined. Satanists will do anything the mind can conceive to desecrate the name of Jesus. The more flagrant the abuse, the more pleased, they believe, satan will be with them. They hate the Name of Jesus. Although they profess that satan has the greatest power, they possess a mortal fear of Jesus and the presence of Light.

Some of the most horrendous and standard parts of a satanic ritual are the gross, multiple sexual acts done to little children, little girls primarily, but some little boys as well; those between the ages of two and six are most frequently used. The violations are perpetrated by women as well as men and often simultaneously.

Enough of what happens in ritual. It is too gross to further describe here. Our concern is what happens to these little children, the ones who survive, when they are cast off. They grow into adulthood with deeply shattered lives. In many cases their minds, their bodies, and their emotions are so splintered it is virtually impossible for them to live a healthy and productive life. We meet these women and a few men in their thirties, forties, and fifties. In almost all cases they have been to counselor after counselor seeking help and answers. Most of them have found none.

Satanic ritual abuse is well known and documented, especially in the secular and professional community, where police forces are trained to recognize satanic crimes. What is shocking is how few Christians, churches, counselors, and pastors have any knowledge of its existence. Even worse is the number of Christians who prefer to turn their heads the other way and pretend it doesn't exist. Yet there is hardly a church congregation that doesn't have at least one adult victim of childhood satanic ritual abuse.

In the past three years we have prayed with more than sixty individuals whose violations in these orgies were clearly revealed. In ministering to these victims, we learned both the nature of the violations and the resulting adult symptoms. The understanding of these clear symptoms has enabled us to further identify approximately one hundred additional victims. Those with whom we have personally spoken or ministered to are only a minute fraction of the vast number who have endured such abuse. We are convinced that if all the people who have been violated in satanic ritual (that is, those who are aware of it, as well as those whose memories are suppressed) were convened they would overflow the Rose Bowl in Pasadena, California, which seats a hundred thousand in the stands! This is a huge problem. Literally thousands upon thousands of adults are suffering from the effects of this horrific trauma.

We are fully aware that there exists a very small but very dedicated group who are doing everything they can to discredit the truth. They have been successful in planting magazine articles in credible Christian magazines, in getting books removed from store shelves, and in disparaging those few who have been willing to publicly testify to their experiences. The minds of these few are shut tight.

We can think of only four reasons why any Christian would promote such a dogmatic position:

1. They have been so totally deluded by satan himself, or his followers, that they cannot see the light.

2. They have a hidden agenda of their own.

3. They themselves are victims of this abuse but are in such denial their only coping mechanism is to refute its very existence.

4. They in fact serve a different master. Did not the Lord Himself warn us to "Beware of false prophets, who come to you in sheep's clothing, but inwardly they are ravenous wolves" (Matt. 7:15)?

It is now possible to quickly and accurately identify the evidence of childhood satanic ritual abuse. Henceforth we will refer to it by its common term, SRA. By knowing the disease that afflicts a patient a doctor can be much more effective in treating it; otherwise he or she might just as well prescribe aspirin for every problem. In the same way, in dealing with the effects of SRA, it is important to know what the real issues are. They are painful. They are traumatic. They are real.

The atrocities committed were so damaging that the young victim either consciously suppressed knowledge of the experience, or the Lord graciously permitted that suppression of memories. This is God's ordained escape mechanism according to 1 Corinthians 10:13: "God...will not allow you to be tempted (tested, tried) beyond what you are able, but with the temptation will also make the way of escape, that you may be able to bear it." In addition, the satanists themselves, for their own protection, use mind-control techniques, perfected over literally centuries, that enable them to preclude the child from ever having the knowledge of the experience.

Thus, most adults who were used as children in these rituals have no present-day knowledge. These memories are gradually being recovered today by secular professionals with the numerous and varied psychological means available to them. But only Christians have access to the awesome capability of the Holy Spirit to immediately bring back to remembrance whatever the Lord knows these former victims are ready to receive, according to the promise of John 14:26.

Adults who were discovered to have suffered satanic ritual abuse have amazingly similar patterns of childhood experiences. Later adult symptoms, struggles, and fears also follow a pattern. These consistent validations made it possible to conclusively predetermine the emotional responses to a series of questions, whether or not an adult was indeed a victim of childhood ritual.

The first indication of the possibility of SRA may have been found in Chapter 11, "How Can I Know If I Was Sexually Violated As a Child?" Those who checked several lines in the fourth column of the Survey of Emotions and Experiences in that chapter, indicating group abuse, may be surprised to learn that abuse in satanic ritual is the predominant form of group violation.

Edith was an alum at one of our recent CLASS training sessions. The year before she asked Fred if she could meet with him privately. From reading *Freeing Your Mind from Memories that Bind* she had already sensed that someone in her childhood must have violated her. The symptoms and struggles she had faced for fifty-six years were too evident to deny.

Edith asked Fred, "Can we pray together to retrieve my memories?" Within seconds, she found herself "sleeping over" at her piano teacher's house at the age of six. She was in bed, the door opened. Her teacher's husband came in, shut the door, and got under the covers with her. He began touching her body. She froze, but did not cry out. She said nothing to him. She felt powerless as he took more and more liberties with her. Suddenly the door opened, the light was turned on, and she heard her teacher yell, "Get out of here!" She had been rescued by the fortuitous intervention.

Edith was amazed at the reality of the scene. The Holy Spirit had guided her into the truth, and she felt remarkably free. Even though this memory had been totally suppressed, the retrieval took no more than five minutes.

At the next CLASS seminar a year later, Edith came to Fred and said, "I think there's more. Would there be a time that you could pray with me again?"

This time Fred felt she should go through the Survey of Emotions and Experiences. Fred later reported that as he read the fifty-eight items to her she responded to three of them in the fourth column, indicating group abuse. He was surprised. Yet Edith did not have a high total on the whole survey, and in the several years we had known her before she even came to CLASS to polish her speaking skills she had never seemed to exhibit any of the traits we frequently see with people who have endured SRA. Nevertheless, Fred thought Edith should go through the Sarita Questionnaire, which we had developed during the previous year and which is included later in this chapter. It, too, proved to be amazingly accurate and revealing.

Fred asked Edith all of the questions on the Sarita Questionnaire. She answered Yes to twelve of them, but none of them evoked any strong emotion or reaction. When he explained to Edith the significance of her answers, she was dumbfounded. She was not denying the possibility; she just couldn't imagine when or how it could have happened. She was certain it could not have been her parents as they rarely left her with anyone else when she was a child. Fred could not comprehend or explain anything to her. He only knew two things: She had answered Yes twelve times, and if it were true, the Holy Spirit had the power to reveal it to her.

As Fred and Edith talked about the significance of her answers, Edith did remember one time when she was six; her parents went away for a week on vacation and left her with a nice lady who took care of children. She did know she hated it there because when she didn't sit up straight at the table the lady tied her arms to a broomstick behind her back, and the other kids laughed and made fun of her. This had been fifty years ago.

First Edith prayed. She asked God to reveal to her if there was any ritual abuse at any time in her childhood. Then Fred followed Edith in prayer and asked the Lord to fulfill His promise of John 8:32: "You shall know the truth, and the truth shall make you free," and to show her whatever He wanted her to see from her childhood (see John 16:13–14).

After Fred and Edith had both prayed, Fred simply asked Edith to shut her eyes and tell him anything that the Lord revealed to her. In an awesome demonstration of His power to reveal truth, Edith immediately responded, "I'm sitting at the table in the lady's house. I'm six years old. There are other kids at the table. She's angry at me, 'cause I'm not sitting up straight. She's tying my arms behind my back to a broomstick. The other kids are laughing at me. I'm crying. She's really angry with me now. She's carrying me down-stairs to the basement. It's dark down here. She's putting me in a box on the floor. She's scolding me. She says if I cry it will be even worse for me. Now she's closing the lid on top of me. I'm scared, but I don't dare make a sound. I think I'm falling asleep." Edith was then quiet for a little while. Fred asked her, "Edith, what is happening now?"

"I think she's coming back. Yes, she's opening the lid. I'm glad to see her; maybe she'll let me out."

"Edith, can you see anything in the room?"

"Yes, I see a candle, just one candle."

"Edith, can you see anyone else in the room?"

"Yes, there are some people there. They seem to have black robes on. . . . Someone's picking me up and laying me down on a table"

"What are you wearing?"

"I don't seem to have anything on. No, I don't have anything on. They're standing around me in a circle. They're saying something. I can't understand what they're saying. They seem to be chanting. . . . Somebody just said, 'Hail, satan!'"

"Edith, look at them. Are they men or women? Can you tell?"

"They're mostly men. Oh-oh, they don't have any clothes on now. Oh, I'm scared!

"Somebody is holding me down. A man is telling me to 'Be quiet!' Oh, somebody's putting something in my mouth. It's big and it's hard; it hurts. Oh, it tastes terrible . . ."

There was more. Little Edith was sexually violated over and over again. There was nothing she could do. She couldn't run away. She wasn't even allowed to cry. Her parents would never know. Even Edith would never know because it was so horrific. God allowed her to completely repress this trauma into her subconscious.

Edith was luckier than many. She clearly knew that neither her parents nor any relatives had anything to do with it. The abuse had happened only one time, during that one week when her parents entrusted her to that nice lady who took care of children. Today she is more vibrant and vital in her ministry to others in the name of the Lord Jesus. Who can guess how many little girls, and perhaps some boys as well, may have had to endure this same type of satanic abuse in this woman's basement?

Recently, we received a letter from Edith in response to our request to tell the above story here. Her response beautifully demonstrates the power of memory retrieval.

"Dear Fred and Florence," Edith writes, "I found the letter from you in my mailbox this morning. I was startled by my reaction. Racking sobs poured from my innermost being as I read the manuscript and relived the horror of what happened to me at age six. This confirmed, without any doubt, the revelation from the Holy Spirit during my session with Fred. I sat in the car and wept it out, then prayed a long time for God's cleansing and refreshing. I used to have terrible nightmares of being abandoned—often war themes—and I would be on one side of a chasm, all alone and was unable to get across, but trying to escape from someone. I have never once had these nightmares since Fred prayed for me and we retrieved the SRA memory.

"Because many people chalk up these types of memories to vivid imagination, I thank the Holy Spirit for confirmation of their validity... as well as for His cleansing and healing power.

"Isn't it wonderful that God can take the darkest moments of our lives, turn them around, and use these experiences to minister to others. Praise God!"

Based on the facts given us by several ex-satanists, we know there are eight high holy days or sabbats each year. There are also special ritual days that celebrate seasons, moons, and other signs. Christmas Eve and Halloween are times of significance and destruction. For an average coven ten children per year would be a fairly accurate estimate, and many children are used repeatedly over a period of several years. If we were to presume that this might have gone on for twenty years in any one coven, which is probably a conservative estimate, we can quickly see that more than two hundred little children were likely to have been used and abused in that one coven!

How many covens are there in the United States alone? Literally thousands—no one really knows. They are just as prevalent all around the world. We ourselves, in praying with women and men who have been satanically victimized, have found the practice to be equally common in Canada, Australia, New Zealand, England, and virtually all of Europe.

In the United States alone, we estimate there is an average number of five hundred covens in each of the fifty states, and many states surely have significantly more. That would mean:

- 25,000 such covens exist in the United States today,

- 250,000 little children are violated in ritual each year, and

- 5,000,000 children are used in any twenty-year period.

These are frightening figures. The worst part is they may be too conservative.

Where are these children today, who, like Edith, were used and abused twenty, thirty, forty, or fifty years ago? They are all now adults struggling to live normal, healthy, and productive lives. Many have sought relief by turning to drugs and alcohol. Many have sought relief by coming to the Savior. They are in our churches today, where no one seems to understand why:

- They feel ashamed and dirty.
- They feel God doesn't love them.
- They find it very hard to pray consistently.
- They have night terrors and bad dreams.
- They suffer from depression, anxiety attacks, and fears.
- They struggle in their marriage relationships.
- They are married to abusive or controlling mates.
- They've been to the altar, they've been to the pastor, they've been in counseling, they've been in therapy—and they don't seem to get any better.
- They feel people in church are tired of hearing about their problems and as a result, they feel hopeless.

Fortunately, now through the resources that God has given us, it is readily possible to determine the cause and discover the roots of these kinds of adult emotional, physical, and spiritual issues. Once we know what the real problem is rather than the "presenting problem," we can deal with the central cause rather than the peripheral symptoms.

The Sarita Questionnaire will enable you to discover if there is a possibility of totally suppressed satanic ritual abuse in your childhood. It is best if a trusted friend or professional helper can read the questions to you and record your responses.

Sarita Questionnaire

Some of these questions will evoke an emotional reaction. This is exactly what we are looking for, not "intellectual" answers. Place a check in front of each question to which you (or the seeker if you are reading the test to him or her) react affirmatively. Place two checks if a strong reaction occurs.

_____ 1. How do you feel about snakes? How would you react if you saw one coiled up over there in the corner and it started to move?

_____ 2. Do spiders bother you, particularly big hairy black ones?

_____ 3. How would you feel if you walked into a darkened room and saw nothing but candles?

_____ 4. Have you ever been chased in a dream? If yes, was it by one person or more than one?

_____ 5. If you answered "more than one" in question 4, what did they look like or what were they wearing?

_____ 6. Have you ever seen people in robes, hoods, or blankets in your dreams?

_____ 7. Have you ever heard chanting or wicked laughing in your dreams?

_____ 8. Have you ever sensed a black presence in your bedroom?

_____ 9. As a child, did you ever wake up during the night and think there were people or forms in black standing around your bed?

_____ 10. Do you ever die or have an intense fear of dying in your dreams?

_____ 11. How do you feel about knives or scissors? Have they ever been in your dreams?

_____ 12. How do you feel about blood? Do you ever see blood in your dreams?

_____ 13. Do any of your dreams take place in graveyards?

_____ 14. Do you ever see dead bodies in your dreams?

_____ 15. How do you feel about the full moon?

_____ 16. How do you feel about Halloween?

_____ 17. How do you feel about Christmas Eve?

_____ 18. How do you feel about your birthday?

_____ 19. How do you feel about Friday the thirteenth?

_____ 20. How do you feel about big or black dogs?

_____ 21. Are you ever bothered by bells, chimes, gongs, or loud noises?

_____ 22. How do you feel about roses or their smell?

_____ 23. Do you ever have strange feelings about the cross? If so, how would you feel if you looked over there and saw a cross upside down on the wall?

_____ 24. Have you ever been afraid of darkness?

_____ 25. Do you ever feel as though voices are speaking to you, saying bad things to you?

_____ 26. Do you tend to find yourself somewhere and have no idea how you got there?

_____ 27. Have you ever had a fear of "spirits"?

_____ 28. How do you feel about the occult?

_____ 29. What is your feeling about being hypnotized?

_____ 30. Do you know what guided imagery is? How do you feel about it?

_____ 31. Do you sometimes hesitate to take drugs or vitamins?

_____ 32. Do you know what a pentagram is? How would you feel if you saw one?

_____ 33. Do bright lights ever bother you?

_____ 34. How do you feel about hypodermic needles?

_____ 35. How would you feel if you found yourself in a wooden box?

_____ 36. How do you feel about bonfires?

_____ 37. How do you feel about having your picture taken?

_____ 38. Have you ever felt as though you were outside of your body?

_____ 39. How would you feel about receiving electroshock therapy?

_____ 40. Have you ever had "night terrors"?

_____ 41. How would you feel if you smelled incense?

_____ 42. Have you ever had a problem in cutting raw meat?

_____ 43. Have you ever been told you have vaginal or uterine scar tissue?

_____ 44. How would you feel if you were in a doctor's office for an examination and you saw several big gold rings on his fingers?

_____ 45. Do you sometimes react when communion is being served?

_____ 46. Have you ever been told, or felt, that your emotions were dead or frozen?

_____ 47. Have you ever reacted to seeing the temple of a fraternal order?

_____ 48. Have you suffered from sleep disorder?

_____ 49. Are you apt to be bothered by a baby dedication?

_____ 50. Have masks, ghosts, or "faces" ever upset you?

SCORING YOUR RESPONSES TO THE SARITA QUESTIONNAIRE

Each of the fifty questions relates to either a specific adult symptom of satanic ritual abuse (SRA) or to one of the actions or activities connected with satanic ritual.

A person who has answered yes or given affirmative responses to as few as ten or twelve questions is very likely giving evidence of having been used, and most probably sexually violated, in ritual. The more questions that are affirmed the more certain are the conclusions. Higher totals also tend to indicate increased frequency and longevity of the victimization.

Strong emotional reactions to certain questions would tend to indicate that the individual may have had this particular experience at some time in a ritual. These are generally during early childhood; however, we know of a few individuals who were used in ritual during their early-adult years, ages eighteen to twenty-five.

The first thing you may need to do is to completely wash away the concept that these things never happen:

a. Because you have never heard of them before, or

b. Because you have read that they never happen, or

c. Because your church does not believe there is any such thing.

The simple facts are that there are millions, yes, literally millions of adults living today in the United States alone (see page 214) who bear in their minds, emotions, and bodies the scars of the vile acts that were committed against them as little children. These atrocities do happen, they have been happening since biblical times, they are happening now, they will continue as long as there are evil men and women on the earth. Obviously, those perpetrating these crimes have learned over the centuries how to function in absolute secrecy. They are experts in what they do and in how to leave no traces whatsoever.

However, as in every "perfect crime," there is one slipup, one type of physical evidence, that can never be disputed: the bodily scars of what is termed "satanic circumcision"; these marks or scars never disappear. They are most frequently, but not exclusively, made on the child's labia, often on one side only. We have personally spoken to over fifty women and one man, who upon self-examination, confirmed that they did indeed have such a mark!

Let there be no doubt, we are talking about sexual horrors that are perpetrated in very real, but very secret, circumstances by people who look perfectly normal and respectable. These are people who occupy high positions in the community, the professions, even the church, and in national and international government.

Without attempting to go into too much detail of the horror of the abuse and torture that takes place in satanic ritual, we will briefly describe the significance of the preceding questions. This will help you understand why a person might emotionally react when going through the Sarita Questionnaire.

SIGNIFICANCE OF RESPONSES

The following statements relate to the corresponding question on the Sarita Questionnaire:

1. Snakes. In addition to being symbolic of oral violation by an adult male (very common in SRA as previously described in the Chapter 11 discussion about dreams of snakes), snakes are frequently used as part of the mind-control techniques developed by satanists. It is not uncommon for a child to be placed in a hole or a box with a snake to frighten the child into total submission or obedience. This can also cause the child to have a misplaced trust in the person who eventually "rescues" him or her from this temporary tomb, further bending the will of the child to trust those who would use him or her.

2. Spiders. Whether they appear in your dreams or you have an irrational fear of them or you are obsessed with them, spiders are also symbolic of oral male abuse. They can also represent oral abuse by an adult female.

3. Candles. Because candles are an important part of most satanic rituals the sight of candles or merely being asked a question about them may trigger a reaction, even though the memory of the ritual may be lost. When asked about the significance of candles, healthy (non-abused) people would answer, "Nothing special," or "I'd think it was romantic," or "Why all the candles?" These are non-emotional answers.

Not long ago Fred was asking the list of questions on the Sarita Questionnaire to a young mother whose life was full of struggles; she had shown SRA indications on the Survey of Emotions and Experiences. She answered in the affirmative to questions about both snakes and spiders. When Fred asked her, "How would you feel if you walked into a darkened room and saw nothing but candles?" she began to sob. The question had triggered repressed memories of her ritual abuse. There was now an explanation for many of her emotionally crippling symptoms.

4. Being chased. Having dreams in which you are being chased is a key indicator of childhood sexual abuse. Often people are aware of who or what was chasing them. One person doing the chasing usually indicates violation by a single person (but not necessarily a single occurrence). Being chased by a group indicates group violation and as we said earlier, SRA is a most significant form of this.

5 and 6. What did they look like, or what were they wearing? It is not unusual for adults to have a very clear sense of what was worn by the people who were chasing them in their dream. Often the answer is black robes, uniforms, cloaks, or monster faces that relate to actual satanic practices.

7. Chanting or wicked laughing. This is a regular part of satanic ritual. Often the person who has heard such chanting or laughing in dreams will be able to further identify that the persons in the dreams were wearing black robes! Remember: One of the roles of dreams is the release of subconscious memories and emotions.

8 and 9. A black presence in the childhood bedroom. This is often sensed, and frequently seen, by the child while he or she is awake, especially after a bad dream. This is the very real presence of evil, or of satanic forces. Every Christian, but especially a parent, can immediately rebuke and dispatch that presence by invoking the name of Jesus Christ, the authority of Luke 10:17–19. (See also James 4:7.) He will flee—he *must* flee, because he has no choice!

10 and 11. Dying in dreams or a great fear of dying. To force obedience and compliance, the child is not only threatened with death, but also may have witnessed the sacrifice of animals or the death of humans. The child fully understands what disobedience could mean.

11 and 12. Knives and blood. Used regularly in satanic rites, knives are used for drawing blood for communion, for marking, and for sacrifice. A child who has been repeatedly involved in ritual will have seen this enough to leave an indelible mark on his or her emotions, even without any conscious memories of it.

13. Graveyards. Cemeteries are often the sites of nighttime satanic rituals. Dreams of graveyards represent the replaying of long-suppressed actual experiences.

14. Dead bodies. In dreams dead bodies are often-seen symptoms of those who were used in ritual over an extended time. The dreams replicate previous actual experience. They are especially significant when there is emotional reaction with the answer, when it is *bodies* and not *body*, or when blood is also mentioned. Generally, it would not be the type of dream a child would have after Grandma died, for instance, and the child saw her in a casket.

15. Full moon. Because a full moon is a high day of satanic observance, it is likely to evoke fear or emotions in one who has been abused in rituals. In contrast, a healthy person's response to a full moon might be, "Oh, I think it's romantic."

16. Halloween. Also called All Hallows Eve, Halloween is one of the eight most important satanic sabbats, or sacred holidays. Children violated in ritual abuse have learned to fear that night that some children see as a fun time of costumes and begging. The other and non-emotional response to this question from a Christian adult would be "I don't agree with it" or "I don't like it because I know what it stands for." A moral opinion doesn't indicate abuse.

17. Christmas Eve. December 24 is another favorite day of devil worship. It is important to remember that followers of the prince of darkness will do everything they can to desecrate and profane the name of the Lord Jesus. They hate this name and what He stands for. While professing satan's power as the greatest, they are deathly afraid of Jesus!

18. Your birthday. Most people will respond positively to a question about their birthdays. Even a negative response will be non-emotional such as, "Well, I never liked it much because it was too near Christmas and I never got many presents." An emotional response may indicate that the child was used in a ritual arranged especially for his or her birthday. There would also be a strong likelihood that someone who was part of the child's support was a satanist and therefore knew his or her birthday.

19. Friday the thirteenth. This also represents a special date of satanic worship, and is apt to bring a reaction when a person has been used in SRA.

20. Big or black dogs. These animals are commonly used in acts of bestiality. Little children, especially girls, may be forced to engage in any and every conceivable sex act with a large dog and even more, a black dog. It would not be unusual for the child to be forced afterward to participate in the sacrifice of the animal! When this question is affirmed as well as a number of others, it takes on important significance.

21. Bells, chimes, and gongs. These instruments are often used in certain rituals. These sounds may trigger long-suppressed fears relating to ritual experiences. *Loud noises* are apt to have been used in some of the mind-control techniques, once again eliciting deep and even unknown fears.

22. Roses or their smell. In interviewing people about smells and odors that bother them, a number mentioned roses. How could anyone not like roses? This was explained to us by an ex-satanist.

Who is the "Rose of Sharon"? Song of Solomon 2:1 answers the question: "I AM the rose of Sharon."

Remember these evil people will do anything they can to profane the Lord Jesus. They will crush "the Rose" (preferably a white rose for purity or a red rose for blood) by thrusting it inside a little girl. The thorns will be used to draw blood for their "communion." Is it any wonder these little victims grow up hating roses and never know why?

23. The cross. In satanic rituals the cross is usually shown in an upside-down position. But that is not all. As another means of desecrating our Lord, a cold, hard, metal cross, long end first, may be used in the same way and for the same purposes as a rose blossom. There is an additional purpose in the use of the cross. How can a child who has endured such an atrocity ever trust the One who said He died on that cross for her to save her?

24. Fear of darkness. This symptom alone would not be significant. However, when connected to many other symptoms on the questionnaire the reactions to or fear of darkness can be readily understood because almost all rituals are performed at night.

25. Voices speaking. Demons and demonic spirits are an integral part of ritual. The child has learned to know them, to fear them, and to obey them. When they work their way into the child's body or mind, they will speak to the person for years, often telling them to do evil or risky things.

26. Lost time. Finding yourself somewhere with no idea of how or why you are there is usually an indication of the presence of alter personalities. The creation of alters is a direct result of ritual violation. (See Chapter 14.)

27. Fear of spirits. This fear taps into the suppressed memories and emotions of the involvement of evil spirits in ritual. Most of us have little concept of how those involved in the world of darkness rely on spirits. An authority and former satanist told us that to the Christian, the material realm, which we can see, touch, and feel, is 80 percent of reality and the spiritual realm is 20 percent. To the satanist the material realm is only 20 percent of reality and the spiritual realm is 80 percent. They have, therefore, a much more highly developed sense of how to exercise spiritual powers than we do.

28. The occult. This question often triggers deep response, even when an individual has no knowledge of ever having been involved in an occult or ritual activity.

29. Hypnotism. Hypnotism is a well-understood technique to satanists. It may be used (1) to confuse or control victims, (2) to suppress any knowledge of the torment or torture to which the victim child has been exposed, or (3) to create multiple personality disorder (see Chapter 14). Consider a child who has been hypnotized into a non-cognitive state and then used in the ritual. Upon return to normal awareness, the child will have no knowledge of what has transpired. In this way cultists create alter personalities. An adult who has no knowledge of these childhood experiences is very apt to emotionally react to this question. *Our emotions remember what our mind has forgotten.*

30. Guided imagery. This is a technique used by professional therapists in helping people to resolve the pains of their past. At a recent Christian abuse-recovery workshop, a guest speaker was describing how she used this technique without even naming it. A number of people in the audience became restless, then upset, at what they were hearing. Several had to leave the room due to their emotional distress. We learned the next day that every single one of them—about twelve in all out of a group of forty-five—had been victims of SRA and had experienced similar treatment in setting them up for ritual abuse.

31 and 34. Drugs and hypodermic needles. Ritualists often use drugs and hypodermic needles to prepare a child to satisfy their desires. There are frequently people in covens with wide knowledge of drugs and their use. Here, in part, is the dialogue of one of the first young women with whom we uncovered SRA through memory-retrieval prayer:

(Speaking in her childlike voice of this experience at three years of age) "He's taking my clothes off . . . ! Oh, somebody's holding my arm. He's pinching my arm. . . . Oooh, that hurts. Oh, I feel so drowsy . . ."

Even though the child had been given some kind of sedative to make her completely compliant and unaware of her surroundings, the Holy Spirit was not bound by the drug. We were able to see the whole ritual and violations, including the child's being driven back to the babysitter, a woman who had sent her off for this purpose. The little girl had been staying overnight while her parents were taking night classes at Bible college! Satanists love to victimize the children of Christians.

32. The pentagram. This inverted five pointed star is one of the most significant satanic symbols. Most people know what a pentagram is but have no reaction to seeing or thinking of one. Ask this question to a person who has suffered SRA and you will get a strong answer, if not an emotional response.

33. Bright lights. Sometimes bright lights are used in rituals to confuse or control the child. They may be direct overhead lights or blinking lights. The child may have no memories but her emotions "feel" that bright or blinking lights are associated with bad things.

35. Wooden box. This question about a wooden box evokes some of the strongest emotions. Note that the question, "How would you feel if you found yourself in a wooden box?" is nonspecific. There is no indication of whether it is a good box or a bad box, whether it is horizontal or vertical, whether there is a lid or door on it, whether it is big or small. There is nothing in the question to indicate whether it is scary or not or if you were in it as an adult or a child. However, the ritual victim always has a mind's image of being in a small horizontal box with the lid shut tight.

36. Bonfires. Bonfires are an integral part of outdoor rituals. Without going into detail as to the role they may play, it is clear that the image of a bonfire could be very threatening to an SRA victim. To a non-victim the response might be, "I think of toasting marshmallows at a campfire."

37. Having your picture taken. Don't we all like to have our pictures taken, especially those of us with Sanguine personalities? The answer is an unqualified *No*. Since satanism, the Mafia, and child pornography are all closely interrelated, often the same children used in satanic ritual will also be used in child pornography. Sometimes the pictures are taken during rituals. Numerous times in memory retrieval the person seeking truth will report seeing lights flash during the ritual. Kitty, a young woman in Florida, has many memories of being used in ritual, even up to her adult years. She is fully aware that she was used for pornographic filming in her early teens.

38. Out-of-body experiences. These experiences are not unusual for a person who has been used in cultic ritual. These experiences can occur in basically two ways:

a. They can be created by the cultists through the spiritual powers of darkness, and

b. The child may consciously choose to leave her body as the only means of coping with the pain of the trauma and torture.

39. Electroshock therapy. This question triggers the feelings of electric shock that may have been used in ritual to force compliance and obedience. Two women associated with our ministry, both victims of long periods of satanic ritual abuse, have told us that for years they "had a real problem in pulling a plug out of a wall socket for fear of the sparks that might come out."

40. Night terrors. More than bad dreams, night terrors are the kind of experiences from which a child or an adult awakens petrified with fear, in a cold sweat, or with their hearts pounding. Although not exclusively related to SRA, they are often experienced by those who have been subjected to continuing ritual abuse.

41. Incense. This may also be used in rituals, so the question may trigger a negative reaction in those who have been subject to it.

42. Cutting raw meat. Due to the sensitive emotions this might evoke in some people, we will avoid further discussion. Suffice it to say that this could be a very important symptom.

43. Vaginal or uterine scar tissue. These scars can be the result of satanic circumcision. Not long ago Fred met a retired OB/GYN physician. He told Fred that during his forty years of practice he had birthed fourteen thousand babies. Fred asked him if he had ever noticed any of his patients with labial scars. "Oh, yes," he replied.

"Did you ever discuss it with the patients or ask them how they got the scars?"

"No, I just figured it was from some kind of accident."

The vast majority are no accident.

44. Big rings on a doctor. This question surprises people. It would not be unusual for the high priest in a ritual to be wearing several large rings on his fingers, especially on his left hand. A woman who reacts to this question might be relating to what she had actually seen while lying on a ritual altar.

Satanists tend to do everything they can with the left hand; they emphasize the left side. Remember they try as much as possible to do just the opposite of Christ. In Scripture Moses parted the Red Sea with his right arm (Isa. 63:12). The Psalms also talk about God's protection: "Your right hand shall hold me" (Ps. 139:10). "Your right hand, O LORD, has become glorious in power" (Exod. 15:6). And Jesus is pictured as sitting on the right hand of God: "You will see the Son of Man sitting at the right hand of the Power" (Matt. 26:64), and "He . . . sat down at the right hand of the Majesty on high" (Heb. 1:3). Finally, God separates the good and the evil and places them on specific sides: "He will set the sheep on His right hand, but the goats on the left" (Matt. 25:33). The goat head is a favorite symbol of the satanists!

45. Communion. A regular part of satanic ritual, communion involves a single cup, often highly decorated and sacred, that is passed from one person to another as part of the worship and commitment. The element, however, is very different. It is blood that has been drawn from animals or humans and mixed with other body fluids. The child on the altar not only sees this ritual, he or she is forced to participate. Is it any wonder that, as an adult, church communion could be difficult for this person?

46. Dead or frozen emotions. One of the requirements of the child used in ritual is absolute silence. The various mind-control techniques teach this to the child. These are reinforced both by threats and the carrying out of those threats if the child is stubborn or disobeys. During memory-retrieval prayer, Betty remembered being on an altar at the age of three. She was understandably crying. Her father told her to be quiet or a (male organ) would be put in her mouth to make her shut up. Betty hadn't learned. She was scared. She continued to cry. The threat was carried out. She couldn't cry! She learned to never show her feelings or emotions. "I will never feel again."

47. Fraternal Order. These centers are often the locale for SRA. At a Promise of Healing workshop in Australia a woman named Marian had volunteered for a demonstration of memory retrieval in front of the whole group. The Lord revealed her being taken at the age of five into a big room of a temple, with her father and a man she recognized as a neighbor, to perform sexual acts for and in front of the men gathered there.

48. Sleep disorder. Sleep interruption is a standard means of disorienting the child for ritual use and mind control. The result is often a sleep disorder that continues long after the abuse ends.

49. Baby dedications. Baby dedications in church are not unlike the dedication of an infant to satan, an act a little child may have observed. The child herself or himself may be dedicated to satan; some at slightly later ages are "married" to satan. This is particularly true when the child is being trained for later "high" value to satan. These children are called "vitals." Those used only for a short time and then cast off are known as "trinkets."

50. Masks, ghosts, or faces. Because these items are a frequent part of rituals they are apt to cause distress to an adult victim. Imagine the reaction that a mother, not knowing she is an SRA victim, might have upon going to the door on a dark Halloween night and seeing bigger and older children in ghostly masks!

You may remember the time we spent with Anne and Joy after the Mount Shasta retreat. Anne promised Joy she would keep in touch with her as well as with us. They became prayer partners and after a few months Joy felt ready to pray for her repressed memories. They brought in a friend to be the prayer support and witness. As they asked the Lord to reveal what Joy needed to know to be free, Jesus showed Joy memories of a church basement. She was lying naked on a table. As she looked around there were people in hoods who took turns violating her. She could identify the church, her age, and a priest who was participating in the ritual. There is no need to describe what she was put through, except to say that it fit many of the experiences that we have just explained.

Joy felt some immediate relief, but she knew there was more. Anne wisely postponed more exposure until Joy had time to accept what she had seen and prayerfully prepare herself for more. She ultimately found out that her ex-husband had been involved in ritual and that he had abused one of their sons.

Joy could now see why her victimized past kept her from objecting to her husband's physical and sexual abuse. She thought she was a "hopeless case" because she allowed him to use her. She could see why she felt so rejected and looked for people who would continue to reject her.

Anne took a great step in her own faith when she saw that God could use her, a victim herself, to help Joy deal with her pain. Anne told us Joy looks so much better now. "She even stands up straight and can look you in the eye," she said. Joy has a new job and feels good about herself. She is writing her prayers daily and is interceding for her children, asking for their healing. Her spirits are up and her new desire is to get healed enough to help others in similar situations.

14

What Is MPD?

Where do multiple personalities come from? Is this a disorder, as it is often called (multiple personality disorder, or MPD), and is it permanent? Or is it just a psychological diagnosis that we should avoid or deny?

These are very real and valid questions that people are asking today. With the proliferation of television programs and books on this subject there has been a heightened interest in finding the truth. Is it fact or fiction?

We will try to answer these questions to the best of our ability and knowledge. We do not pretend to be experts. Even the experts question the conclusions and premises of other experts.

We will not avoid the issue because it may be controversial. Our desire is to help people find answers and explanations for the way they feel or for the struggles they are facing. Let's look first at the questions.

WHAT ARE MULTIPLE PERSONALITIES?

Perhaps the hardest thing to comprehend for people who are not affected with this problem is that there could be such a thing. It just doesn't fit into any of our preconceptions of who people are or how they function. How could a person be fractured into different personalities or "parts," as they are frequently called?

Perhaps the best way to identify with multiple personalities is to picture a girls' college dormitory bedroom packed full of friends in their pajamas or nightgowns. They all have different names, look different, dress differently, and *act* differently. The one thing they have in common is that they are all friends of, or are somehow connected to, the one girl who lives in the room. Now try to transfer this picture of all these girls in the dorm room to being inside the head of the one girl, who we'll call the host personality.

People who are struggling with multiple personalities deal with anywhere from one or two, to a dozen, to possibly hundreds of parts who often want to be in control or to be heard. Sometimes the parts work very harmoniously together, each doing its own assigned or specific function. Some are quiet, some are loud, some are happy, some are mean. Some are afraid, and some help those who are afraid. Some are very young; some are like mothers to the others. Some have names; some have none. Some are leaders; some only follow. Different ones hold different memories. Some of these memories are bad, so some parts protect others so they won't know about the "bad stuff." Some parts carry these black memories so the host personality won't have to because she may not be able to handle them emotionally.

Multiple personalities comprise an internal system that enables the host to cope with life without becoming totally dysfunctional because of the experiences to which she has been subjected. (We use the feminine pronoun because the vast majority of people with known multiple personality disorders are women.) Little girls also carry these parts, but they are seldom identified until they grow up. The largest number of parts or personalities actually are created in early childhood.

HOW CAN WE DETERMINE THE POSSIBILITY OF MULTIPLE PERSONALITY DISORDER?

Perhaps the simplest and quickest answer to this question would be to take the Dissociation/Amnesia Response Survey that follows. It was developed by Star Cole of Hope and Restoration Ministries in Anaheim, California, after doing extensive research from available resources and then factoring in her own experiences and the struggles she has faced herself. In her comprehensive questionnaire you have the benefit of known wisdom as well as the personal understanding of someone who has been there herself.

The survey may not apply to you. For some it may prove to be the first indication for them to think, *I'm not crazy!* Others who read it may soon find that God will put someone on your mind for whom it would be uniquely helpful. If you found Chapter 13 on satanic ritual abuse significant to you, we would recommend that you proceed with this survey.

THE DISSOCIATION/AMNESIA RESPONSE SURVEY

This survey is best taken by having someone read the questions to you and marking your responses.

To the reader of the survey: Read each question quickly and simply without adding personal comment. Do not encourage comments from the one taking the survey. Put one checkmark or tick on the line corresponding to each question for each Yes answer. If a question gets a strong reaction, make two checkmarks or ticks. Leave blank any lines that are answered No. Count up the total checks at the end of the survey.

To the taker of the survey: Listen to each question and answer simply and honestly. There are no right or wrong answers. These questions are designed to help you understand things about yourself. You do not have to explain your answers. After taking the survey read the "Explanation" section, which follows.

_____ 1. Have tests revealed or do others seem to believe you are smarter or more intelligent than YOU think you are?

_____   Were your achievements in school uneven or sporadic throughout your education?

_____ 2. Do you have an intense interest in or do you possess an ability or gift in creative activities such as writing, music, art, drama, etc. (whether or not you actively engage in them)?

_____ Do you have a natural gift of imagination? (Can you easily create a picture in your head if something is described to you verbally?)

_____ 3. Do you constantly find it difficult to stay focused on one project?

_____ Are you frequently "side-tracked" before completing a task?

_____ Does time seem to fly by too quickly, creating a sense of urgency about your goals and projects, or about life in general?

_____ 4. Do you make numerous lists and feel you would not accomplish anything without lists?

*_____ Do you often misplace or forget your lists?

_____ Do you complete the tasks on your lists?

_____ 5. Is there a notable difference in your printing/penmanship between or within notes, letters, diaries and journals?

_____ 6. Do you often feel disoriented, dazed or "spaced out"?

_____ 7. Do others feel that you overreact or underreact to situations?

_____ Do you feel your responses are often disproportionate (+ /-) to the circumstances?

_____ 8. Do you find it difficult to understand the behavior of those around you?

_____ Are many of your relationships typically unpredictable, "stormy," and volatile?

_____ 9. Do you feel you are somehow "different" from others?

_____ Do you feel that your mind works differently or that you experience things differently than others?

_____ 10. Do other people comment, or have you noticed, that your mood or tone of voice sometimes shifts or changes suddenly?

_____ Does your manner of speech change regularly, including changes in pitch, vocabulary or use of profanity?

_____ Have you, or family/friends, assigned descriptions, titles, or nicknames to specific moods you experience?

_____ 11. Do you find yourself saying words you hadn't planned to say and weren't aware of thinking?

_____ Do you sometimes feel as though someone else controls your thoughts?

_____ Do you often lose track of your thoughts, the next words you intended to say, or what you were doing?

_____ 12. Do you often protect yourself by altering the facts or modifying events of your life when relating them to others, particularly when you have been asked a personal question that you feel uncomfortable or unsure about or that you do not clearly remember?

_____ 13. Do you struggle with chronic insomnia or does your need for sleep vary widely (4 - 5 hours for a while to 10 - 11 hours for a while, because of body requirement for sleep)?

_____ 14. Do you experience any of these physical symptoms but a specific physical disorder has not been found to account for the symptom:

_____ hyperventilation

_____ shortness of breath, heart racing/palpitations

_____ chest pain/pressure

_____ gastrointestinal problems: especially, nausea/vomiting (other than motion sickness) or peptic ulcers

_____ general chronic poor health; frequent colds, flu, bronchitis, sinusitis, etc.

_____ unexplained aches/pains; abdominal, back, genital or joint pain, pain in hands or feet, urinary difficulty/pain/retention

_____ responses to Rx unpredictable

_____ ability to endure pain unpredictable

_____ menstrual irregularities/pain/excessive bleeding.

_____ Have you had many physical problems for several years prior to age 30 or have you ever had other serious physical symptoms that doctors could not explain?

_____ 15. Do you have sexual difficulties that you cannot adequately explain?

_____ Does your sexual interest seem to vary from interest and enjoyment to disinterest and revulsion?

_____ Do you have an internal conflict regarding your sexual orientation (i.e., do you feel sexually attracted to the same gender)?

_____ 16. Do you find that your symptoms and ability to function tend to fluctuate unexpectedly?

_____ 17. In seeking professional help for your troubles have you been given more than three different diagnoses (i.e., depression, anxiety disorder, psychogenic amnesia, dissociative disorder, manic/depressive disorder, borderline personality disorder, schizophrenia (or paranoid schizophrenia), post-traumatic stress disorder, etc.)?

_____ 18. Have you frequently wanted to run away, or did you run away?

_____ Do you fantasize about having a secret safe place away from contact with all other people?

_____ 19. Have you struggled with impulses or attempts to hurt yourself by abusing drugs/alcohol, hitting, cutting, or burning yourself to feel better?

_____ Have you struggled with thoughts, impulses or attempts to kill yourself?

*_____ Do you struggle with other compulsions or obsessions?

_____ 20. Do you struggle with many different fears?

_____ Do you tremble easily?

_____ Do you have a fear of choking or dying you can't explain?

_____ Do you struggle with anxiety or panic attacks?

*_____ Do you experience terror or panic related to objects or circumstances you cannot adequately explain?

*_____ Do you suddenly relive painful or traumatic events?

21. Do you suddenly experience:

_____ confusion

_____ disorientation

_____ dizziness

_____ headaches or

*_____ blackouts, especially when talking or hearing about painful or upsetting issues?

*_____ 22. Do you find it difficult to remember large portions of your personal history (childhood and/or adult)?

*_____ Do you remember little or nothing of your childhood before age 5?

*_____ Between the ages of 2 - 15, do there appear to be blocks of time where you have very little or no memory of events in your life?

*_____ Are there significant events in your childhood, which others relate to you, that you do not have real memories of; do you see pictures of yourself from childhood and only remember the event because there is a picture, not because you recall the event?

_____ 23. Does it take you "forever" to decide what to wear?

*_____ Do you change your mind (or your clothes) several times before making a final decision?

*_____ Do you sometimes find that you hate the choice you made or seem puzzled by your selection of wardrobe later that day?

_____ Is there a marked difference in styles/fashion within your wardrobe (ex: sexy, conservative, Victorian, exotic, sophisticated, and casual)?

*_____ 24. Do you have difficulty locating your parked car or find you're not certain which car you are driving?

*_____ Do you always park in the same place at shopping centers, malls, etc., so you'll know where your car will be?

*_____ 25. Do you frequently find that you don't recall information or experiences that others seem to believe you should know or remember (not counting substance use)?

*_____ Do people accuse you of having said or done things you know you didn't do (not counting substance use)?

*_____ Do people ever begin talking to you as though they know you but you don't know them, or you recognize them only faintly?

*_____ 26. Do you have difficulty recalling daily events?

*_____ Do you ever fail to remember where you have been during certain periods in the day or are you ever unable to account for several hours or portions of the day?

*_____ Do calendars or clocks confuse or puzzle you sometimes?

*_____ Do you sometimes discover things you don't remember buying, making, or writing, or that you don't recognize?

*_____ Do you make plans to go somewhere or do something and realize you have arrived or finished and do not clearly recall the trip or the process?

_____ 27. Have you ever felt as though you were observing yourself or listening to yourself from inside?

*_____ 28. Do you talk to yourself in your head?

_____   Are you aware of internal voices carrying on conversations in your head?

_____   Do these voices ever seem to argue or disagree with one another?

_____   Do you talk to yourself as "you" or refer to yourself as "we" or "she/he" (ex: "You need to sleep now" or, "We like ice cream" or, "She always says that," meaning yourself)?

_____ TOTAL parts of questions: 80 possible

THIS IS NOT A DIAGNOSIS.

Survey prepared by Star Cole, Hope and Restoration Ministries, P.O. Box 6800, Corona, California 91718-6800. ALL RIGHTS RESERVED. THIS FORM MAY BE REPRODUCED. NOT INTENDED FOR DIAGNOSTIC PURPOSES.

EXPLANATION

If I were to tell you that you MAY be dealing with Multiple Personality Disorder (MPD), would you (circle one):

A. Feel terror, or panic that you may be "crazy"?

B. Feel relieved because that would certainly explain a lot of things?

C. Not have a clue what I'm talking about?

D. Not be concerned? Or

E. _____

Forty or more Yes answers to these questions may be indicative of periods of dissociation or amnesia. Your responses here should help you understand that you are not alone in the issues that confront you and in your search for wholeness. Many people giving Yes answers to this survey say they feel relieved because it would explain a lot of things. Questions on the survey that have asterisks next to them may indicate possible amnesiac experiences.

HOW DOES MULTIPLE PERSONALITY DISORDER HAPPEN?

As mentioned earlier, MPD develops as a means of coping with life's traumatic experiences, which may include repeated sexual violations. The "part" becomes the victim of trauma the child could otherwise not endure. The child survives because the trauma is unknown or unfelt; it is "not happening to me, but to her." We do not believe God creates this part, but He may permit it.

A part can also be specifically and intentionally created in satanic ritual by the coven. This frequently occurs through the use of hypnosis, drugs, electrical shock, sensory deprivation, and similar mind control techniques. The purpose of the part in this case is to protect the coven members, not to protect child! A child who "knows nothing" cannot speak out, even as an adult.

One thing about which most professionals agree is that 85 to 90 percent of people with MPD are also victims of satanic ritual abuse. Because we can now frequently predetermine who might be an SRA victim by use of the Sarita Questionnaire and we can find valid confirmation through memory-retrieval prayer, we suspect it may be even higher. Along with others associated with our ministry to the sexually victimized, we have met and identified many people who experience multiple personality disorder. Virtually every one of them have also uncovered memories of satanic ritual abuse.

IS IT FACT OR FICTION?

Just as satanic ritual abuse is a certainty, multiple personality disorder is an undisputable fact. Over the past few years, Fred has ministered to a number of women with multiple personalities. Much of this has been by telephone. With these persons it is not uncommon for the host to "switch" to a part and later to switch back again. The conversation completely changes, and often the sound of the voice is different. When there is no "co-consciousness" (communication or hearing between the parts), the host personality will have no knowledge of his or her conversation with the part!

IS IT A DISORDER? IS IT PERMANENT?

Disorder is a clinical term that implies a state of being for which there is little hope, aside from medication. Most people with multiple personalities or parts don't ever know it, and they function relatively successfully in their daily lives. Having parts, therefore, is not a social stigma, and does not make you an outcast or one without hope. It does mean that you cope each day with certain situations in life that others have never even heard of.

One thing we can be sure of, God did not create us with multiple personalities, according to Genesis 1:24. They are the result of what has happened or been done to us. Therefore our answer is yes, there is healing and no, the condition does not have to be permanent. There is hope!

In John, chapter 5, a man paralyzed for thirty-eight years waited at the pool of Bethesda for the angel to stir up the waters. He knew that the first person into the moving water would be healed of his affliction. When Jesus asked the man, "Do you want to be made well?" the man replied, "Sir, I have no man to put me into the pool when the water is stirred up; but while I am coming, another steps down before me" (vv. 6-7). Jesus then healed the man immediately.

This man needed help to find healing for his condition, as do many persons with multiple personalities. Help is available today:

1. Professional psychological therapy for MPD is a growing specialty. The prospects are often five to ten years of expensive weekly therapy, usually without guarantees or assurance of integration or healing. In considering such therapy, be sure the practitioner is highly experienced and knowledgeable, an expert with a good success record. We would be very hesitant to ever recommend a non-Christian therapist to a Christian.

2. Christian prayer therapy is available but may be hard to find. In prayer therapy each part gives up its pain or hurt, its memory, to the Lord and goes to a safe place. Once the parts' issues have been resolved, the part can be merged, and the Lord will bring true healing.

One lovely Christian lady whom we know very well has fully integrated, one by one, many different and named personalities in less than a year of professional prayer therapy. This has required her to be willing to invest twice a week in lengthy prayer sessions with her prayer therapist. Because of the distance involved, much of this has been by telephone. This has taken dedication and commitment, not only on both of their parts but from those of their families as well.

3. Unification occurs through prayer. This is somewhat different from prayer therapy in that each part is not identified and prayed with individually; instead, the whole issue is brought to the Lord for cleansing and healing. This, too, is a process and, in the Lord's time, complete unification takes place. We must never doubt the power of the Sovereign God to work His will as He purposes.

One recommendation we strongly make to persons with multiple personality disorder is to get connected and bonded if possible to another like person. This mutual encouragement and empathy can be invaluable. Just to find another person who has experienced similar childhood trauma and now as an adult contends with the same hurdles on the healing journey is of great comfort.

Whatever the form of therapy that God leads you to, there are no shortcuts to healing. There is only One who can heal you. He is the One who said, "[I have come] to heal the brokenhearted, / To proclaim liberty to the captives" (Luke 4:18).

"All the king's horses and all the king's men can't put you together again—but the King can!" (Star Cole).

PART FOUR

———— ◆ ————

*A Solution
in the Future*

15

How Can I Plug In to the Power?

T here isn't the money and there isn't the manpower to reach all the people who need help." So writes psychiatrist Christ Zois in his insightful book, *Think Like a Shrink,* in which he suggests that people should try to solve some of their own problems. The reason many of us are not successful in this is that we have no confidence in our own ability and we don't want to go through the hurtful process of uncovering our buried emotions. Instead we build defenses, excuses, and rationalizations to prevent the pain. He suggests that until we are willing to tolerate some degrees of anxiety we won't get to the heart of our problems.

A Christian psychiatrist told us he takes into his clinic sixty new sex-abuse cases a week. Using all the skill and techniques available plus loving concern, he confesses very limited results. In reviewing the last five years of his practice, he feels only ten people made significant progress and three of them are himself, his wife, and her therapist. "Try as we may, we just don't have the answers," he said.

HOW TO PLUG IN TO THE POWER

As you have taken the tests set up for you in this book, you have in effect become your own counselor. From our experience of

245

twenty-five years in Christian ministry, we have found that many of us *can* solve our own problems if we have tools that are simple enough for us to understand—and if we are willing to pick up those tools and get to work. With the tools must come the belief that Jesus Christ is our Ultimate Healer and with Him we can achieve not only the possible but the impossible (see Luke 18:27).

There are no simple answers to our complex life problems, but we do have Power available to give us hope. Before we go any further in our search for an abundant life, let's make sure we know how to plug in to the real Power. Check Yes or No to the following questions and then read the explanations.

SPIRITUAL INVENTORY

		Yes	No
1.	Would you consider yourself to be a relatively religious person?	____	____
2.	Have you ever felt a real pull toward spiritual matters?	____	____
3.	As a child did you attend church activities?	____	____
4.	Can you remember when you first asked the Lord Jesus into your life?	____	____
5.	Did this commitment make a difference in your behavior and lifestyle?	____	____
6.	Do you attend a church or Bible study regularly?	____	____
7.	Do you accept that God is the Creator of heaven and earth and is the Father of all true believers?	____	____
8.	Do you believe that Jesus Christ paid a sacrificial price for your sins, arose from the dead, and is still alive today, making intercession for you and me?	____	____
9.	Do you believe the Holy Spirit gives power to your life and can bring recall of forgotten events?	____	____

10. Do you know that when Jesus is in us we
can have a transformed life and that when
Jesus sets us free we are free indeed?   _____   _____

If you have answered Yes to all of these questions and you know you are a believing Christian who accepts the Bible as God's Word for the human race, then you are ready to move on to your goal of emotional health and stability.

If you could not say Yes to most of these questions, let's find out why. Do any of the descriptions below apply to you? Check the ones that do.

_____ The Pharisee

Being religious doesn't prove anything if you are just obeying a set of rules. The Lord Jesus said those who were outwardly religious but also judgmental and unloving were hypocrites, whitewashed sepulchres, religious on the outside but spiritually dead inside. Does this description fit you or anyone you know? Jesus wants us to be vibrant on the inside and on the outside. He desires truth in our innermost parts. He asks us to practice what we preach.

_____ The Nominal Christian

If you grew up in the church and attended regular children's activities as we did, you should understand spiritual matters as an adult, but not necessarily so. Sometimes youthful church attendance causes us to be blasé about the Lord and to never seek a genuine personal relationship. "I'm a good person, go to church, and live by the Golden Rule. Isn't that enough?" you might ask. Sometimes we get too close to some of the people in the church and see their weaknesses. Then we brand them as phonies and never want to be like them. This attitude gives us reason to stay away from the church. Sometimes, if we were required to attend church as children, we rebel when we grow up and determine we will not force our children to go. We say we'll give them—and ourselves—a free choice.

_____ The De Facto Christian

Many people feel they have always been Christians because they weren't raised to be Jews or Muslims. But the Bible tells us we must make a personal commitment to the Lord Jesus, give over our wills to

His control, and ask Him to come into our lives and change us. John 1:12 tells us that "as many as received Him, to them He gave the right to become children of God, to those who believe in His name." He didn't say he would give an abundant life to those who have perfect-attendance buttons or who have never missed a church potluck supper, but to those who believe and receive.

If you are not sure whether you have ever received the Lord Jesus, you don't have to get up and go find a cathedral; you can pray right where you are. You can be creative in your words to Jesus or you can read the following prayer with personal feeling and heartfelt dedication:

Lord Jesus, I come into Your presence as I am and where I am at this moment. I don't really know You in a personal way and yet I have this hunger for spiritual things. You say that if I believe in You as a real person and reach out to receive You, You will come in and live in me from here on. I ask You to come into my heart right now, make Yourself real in my life, and change me into what You want me to be. I thank You ahead of time for what You will do with me and I pledge to share what You teach me with others who also need help. I pray, believing that You are true to Your word and that You are already at work in my life. In Jesus' precious name, amen.

_____ The Lukewarm Christian

If you made this commitment in the past, has there been a change in your life? If you prayed just now, do you have a new wave of peace washing over you? The Lord is only as active in our lives as we allow Him to be. He is not pushy; He is always gentle. He gives us a new nature and He changes our desires. He does not send a man dressed like Moses to our doorsteps carrying a big tablet saying, "Thou shalt not have fun ever again." He just quietly goes about rebuilding the parts of our lives that have been torn down. Oswald Chambers wrote, "Our Lord never patches up our natural virtues, He remakes the whole man on the inside."[1]

_____ The Christian Who Lacks the Power of the Holy Spirit

As children we may have known no more of the Holy Spirit than the line at the end of formal prayers: "in the name of the Father, the Son, and the Holy Ghost." Was He someone spooky who hovered over us or was He someone who peeked at us through the venetian blinds?

As we began to study God's Word we found that the Holy Ghost, also known as the Holy Spirit, was the third member of the Trinity, and He is the One who gives us the power to change. What a blessing for those of us who flunked charm school and who feel we can't win friends or influence people! The Holy Spirit can do what we have failed at doing. For some, transformation comes quickly, but for most of us the changes are gradual. One day, out of the blue, we notice that we no longer think or behave as we used to. Our temper hasn't flared up, our anger has diminished, and we're no longer procrastinating. The power of the Spirit has changed us. Chambers said, "When we are born again the Holy Spirit begins to work His new creation in us and there will come a time when there's not a bit of the old order left."[2]

Look again at the story in John 5 about the man, paralyzed for thirty-eight years, who waited beside Bethesda Pool to be healed. When Jesus came along He told the man to pick up his bed—his place of confinement—and walk. When the man did what Jesus told him he was able to walk.

Jesus didn't stay around to take credit for the miracle; He just slipped away through the crowd. Later, the Lord found him in the temple and said, "You have been made well. Sin no more" (John 5:14). The man went away and told the people it was Jesus who had made him well.

In this simple story are some basic principles we need to accept before we will get any healing.

1. Realize we have a problem. The man knew he was lame. Many of us have needs that we deny, hurts that we refuse to look at. Until we are willing to admit we have a problem we won't get well. Some people suffer from headaches, stomach problems, and other illnesses their doctors can't heal because the suffering people won't admit they have a problem that is not physiological.

2. Go where there is help. The lame man knew that people got healed at the pool, so he went there every day. He waited thirty-eight years in faith, believing that if he went to the place of healing, ultimately he'd be made well. Let's hope we don't have to wait thirty-eight years for healing!

3. Do what Jesus says. Once Jesus knows we want help and we have made a move to receive it, He is willing to give instructions. He told the man to get up and walk. The man didn't argue or say it's impossible; he took the first step. Do we want healing enough to move on it today?

Some of us don't think our problems are big enough for Jesus to notice or to heal. We don't think there's any hope so we don't go to find help. The lame man didn't give up; he went every day for thirty-eight years.

For some of us the "place" of help is a church, a counselor, a friend, or a book. As we listen or read we have to be tuned in to the voice of Jesus so that we will hear Him when He speaks.

The Spiritual Variations in the Personalities table may help you

SPIRITUAL VARIATIONS IN THE PERSONALITIES

		Barrier to becoming a Christian	Spiritual hangups	Favorite type of church	Favorite hymn and verse
POPULAR	SANGUINE	It doesn't sound like fun and those people are too serious	Trouble with idea of holiness and purity. Too many strict rules and commandments.	One with fun, action, lively choir, dancing in the aisles with tambourines. Likes short, humorous sermons full of stories.	"Oh for a thousand tongues" "A merry heart does good, like medicine" (Prov. 17:22)
PERFECT	MELANCHOLY	I could never be perfect enough to please God	Trouble with forgiveness for those who don't deserve it. Too much unconditional love.	One with serious liturgy and dignified presentation. Likes detailed bulletins. Admires intellectual, spiritual, deep sermons with reference to Greek derivatives.	"When the Roll Is Called Up Yonder I'll Be There" "Therefore you shall be perfect" (Matt. 5:48)
POWERFUL	CHOLERIC	I couldn't give up control to someone I can't even see.	Trouble with authority of God. Too little control of one's own destiny.	One with obvious order and organization. Wants service to move right along and be practical. Likes brief sermons that apply to others.	"Onward Christian Soldiers" "Let all things be done decently and in order" (1 Cor. 14:40)
PEACEFUL	PHLEGMATIC	Would it mean I'd have to change?	Trouble with truth and responsibility before God. Too much emphasis on good works.	One with a relaxed atmosphere—not too dressy or demanding. Likes pleasant, brief sermons with no mention of hellfire and brimstone.	"Leaning on the Everlasting Arms" "Blessed are the peacemakers" (Matt. 5:9)

achieve healing by giving you insight into additional spiritual variations that occur in the various personalities. Knowing which traits can become problems for you may help you overcome them; knowing which traits make certain components more appealing may help you find them more easily.

If you do not already attend a church and/or Bible study, you will now want to find a place where God's inspired Word is taught and honored and where you see the love of the Lord reflected in the eyes of the people. Be wary of a situation where the pastor or teacher is being worshiped instead of where the Lord is being lifted up and watch out for groups who try to take control of you, your finances, or your family. Pray for discernment from the Lord as to where you should attend and how involved you should become. Remember that the church is full of imperfect people; don't get disillusioned when one of them behaves in a totally unspiritual way.

For some of us the voice of the Lord will be clear and the instructions life-changing, but others of us will turn away and say it all sounds too much like work. For many people healing is a difficult process, but Jesus is faithful when we are willing to pick up our bed and walk.

We must remember what the lame man said when his friends asked him about his healing. He stood publicly and stated, "Jesus made me well."

No matter what our difficulties are, ranging from personality problems, troubled relationships, poor communication, rejection, or childhood trauma, Jesus can make us well. We must first be plugged in to the Power before we can shine. To help you make the connection, picture for a moment an elegant living room. Perhaps it's your own or one you visited recently. There is a long, plush sofa against the wall with an ornate table at each end. On each table is an expensive lamp with a handsome base and a pleated silk shade.

As the sun sets you reach over and turn on one of these lamps and nothing happens. You check to see if it has a bulb and it does. What could be wrong? The lamp looks perfect but it doesn't work. You follow the cord down the back of the table and you find the problem. The lamp wasn't plugged in; it has no power. Once it's plugged in to the source, it shines brightly as it was created to do.

How about you? Do you have a handsome base and a silk shade? Do you have a bulb that would allow you to shine as a light in the world, but you're not plugged in to the source? Today is the turning point for you. You now have the Power to use in rebuilding a life without the strife.

16

How Do I Know If I Need Counseling?

Let's assume you started reading this book because you had some relationship problems, some emotional stress, and some physical symptoms. You needed some help but you didn't know where to turn. Someone suggested this book and you started to read. We assume by now you have taken all the tests set up for your self-analysis, and you have uncovered a few surprising facts.

You've examined your personality, perhaps for the first time, and have found out that you've been trying to be like other people you admire and have missed who it is that God wants you to be. Perhaps you've found out that your emotional needs were never met as a child, and you've been trying to get them out of your mate, who has no idea what you're looking for. We hope you have given some prayerful thought to your own personality in order to enhance your strengths, to work toward overcoming your weaknesses, and to stop trying to be someone else. You've explained to your mate and friends that you realize why you've been so emotionally needy and you've thanked them for anything positive they've ever done to bolster your feelings of insecurity.

If you are a Popular Sanguine, thank your spouse and your friends for laughing at your stories, for loving you as you are, and for complimenting you on your looks.

253

If you are a Perfect Melancholy, thank any who have had even the slightest sensitivity to your feelings and who respect your need for space and silence.

If you are a Powerful Choleric, thank those who have noticed how hard you work, who have appreciated all you've done for them, and who have been loyal to you in spite of opposition.

If you are a Peaceful Phlegmatic, thank those who have noticed the quiet behind-the-scenes deeds you have done, those who have appreciated your skills at mediating problems, and those who have commented on your balanced emotions and peaceful nature.

By now you have probably begun to use your new personality knowledge to understand those who are nothing like you, and you are looking at your children in a whole new light. One mother wrote, "I had always thought Proverbs 22:6 was a promise that if we kept our children in church, they'd turn out all right. Now I see that we are to train them with wisdom according to their inborn personalities, not according to how we want them to be. Then when they get older, they'll have some idea of who they are and will make career choices that fit their personality strengths, not their weaknesses."

Unless you are in a very serious emotional state at the moment, do not run to the Yellow Pages and dial the local mental health hospital. If you have gone through the questions in this book and found that your life has some strife, you can now narrow your problems down to a specific source. You believe that God has a plan for you, that Jesus Christ is your Healer-Counselor-Physician, and that the Holy Spirit can give the power tools that you need to build a new life. Before seeking human help, pave the way with daily written prayer, as Fred did. Give yourself a month of coming to the Lord in writing and asking Him for direction. Ask Him to show you what kind of help you might need and to send someone to you who knows a helpful counselor. As you come to the Lord in listening prayer—writing your questions and waiting for an answer—you will sense what the Lord is directing you to do. It is never a mistake to start a healing journey with prayer; this may be what you need to change your direction and outlook on life.

In the eighties Norman Cousins chronicled the healing power of laughter, showing the connection between our emotional status and our pain. His theories were widely publicized and practiced. In 1993 Bill Moyers, one of the country's most respected journalists, wrote a book, *Healing and the Mind,* in which he explains the "new" scientific evidence linking emotions to body chemistry. Neuroscientist Candace Pert says the mind is everywhere in the body. She calls this theory the "mind body: the biochemicals of emotions."

Start with the power tools that cost you little but time before you seek outside help. Sometimes you may need professional help. Experts say that 40 percent of all Americans will enter psychotherapy at some point in their lives.[1] If this figure is close to accurate, many of you who are reading this book will seek the advice of a counselor, pastor, or physician. Although we have seen lasting healing from coming to the Lord daily in prayer, as our previous chapter outlined, we know that for some the personal eye-to-eye contact with a person who cares is beneficial.

Florence had a counselor-friend with her when she confronted Fred and he was willing to go for two weeks of intensive therapy to find the root of his childhood problems. Before he went, he started writing his prayers for an hour a day, and he feels this is why he made such fast progress. He did not uncover his abuse in this time of therapy, but the psychologist did start him in the right direction. Working with one of the prayer directors he had previously trained, Fred uncovered his molestations by both a female and a male. If he had known at that time what we know now, he could have possibly saved himself an expensive two weeks of therapy.

Now that you have worked through this book and have found your area of need, you should make a decision as to what to do next. You can probably handle the areas of personality, masking, emotional needs, stress, maturity, and communications. In the back of the book, we have given you suggested reading material that will help you once you've spotted a problem area. But in other areas you may need professional assistance. In confronting your mate, for example, you will be safer with a friend or counselor. Some people need help in dealing with grief situations, especially if true feelings have been repressed, and many need guidance in finding the source of their rejections. You can certainly analyze your pictures by yourself, but if you go to a counselor, that person will often ask for your childhood photos.

When you enter into the area of possible abuse, it would be helpful to have a professional available, even though some people have been able to find healing through coming to the Lord daily in prayer. Not every counselor has experience in dealing with child-hood abuse, especially in the area of memory retrieval, and even fewer know how to uncover and work with ritual abuse. As we have mentioned, some even deny there is any such thing. By the time you get to MPD, there are few who have training in this area so you will need to find one who has experience.

Now that you have narrowed down your own symptoms you will know what to ask before going to someone for help. A counselor without experience in these last areas could do you more harm than good.

We have put together some checklists for you to review before selecting a person to guide you in your healing.

HOW DO I FIND A COUNSELOR?

Once you recognize that you have a need you may have no idea where to turn for help. What do you do now?

1. Ask your friends. The best way to find a person who is tried and true is to ask friends who have had counseling. They can tell you ones who helped them, those who were pleasant but seemed to miss their point, and those who made them feel worse.

2. Check with your church or large churches in your area. Many churches have realized the need for Christian counseling and have established centers in their churches or have compiled refer-ence lists of local counselors. Let them know the type of problem you perceive you have and see what they suggest, since there is a big difference between marriage problems and addictions.

3. Go to seminars. Frequently local counselors will speak at churches and explain what they do. If you listen you can usually tell whether this person understands your area of need.

4. Call local agencies. Check in your phonebook for counseling agencies. They may refer you to one of their people or even to another group if they know a specific person who specializes in your problem.

5. Call or write national agencies. The American Association for Marriage and Family Therapy can provide lists of counselors and will send you a copy of their *Consumer's Guide to Marriage and Family Therapy*. Send a stamped self-addressed envelope to: AAMF and Referrals, 1100 17th Street, N.W., Tenth Floor, Washington, D.C. 20036. Their toll-free number is 1-800-374-2638. Other sources of help include:

Minirth-Meier Clinics, 1-800-545-1819

New Life Treatment Centers, 1-800-NEW-LIFE

Rapha Treatment Centers, 1-800-383-HOPE

WHAT IS A CHRISTIAN COUNSELOR?

There are many kinds of Christian counselors. Some have no more personal relationship with the Lord except that their offices are in churches. Some use a verse here and there to establish a speaking acquaintance with God the Father. Some start and end each session with a perfunctory prayer that is somewhat akin to "Now I lay me down to sleep." At the other extreme are the pastors who don't believe in any form of counseling. They say, "If you were reading your Bible each day, coming to prayer meeting, and tithing to the church you wouldn't have problems" or "Perhaps there is sin in your life and that's why you feel guilty. Confess it and move on." When someone is desperate these Christian clichés are of little help.

A woman named Laura wrote, "I was in tears and suicidal when I phoned the pastor. I thought I was going out of my mind when I called out 'Help me, Pastor, help me!' He paused and asked, 'Did you read your Bible today and have your quiet time with the Lord?' I told him I couldn't read. I couldn't pray. I couldn't even think.

'That's your problem,' he replied. 'You need to spend time with the Lord.'

"I held my breath, with my face washed in tears, my nose running. God was putting me through this because I didn't read a verse today? What kind of a God is that?"

We know this kind of counsel is not the rule, but if you receive legalistic Christian platitudes that add to your guilt, look elsewhere for help.

Now that we have seen the negative extremes, what are some of the things a competent Bible-believing counselor should do?

1. Establish your mutual faith in the Lord. Before we pray with anyone, we make sure he or she is a believing Christian who knows that the Lord can heal. When we find that the person is not sure, we lead him or her to the Lord in a prayer of commitment before praying for the lost memories. One man asked if we thought abuse could have happened to him in one of his past lives! There would be little chance that this man, out on a limb as he was, would be healed by the Lord by his calling out to the spirits of his past lives.

2. Believe that sincere, seeking prayer will be answered. If the counselor doesn't pray with you specifically for the root of your problem and lead you closer to the Lord and His power, then you are both functioning in your human strength. You may make some determined progress but chances are you won't be healed quickly. The best advice achieves little without the Power to put it into practice. Find out if the person you are considering believes in using prayer. If he or she responds, "Well, what do you mean?" or "We always pray at the end for a few minutes," perhaps this is not the one for you. If you are aware that you have some hidden trauma from your past that needs to be uncovered, you need a counselor who understands how to pray with you for these memories and who believes that God answers the sincere prayers of His people.

WHAT DO I ASK A COUNSELOR?

When you are seeking help you need to know some answers up-front. Ask a potential counselor these questions when interviewing him or her by telephone:

1. Are you a believing Christian who has asked Jesus to be your Lord over all of your life?

2. Do you use prayer in healing?

3. How do you utilize the Scriptures?

4. How often do most people come to you?

5. How much do the sessions cost?

6. How many minutes are in a session?

7. Do you accept insurance?

8. Do you deal with my type of problem?

9. What has been your experience in this area?

10. Do you provide group therapy?

11. Are there followup support groups?

You may have other questions that are personal, but this list gives you some ideas. Many people we meet went to counseling without asking any of these questions—and received some rude surprises.

WHAT CAN I EXPECT FROM COUNSELING?

If you feel you need counseling, don't think you are a failure. Many of us need an outside helper at crucial times. In 1 Samuel 8 the people explained why they wanted a king: They wanted to be like everyone else. Doesn't that sound like us? We don't want to be strange or peculiar. We want to have the current clothes, the "in" car, and the charming personality that is expected in our circle of friends.

The Israelites' second reason was that they wanted a leader who was at hand, one who would listen to their problems, one who would face them eye-to-eye, one who cared. Isn't that why we seek counseling? We want a physical presence, an authority figure, whom we can talk to, who will listen and not put us down— someone who cares about us and will be on our side.

Also, the people were looking for someone who would fight their battles for them. That also sounds like us. In this day of instant everything we want a pill to lose weight, a shot to relieve pain, and emotional healing with no work on our part. We want someone to fight our battles for us.

The people of Israel got that person. King Saul came in with great promise, but the people learned there was no free lunch. The help cost them plenty!

Going to a counselor takes time and usually money, but the trip doesn't guarantee magic tricks or instant healing. The counselor is not God. He or she can look you in the eye, pat you on the shoulder, give you words of encouragement, offer guidelines, but cannot fight your battles for you. You have to do the work!

WHAT CAN A COUNSELOR DO FOR ME?

A counselor can help you in several ways, including some you might not be considering:

1. Offer hope. For the distressed person, an outsider who will listen may give you the first ray of hope you've had in years. Just the fact that a caring person will let you finish a complete sentence and won't tell you you're stupid will be a blessing.

2. Be objective. "Am I crazy or what?" So often people ask us that question. They have been told for so long that it's all in their heads, they feel they must be losing their minds. Their mothers put them down, their mates proclaimed them hopeless, and their children have not been calling them blessed. *Am I really a mental case?* they wonder.

A counselor can calm you down, let you know you are not crazy, and give you an objective opinion that's not colored by family hysteria. One woman wrote, "At that point I would have paid a hundred dollars for one sentence from a counselor who said, 'You are not crazy!'" Sometimes that assurance alone is worth the trip.

3. Set boundaries. Sometimes we need an outsider to show us where we are out of line and what is reasonable. People who have been victimized want so desperately to please that they often get taken advantage of. Since they have little ability to say no, they need someone to say, "This is ridiculous. You cannot continue to kill yourself this way." Sometimes your parents are demanding that you call them each morning, spend Christmas with them or you'll be disinherited, or telling you to go to their church or you're not really a Christian. Sometimes the boundaries need to be set on how often you see the perpetrator of your past victimization. What do you do when one parent denies the possibility that the other could have done you wrong? Questions like these can be handled by an objective helper who has experience in dealing with these problems.

4. Relieve guilt. Anyone who has been victimized in any way feels guilty. When we gave birth to our second brain-damaged son, we felt we were total failures as parents. We thought we must somehow be to blame. People inferred maybe Florence didn't eat right or maybe there was a curse on us or maybe we'd dropped the babies and didn't want to own up. When we look at that period of guilt, added to our grief, we wonder that we pulled through at all! We could surely have used a counselor who said, "It's not your fault." A competent therapist can relieve your guilt when it's not your fault, place responsibility when you need to change, and know the difference.

5. Keep you moving. Because we are usually a little lazy when it comes to working on our own issues, we often need someone who will keep us accountable and see that we don't give up. We have so many necessary things to do that we neglect the most important: getting ourselves on an even emotional keel so that we can cope with all these other things that are pressing down on us. The reason weight-loss centers are popular is not so much that we can't lose weight on our own, but that when we go there the counselor tells us we've done a great job to lose two pounds. His or her affirmation makes it worth starving for another week. In the same way, going to a counselor and reporting how we've done often disciplines us to move on.

6. Find reality. One of the greatest services a counselor can provide is to get you in touch with reality—the truth of what has happened to you versus denial of the facts. So many of us want someone to say that bad things don't happen to good people. But they do. Your father really wasn't the great saint he and your mother have made him to be. Your son really is on drugs and needs help. You were sexually abused as a child. Sometimes the most important blessing the counselor can bestow is to break the happy-ever-after fairy-tale illusions. This is never a popular step and is not the first thing a counselor will do, but sooner or later he or she must bring you in touch with reality, unpleasant though it may be. Coming out of denial is painful, but unless this happens there is little hope of recovery.

7. Help you forgive. We often meet distraught people who were told by their pastor or counselor that their problem was that they hadn't forgiven their offenders. Once they could say, "I forgive him (or her)" their problems would be over, these helpers said. But since the victims couldn't muster up the willingness to do this, more guilt was added to their pain.

We know that forgiveness is an essential part of the healing process but it is usually not the first step. We have learned that when victims come to the Lord daily in prayer and have some measure of healing, the desire to forgive will come upon them and they can truly forgive the perpetrators, not just mouth the words. When this happens the release is so freeing that people wonder why they didn't do it before. The Lord's timing is perfect and He will bring the victim to genuine forgiveness when the time is right. One line of real forgiveness is worth a paragraph of false pronouncements.

8. Establish a plan. So many of us can't see beyond today when we are upset. We need some objective person who can lay out a plan for our healing so that we can see a light at the end of the long, dark tunnel. We don't need forty-two steps to success on our first visit but we do need the assurance that the counselor has a way to lead us into possible solutions. When we are ready to hear it, the helper will show us the steps of progression and establish a plan for healing. This healing will only take place if we are willing to do our homework, not just show up for an hour once a week.

Don't expect a counselor to solve your life problems in three easy lessons and don't expect that he or she will be available to you twenty-four hours a day. Counselors have a life that may also include some strife.

WHAT SHOULD I WATCH OUT FOR?

Realize that no counselor is perfect, and that even the best ones can't wave a magic wand. However, be wary of a counselor who:

- Spends too much time talking about himself or herself.
- Seems more concerned with his or her life than yours.
- Becomes possessive of you.
- Wants to know where you are all the time.
- Forbids you to see family members or friends.
- Doesn't want any outside ideas.
- Scolds you if you go to a seminar he or she didn't recommend.
- Monitors what books you read.
- Talks you into acts you don't feel right about.
- Makes any sexual advances.
- Minimizes your faith in God.
- Puts extra blame on you.
- Ridicules your family or friends.
- Seems to isolate you from others.

- Won't talk about issues that are too painful in his or her own past.
- Exhibits anger at you.
- Makes you feel stupid.
- Is touchy and defensive.
- Says your problem will take years.

These are a few of the warnings we've gathered from the people who have told us about therapists who did them more harm than good. Often these people hung in there out of fear of what the therapist might do if they suggested leaving. Don't allow yourself to be re-victimized. Also realize your therapist can only take you as far as he or she has gone himself or herself, and you may get to a point where you need to move beyond that stage.

WHAT DOES THE COUNSELOR NEED FROM ME?

Without the cooperation of the seeker, the greatest counselor can achieve little. From our own experience and the comments of other counselors we have learned some requirements the counselor needs from his or her clients to bring about results:

1. Be honest. When you hide the truth, you handicap the helper. Even though they may have enough intuition to guess at your problem, it's a lot quicker and cheaper if you lay it out honestly from day one.

2. Don't try to impress. Don't come to counseling and present a list of credentials to impress the counselor. If the individual helping you has any sensitivity to truth, he or she will soon know who you really are, not who you'd like to be.

3. Don't just dump and run. Although it is important to empty out your feelings, you will learn little if you do all the talking and never listen. Successful therapy depends on what is called "transference," the state where the patient transfers people and problems from his life onto the neutral therapist. This comes through a gradual building of trust through a sharing time, not through a dumping of these problems and then running off.

4. Be responsible. One of the biggest complaints we hear from therapists is the immature clients who forget to show up, don't bother to call, don't value the counselor's time, and don't do the assigned work. Part of successful counseling is the client's becoming a responsible adult.

5. Be open. Don't use therapy to validate your opinion, to prove someone else wrong, or to escape the hard reality of life. If you are not open to the wisdom of the counselor, you can find yourself a one-sided friend who will be much cheaper. To achieve results you have to be more interested in being open than in laying blame.

6. Don't set yourself up for rejection. Some people approach counseling as if they were buying the life of a new friend who is being paid to love them. We know one girl who gives lavish gifts to every helper, sends cards of love and devotion, and is then crushed when the counselor tends to pull back. When you smother the therapist with too much attention because of your own needs, you are ultimately headed for feelings of rejection.

7. Don't make the counselor your god. No matter how excellent your counselor may be, this person is not God. If you rave about the counselor to everyone and put him or her on a pedestal, someday he or she will fall off and then you will be devastated. This hero worship approach is embarrassing for the counselor and replaces real progress with fairy tales.

8. Don't fantasize. According to a survey done by psychologist Kenneth Pope, 87 percent of the psychologists he surveyed admitted to being sexually attracted to their patients at some time. If this is anywhere close to true, it confirms why we must be sure to do nothing provocative that might be a come-on to our therapist.

When we fantasize romantic vacations or sexual acts we are asking for trouble because our words and looks show what we are thinking.

9. Trust your intuition. If you don't feel right about the way your counseling is going, pray about it and see if the Lord validates your concern. We've seen many people who stayed in a negative situation because they didn't want to hurt the counselor's feelings. Your intuition is usually right.

10. Don't quit too soon. One of the most frustrating experiences in counseling is when a person quits just when he or she is getting close to the root of the problem. Men particularly tend to quit as soon as the therapist shows them where they have to change. "As long as it's her fault I'll go, but don't pin anything on me," they seem to be saying. Work through your situation until you and the therapist know you have gone far enough.

Remember: Your therapist is to be your guide and witness, but you have to walk the path to healing by yourself. No one except the Lord can lift you up and carry you to the other side of the mountain.

> Healing is a process, not an event.
> Psychologists can analyze you.
> Counselors can guide you.
> Pastors can pray with you.
> Family can support you.
> Friends can empathize with you.
> Only Jesus can truly heal you.

17

Is There Always Hope?

People who have struggled for years with the effects of childhood sexual victimization have often given up. Their depression has beaten them down. Those horrible dreams have left them exhausted. Their outbursts of anger have started them hating even themselves. They have become so fearful they are afraid to go out of the house, to go anywhere that they are not comfortable. They are sure that God could never accept them because they are too bad or too dirty. No one could love them. Most of the time these sufferers don't even know why they are struggling so much. Often they tell us they've had years of counseling or therapy, and after thousands of dollars they aren't significantly better. They have lost all hope.

Is there any hope? The answer, without a question or a moment of hesitation, is *Yes,* there is hope! There is not only hope, there is healing—complete healing and restoration. With God all things are possible. We end this book with a letter sent to us by Arlene Hardwick of Auckland, New Zealand, just one of many people who have been healed by the Lord.

Arlene had come to the point where she felt there was no hope. She had given up. Yet she kept searching and searching. Maybe somewhere, someone had an answer, an idea, anything she could cling to that might help. Arlene came to our Promise workshop in

Auckland, and everything changed. We'll let her tell you her own story in her own words:

"For as long as I can remember I desperately wanted to be a boy. I never felt loved as a child although my parents wanted me. I was lonely and couldn't relate well to people. At the same time I thought I had a very happy childhood because that was all I had known and of course there were huge gaps in my memory.

"As I moved into my teenage years, life became even more difficult for me. I noticed that people were not taking much notice of me. I began to crave love and attention, but for some reason it wasn't there. Life was even lonelier and I felt like a real misfit. I consequently shut down my emotions and just began to exist. I then turned my affections towards dogs, of which I had previously been terrified as a child. I started to get a very strong attraction to other girls who were a little older than me. This was all done from a distance as the problem was kept within my own emotions and thoughts. This caused a lot of confusion and heartache within me.

"During my teenage years, from the age of thirteen or fourteen, I began to have problems eating. I would take my lunch to school, but I wouldn't eat it. I'd come home and just pick at my dinner. I never realized until years later that I had developed anorexia and at one stage only weighted 6½ stone (approximately ninety pounds) and I am five-feet two-inches tall. This went on for years and not one person stepped in to help me. For three years some of my body functions stopped and then my health began to fall apart.

"Because I didn't feel part of my own family, I left home at an early age and proceeded to look for another family that I could become a part of. This caused much heartache as I already was feeling rejected, and I never found the perfect family who would accept and love me. I ended up moving back home a few years later in a far greater mess than when I had left.

"Emotionally I was a wreck and at the age of twenty-one, I was put into a mental hospital by a lady who I was staying with. I had again gone to look for a family to love and accept me, but after a time I was taken to the hospital and left there all alone and never visited by that family. I stayed there for four months and was diagnosed as a schizophrenic.

"Relationships with males had been very difficult for me but I was in desperate need. I met my husband-to-be and he took me fifty miles each week on the back of his motorcycle to see a psychiatrist. Our relationship then broke up because of rejection feelings and I ended up getting heavily involved in the spiritualist church. I lived with a medium and her family and practiced everything they did.

"From there I was drawn into the lesbian scene, but fortunately for me, never got involved physically. I was emotionally hooked though. Again things fell apart for me and I ended up back with my boyfriend. We decided to get married and did so in the spiritualist church. Six months later we were ready for a divorce. A Christian couple were sent to see us and we committed our lives to Jesus Christ.

"Over the years we had a very, very difficult marriage. In fact at times it was horrific because of emotional, sexual, and mental abuse. I spent years in bed, at home alone, not being able to cope with life.

"Because of the state of our marriage and my mental, physical, and emotional state, I began to look everywhere for help. I read every Christian book I could get on healing, deliverance, and inner healing. I spent many hours listening to tapes. I was taken to healing and deliverance meetings. I tried primal therapy. We had marriage counseling and pastors told us that we wouldn't make it because we were in such a bad way. We went to every traveling ministry that came to the country. In everything we did and all the prayer and counseling, there was always a measure of release. We thought we had been healed, but it never lasted long and things became bad again.

"After fifteen years of marriage and being a Christian, we discovered that I had been sexually abused as a child. At least now we knew what we were dealing with, so again we started the search for freedom. I went to groups and counseling and read books and listened to tapes on the subject. I began to improve as time went on, but then I couldn't seem to go any further.

"Friends told us about the Promise of Healing seminar that was coming to our country. As we read the brochure, we became excited because it covered the areas in which I had struggled all my life: Memory gaps, not feeling loved, health problems, abuse. It looked perfect for us, as my husband had also discovered that he had been sexually abused.

"In preparation for the seminar we read two books, *Freeing Your Mind from Memories that Bind* and *The Promise of Restoration*. The Lord started showing us things that we had both forgotten about our childhoods. Things began to come into focus for us; we saw why we had been dysfunctional, why our marriage and our families had been dysfunctional, why my health had been so bad. I began to experience some very deep emotional pain as I spent time in the Lord's presence. In my counseling I had learned the importance of writing down my feelings, so I was doing that. The pain and the anger were being stirred up from deep within me. I began to get hope because as I read the books, I felt at long last somebody had the answers that we had been so long looking for. The Lord has been very gracious and merciful to us along the way. He helped us to grow and to become free in many areas. He gave us lovely Christian friends to support us and help us along the way, but still the roots of the problems were still there.

"As we went along to the seminar we were both excited and afraid—excited that this could be the answer we'd been searching for but afraid that maybe we'd learn something new, get a measure of help, and have to struggle on again. Also we were afraid of what God was going to reveal to us from our pasts.

"My husband came with me and we went with the prayer director for ministry. We talked for the first hour, then I was ready. We prayed and asked Jesus to show me the truth, and as I shut my eyes I immediately began to see a scene before me. At first it was just the outside of a room that I had been afraid of as a child. This memory came up in one of the questionnaires that we had done. I was standing there, about three years old, feeling afraid and confused. My mother and father were not there; I was with my grandmother. As I entered the room I saw a man that I knew, a close family friend that I called uncle. Nana was talking to him and he was laughing. I just stood by myself and watched him take his pants down and then get up onto the bed. He called me over and asked me to get up with him. I didn't want to so my Nana came and got me and told me to. She took my pants off and my shoes and told me to climb up and lie down."

Arlene went on to describe the entire experience, then she wrote, "The prayer director told me to go back (into the memory) and lie on the bed. I then saw Jesus standing at the door; He walked over to me. I didn't want Him at first because I was afraid and felt awful. Then He picked me up and held me. I saw tears running down His face. He was loving me. He took me outside in the sunshine, put me on the very green grass, and watched me play. He looked at me, smiling all the time.

"I felt very drained afterward. I knew something had happened to me, something very real. I experienced the whole thing.

"I believe that the locked-away memories and pain have been at the root of my problems. I know that this is the beginning of the restoration process and I know that the Lord will bring complete release because He has promised me. He said that He would complete the work that He began in me and that He would enlighten the darkness in me.

"Although my life has been painful, I am thankful to the Lord for His faithfulness and love to me. I am thankful that I don't have to lean on my own understanding because God's wisdom is perfect. He knew me before I was born and the plans He has for me are good. Everything that has and will happen to me, God will use for my ultimate good. Thank you, Father!

"P.S. Over the past two months I have been able to do all of my own housework, shopping, and baking for the first time in twelve years. Since reading the books and writing my prayers, I have been getting up at 5 A.M. to spend time with the Lord and then function in my rightful role for the rest of the day. Praise the Lord, it's been a real miracle."

Notes

Chapter 1—What Is My Personality?

1. Components of this chart are taken from the following sources: Lawrence J. Crabb, Jr., Ph.D., *Basic Principles of Biblical Counseling: The Training Manual* (Winona Lake, IN: Institute of Biblical Counseling, 1978); Gary Smalley and John Trent, *The Two Sides of Love* (Colorado Springs: Focus on the Family Publishers, 1990), 34–36; Carlson Learning Company; Anthony Alesandra and Jim Cathcart, *Relationship Strategies* (Austin, TX: Nightingale-Conant, 1990); Susan Fletcher, "How Do They Manage?" (Merrill-Reid Society Styles), *American Way Magazine,* October 1982, 192–94; Edward D. Bono, M.D., "Creative Thinking," *Voices,* July 1992, 14.

2. Oswald Chambers, *My Utmost for His Highest* (Westwood, N.J.: Barbour, 1987), January 12.

Chapter 6—How Can I Know My Children's Personalities?

1. Alan Chittenden, quoted in the *Brisbane (Australia) Sun,* 27 February 1991.

2. Jerome Kagan's work at Harvard University reported by Daniel Q. Haney, AP science writer in the *San Marcos (California) Blade-Citizen,* 16 March 1991.

3. Dr. T. Berry Brazelton, quoted in *Dallas Morning News,* 8 March 1992.

4. Dr. Stanley Turecki, Head of Beth Israel Hospital's Difficult Child Program and author of *The Difficult Child,* cited in a report in *USA Today,* 11 December 1985.

5. Dr. Albert Stunkard work originally published in the *New England Journal of Medicine,* quoted in *USA Today,* 23 January 1986.

6. Study by Alexander Thomas, Stella Chess, and Herbert Birch, reported in *Ladies' Home Journal,* September 1992.

7. Jerre Levy, professor of psychology at the University of Chicago, quoted in *Time,* 20 January 1992.

8. Studies conducted by the National Institute of Mental Health in Bethesda, Maryland, cited in the *Chicago Tribune,* 15 November 1990.

Chapter 7—Where Do My Feelings of Rejection Originate?

1. Oswald Chambers, *My Utmost for His Highest,* October 21, September 9.

Chapter 8—Why Am I Under All This Stress?

1. Dr. Doyle Carson, cited in "Mind Games and High Stakes," a special advertising section published by *Texas Monthly*, June 1992.

2. Fred Littauer, *The Promise of Healing* (Nashville: Thomas Nelson, 1994), chapter 9.

Chapter 10—Will My Childhood Pictures Help?

1. Fred Littauer, *The Promise of Healing,* 144–53.

2. Oswald Chambers, *My Utmost for His Highest*, April 19, April 30.

Chapter 11—How Can I Know If I Was Sexually Violated as a Child?

1. Fred Littauer, *The Promise of Healing,* chapter 9.

2. C. G. Jung, "Two Essays on Analytical Psychology," Vol. 7, *Collected Works of C. G. Jung* (Princeton: Princeton University Press, 1953).

Chapter 15—How Can I Plug In to the Power?

1. Oswald Chambers, *My Utmost for His Highest,* December 30.

2. Ibid., October 23.

Chapter 16—How Do I Know If I Need Counseling?

1. Catherine Johnson, *When to Say Good-bye to Your Therapist* (New York: Simon and Schuster, 1988), 9.

Bibliography

Burns, David. *Feeling Good: The New Mood Therapy.* New York: Morrow, 1980.

Carter, Dr. Les. *Imperative People.* Nashville: Thomas Nelson, 1991.

Carter, Dr. Les, and Dr. Frank Minirth. *The Anger Workbook.* Nashville: Thomas Nelson, 1993.

Chambers, Oswald. *My Utmost for His Highest.* London: Dodd, Mead & Co., 1985; Westwood, N.J., 1987.

Congo, Janet, Julie Mask, and Jan Meier. *The Woman Within.* Nashville: Thomas Nelson, 1991.

Cousins, Norman. *Anatomy of an Illness as Perceived by the Patient: Reflections on Healing and Regeneration.* New York: Norton, 1979.

Friesen, Ph.D., James G. *More Than Survivors.* Nashville: Thomas Nelson, .

Friesen, Ph.D., James G. *Uncovering the Mystery of MPD.* Nashville: Thomas Nelson, .

Heavilin, Marilyn W. *Roses in December.* Nashville: Thomas Nelson, 1986.

Heavilin, Marilyn W. *When Your Dreams Die.* Nashville: Thomas Nelson, 1990.

Hemfelt, Dr. Robert, Dr. Frank Minirth, and Dr. Paul Meier. *Love Is a Choice.* Nashville: Thomas Nelson, 1989.

Hemfelt, Dr. Robert, Dr. Frank Minirth, Dr. Paul Meier, Dr. Deborah Newman, and Dr. Brian Newman. *Love Is a Choice Workbook.* Nashville: Thomas Nelson, 1991.

Johnson, Catherine. *When to Say Good-bye to Your Therapist.* New York: Simon and Schuster, 1988.

Littauer, Florence. *After Every Wedding Comes a Marriage*. Eugene, Oreg.: Harvest House, 1981.

Littauer, Florence. *Personality Plus*. Old Tappan, N.J.: Revell, 1985.

Littauer, Florence. *Your Personality Tree*. Dallas: Word, 1986.

Littauer, Florence, and Marita Littauer. *Personality Puzzle: Understanding the People You Work With*. Old Tappan, N.J.: Revell, 1992.

Littauer, Fred and Florence. *Freeing Your Mind from Memories that Bind*. San Bernardino, Calif.: Here's Life, 1989.

Littauer, Fred. *The Promise of Healing*. Nashville: Thomas Nelson, 1994.

McClure, Cynthia Rowland. *Food for the Hungry Heart*. Nashville: Thomas Nelson, 1991.

Minirth, Dr. Frank, Dr. Paul Meier, Dr. Robert Hemfelt, and Dr. Sharon Sneed. *Love Hunger*. Nashville: Thomas Nelson, 1990.

Minirth, Dr. Frank, Dr. Paul Meier, Dr. Robert Hemfelt, and Dr. Sharon Sneed. *Love Hunger Weight-Loss Workbook*. Nashville: Thomas Nelson, 1991.

Moyers, Bill. *Healing and the Mind*. Garden City, N.Y.: Doubleday, 1993.

Newman, Dr. Brian, Ted Scheuermann, Larry Stephens, and Bob Dyer. *The Man Within: Daily Devotions for Men in Recovery*. Nashville: Thomas Nelson, 1991.

O'Connor, Karen. *When Spending Takes the Place of Feeling*. Nashville: Thomas Nelson, 1992.

Remuda Ranch. *Beyond the Looking Glass: Daily Devotions for Overcoming Anorexia and Bulimia*. Nashville: Thomas Nelson, 1992.

Samaritan Counseling Center. *A New Beginning: Daily Devotions for Women Survivors of Sexual Abuse*. Nashville: Thomas Nelson, 1992.

Smalley, Gary, and John Trent. *The Two Sides of Love: What Strengthens Affection, Closeness, and Lasting Commitment?* Colorado Springs: Focus on the Family, 1992.

Sneed, Dr. Sharon. *Love Hunger Action Plan*. Nashville: Thomas Nelson, 1993.

Stoop, Dr. David. *Hope for the Perfectionist*. Nashville: Thomas Nelson, 1989.

Turecki, Stanley. *The Difficult Child, rev. ed.* New York: Bantam, 1989.

Vredevelt, Pam, Dr. Deborah Newman, Harry Beverly, and Dr. Frank Minirth. *The Thin Disguise*. Nashville: Thomas Nelson, 1992.

Zois, Christ, and Patricia Fogarty. *Think Like a Shrink: Solve Your Problems Yourself with Short-Term Therapy Techniques*. New York: Warner, 1992.

Other Personality Assessment Tools

Myers-Briggs Type Indicator. Gainesville, FL: Center for Applications of Psychological Type, 1987.

Recommended Resource Order Form

Number
Ordered   **$**   **Total**

_____ 1.	*Personality Plus*, Florence Littauer	9.00 _____
_____ 2.	*Your Personality Tree*, Florence Littauer	9.00 _____
_____ 3.	*Personalities in Power*, Florence Littauer	9.00 _____
_____ 4.	*Personality Puzzle*, Florence Littauer &	10.00 _____
	Marita Littauer	
_____ 5.	*Freeing Your Mind from Memories that Bind*,	10.00 _____
	Fred Littauer & Florence Littauer	
_____ 6.	*The Promise of Restoration/Healing*, Fred Littauer	10.00 _____
_____ 7.	*Raising Christians not Just Children*, Florence Littauer	10.00 _____
_____ 8.	*Hope for Hurting Women*, Florence Littauer	9.00 _____
_____ 9.	*How to Get Along with Difficult People*, Florence Littauer	8.00 _____
_____ 10.	*Silver Boxes*, Florence Littauer Hardback	13.00 _____
_____ 11.	*The Best of Florence Littauer*, compiled by	
	M. Heavilin Hardback	10.00 _____
_____ 12.	*Dare to Dream*, Florence Littauer	10.00 _____
_____ 13.	*Make the Tough Times Count*, Florence Littauer	10.00 _____
_____ 14.	*Too Much is Never Enough*, Marita Littauer	9.00 _____
_____ 15.	*What You Can Say When You Don't Know What to Say*,	7.00 _____
	Lauren Littauer Briggs	
_____ 16.	*Your Personality Tree Video Album*, 8 half-hour lessons	80.00 _____
	with book and Study Guide	
_____ 17.	*Uncovering the Mystery of MPD*,	13.00 _____
	James G. Friesen, Ph.D.	
_____ 18.	*More Than Survivors*, James G. Friesen, Ph.D.	10.00 _____
_____ 19.	*Ritual Abuse*, Los Angeles County Commission	5.00 _____
	for Women	
_____ 20.	*Personality Profile Tests*, Fred Littauer (6 for $5.00)	1.00 _____

Shipping & Handling (Please add $1.50 per book, $5.00 for Video Album)

SUBTOTAL _____

California residents please add 7.75% sales tax _____

TOTAL AMOUNT ENCLOSED (Check or Money Order) _____

CHARGE: Mastercard/Visa # _____

Name on Card _____ Expiration Date _____

Make Checks Payable and Mail To: CLASS BOOK SERVICE
1645 S. Rancho Santa Fe Rd., #102
San Marcos, CA 92069
(619) 471-0233

"Payment Plan" may be made by sending three checks, each for one-third of total amount, one payable currently and the other two dated a month and two months later. International Orders: Please send checks in U.S. funds only and add $5.00 per book for shipping by air.